The Development of Arab-American Identity

The Development of Arab-American Identity

Edited by
Ernest McCarus

Ann Arbor
THE UNIVERSITY OF MICHIGAN PRESS

Copyright © by the University of Michigan 1994
All rights reserved
Published in the United States of America by
The University of Michigan Press
Manufactured in the United States of America

1997   1996   1995   1994   4   3   2   1

*A CIP catalogue record for this book is available
from the British Library.*

Library of Congress Cataloging-in-Publication Data

McCarus, Ernest N. (Ernest Nasseph), 1922–
        The development of Arab-American identity / Ernest McCarus.
            p.   cm.
        Includes bibliographical references and index.
        ISBN 0-472-10439-X (alk. paper)
        1. Arab Americans—Ethnic identity. I. Title.
    E184.A65M37   1994
    305.892'7073—dc20   94-15616
                                                                     CIP

Photographs courtesy of the Arab American Collection, National Museum of
American History, Smithsonian Institution.

Contents

Introduction   **1**
Ernest McCarus

"Coming to America": Dilemmas of Ethnic Groups
since the 1880s   **9**
Éva Veronika Huseby-Darvas

The Early Arab Immigrant Experience   **23**
Alixa Naff

Arab-Americans and the Political Process   **37**
Michael W. Suleiman

Maintaining the Faith of the Fathers: Dilemmas of
Religious Identity in the Christian and Muslim
Arab-American Communities   **61**
Yvonne Yazbeck Haddad

Palestinian Women in American Society: The Interaction of
Social Class, Culture, and Politics   **85**
Louise Cainkar

Issues of Identity: In Theater of Immigrant
Community   **107**
Ala Fa'ik

Ethnic Archetypes and the Arab Image   **119**
Ronald Stockton

Anti-Arab Racism and Violence in the United States **155**
Nabeel Abraham

Contributors **215**

Index **219**

Illustrations *following page* **122**

Introduction

Ernest McCarus

U.S. citizens of Arab origin are today a small but prominent ethnic minority with identifiable personages in all walks of life. While they have historically been primarily from Lebanon, Syria, and Palestine, all Arab countries are today represented in the citizenry of the United States and its neighbors. Along with their increased contributions to American society Arab-Americans have in recent decades received increasing attention and study; the *Arab Studies Quarterly,* for example, devoted a special double issue to "Arab Americans: Continuity & Change" (Vol. 11, nos. 2 and 3, 1989), edited by Michael W. Suleiman and Baha Abu-Laban.

This collection of essays deals in particular with the contemporary scene, bringing the picture up to date. After the historical background has been set, the essays deal with the struggle for religious, political, cultural, and social identity, all of which involve coping with unconscious and conscious stereotyping and marginalization of Arabs and Arab-Americans.

The historical background is provided by Éva Veronika Huseby-Darvas and Alixa Naff. Dr. Huseby-Darvas's "'Coming to America': Dilemmas of Ethnic Groups since the 1880s" provides a conceptual framework of the patterning of European immigrations to the United States as a background against which Arab emigrations can be compared. In her own words, she attempts "to give a broad glimpse of the immigrant encounters and . . . pave the way forward to the comparative exploration of the Arab-American experience, past and present." The millions who came from Eastern and Southern Europe between the 1880s and World War I were largely pushed out by changing conditions, economic or political or both. They conceived of themselves as immigrants and did not attempt to become "American"; they sought economic opportunity, with the eventual goal of returning to their native land. At the turn of the century the concept of the melting pot became current, whereby it was believed that Anglo-Saxon conformity was the ideal goal, and that all minorities would be assimilated into it so producing a homogeneous new race. But in fact, the newcomers were rejected by mainstream society. By World War II the idea of *assimilation*—the total absorption of a minority culture into a dominant one—had begun to yield ground to the concept of *acculturation,* whereby the minority culture takes on select aspects of the majority culture but retains its own identity. Note that the federal government has since the 1970s and 1980s funded the preparation of standard curricula in foreign languages wherever there is a sufficiently large non-English-speaking population in order to promote multicultural diversity. In the second phase of immigration, after World War II, emigrants were generally better educated, politically more sophisticated, and prepared to settle down as permanent residents if not citizens. As will be detailed in the following essays, Arab emigrations followed this pattern. The early Arab immigrants were sojourners who settled in Arab communities and learned only enough English to peddle their wares. Although they had originally come intending to amass wealth and then to return to their homes, for the most part they ended up bringing over their families and becoming permanent residents. After World War II Arab emigrants were generally more highly educated or came for a higher education, and were prepared to settle here permanently. They still encountered overt and covert anti-Arab racism, which even today poses difficult issues for them.

In "The Early Arab Immigrant Experience" Dr. Naff finds that the dilemmas outlined by Huseby-Darvas were encountered as well by the early Arab immigrants. She finds that in the nineteenth century the great majority of them were from Lebanon, and further, that they typically did not emigrate for political reasons but were largely recruited to work in the United States because of mounting labor shortages. They did come intending to work for a few years and then to return to Lebanon with their riches. They formed small communities that served as bases to sustain the itinerant peddlers and small businessmen. The first wave of immigrants was for the most part village farmers or artisans, relatively poor, and poorly schooled. After World War I they began to come from various regions of the Arab world and were politically more sophisticated; after World War II in particular they began to develop an Arab identity, reversing the trend of Arab-Americans to ignore or be unaware of their history as a people. Naff presents the human side of the story, offering insight into the mentality of these immigrants. She paints a picture of community life; thus, she shows that the early immigrants tended to preserve the *millet* system of the Ottoman Empire, with communities subdividing into smaller groups according to religious affiliation or even according to Christian denomination.

The next two chapters deal with political and religious identity. Dr. Michael W. Suleiman, in "Arab-Americans and the Political Process," begins with a rapid survey of the political attitudes of Arab immigrants over the past hundred years. The first wave, which ended with World War I, was characterized by sojourners who never felt that they were full-fledged members of U.S. society; their basic attitude was to be good citizens and to attract as little attention to themselves as possible. The second major wave, which came after World War II, was one of politically sophisticated and active individuals who brought with them a sense of Arab identity; they have joined political parties and have become active in U.S. politics. Suleiman provides a comprehensive picture of the political attitudes and activities of Arab-Americans today, including the results of a survey questionnaire he sent to nearly four hundred politically active Arab-Americans representing a broad cross section of the population. The survey deals with such issues as ethnicity, party orientation, anti-Arab bias, Arab political-cultural organizations, and political activism relative to age of respondent. Suleiman concludes that Arab-Americans today, young and old or first or fourth generation, are more and more finding common ground in their commitment to an Arab identity.

Dr. Yvonne Yazbeck Haddad presents a comprehensive and clear picture of religious affiliations and the role they play in the lives of Arab-Americans in her chapter "Maintaining the Faith of the Fathers: Dilemmas of Religious Identity in the Christian and Muslim Arab-American Communities." It is of course impossible to ignore the role of politics in the life of the community: Haddad correctly points out that it was the June War of 1967 that first awakened most Arab-Americans to this new identity. Before that event most of them were unaware of or unconcerned about their Arab origins—indeed, they were still "Lebanese," "Syrian," or "Palestinian," if anything at all, and the term "Arab-American" had not yet come into general usage. In spite of the influence of political events, religious affiliation is still the determinant of the Arab-American's identity—whether Christian, Muslim, or Jew—and is linked to the degree of assimilation. Dr. Haddad details the different religious communities of the Middle East, including many different Christian sects, the history of their establishment in the United States, and the influence each wields on the attitudes of its practitioners. Particular focus is placed on Islam in the United States, the history of its changing nature as it has changed from an Arab majority to one challenged by non-Arabs, both African-Americans and South Asians. In spite of the centrifugal force of religious particularity, she concludes that the assimilative force is great and that all religious groups are slowly changing and adapting to U.S. society.

Dr. Louise Cainkar's "Palestinian Women in American Society: The Interaction of Social Class, Culture, and Politics" is based on interviews with immigrant Palestinians living in the Chicago area. As one of the rare studies of immigrant women rather than men, it has produced a number of interesting findings. While Palestinian men in the United States enjoy the freedoms that American men exercise, Palestinian women remain attached to their families and under their supervision and control. There are of course differences according to social class: middle- or upper-class women enjoy a measure of freedom denied their lower-class sisters. Since only men work outside of the house among lower-class Palestinian families, it is primarily the Palestinian woman who maintains traditional values and inculcates them in the succeeding generation. Palestinian women also tend to feel that their stay in the United States is temporary and that they must therefore strive even harder to maintain traditional Palestinian values. Cainkar explores the differences in attitudes and behaviors of these Muslim Palestinian women of varying socio-economic classes and concludes that there are several realities for them and that there is no typical Palestinian woman in the United States.

Although an appreciable amount of attention has been afforded

Errata

Acknowledgments for illustrations in "Ethnic Archetypes and the Arab Image," by Ronald Stockton should read as follows:

Fig. 1. *Steve Canyon Magazine,* 1983 (original 1948). Milt Caniff and Field Enterprises, Chicago.

Fig. 2. *Sinbad,* 1989. Adventure Comics, Newbury Park, Calif.

Fig. 3. *Sargent Rock Spectacular,* 1978. DC Comics, New York.

Fig. 4. *"Hawkman,"* 1941.

Fig. 5. *Return of Tarzan,* 1973. Edgar Rice Burroughs, Inc. National Periodical Publishers, New York.

Fig. 6. Scrawls, date unknown.

Fig. 7. Szep, *Boston Globe,* May 18, 1983.

Fig. 8. Oliphant, 1989, Los Angeles Times Syndicate.

Fig. 9. MacNely, 1991.

Fig. 10. Jewish Telegraphic Association, 1989.

Fig. 11. France, 1893.

Fig. 12. *Francis, Brother of the Universe,* 1980. Marvel Comics, New York.

Fig. 13. *Tales of GI Joe,* January, 1988. Marvel Comics, New York.

Fig. 14. *Thrilling Adventure Stories,* 1975. Seaboard Periodicals, New York.

Fig. 15. *Batman: A Death in the Family,* 1988. DC Comics, New York.

Fig. 16. *Star Rider and the Peace Machine,* 1982. Star Rider Productions, Calgary, Canada.

Fig. 17. *Shaloman,* 1989. Mark 1 Comics, Philadelphia.

Fig. 18. *Detroit Free Press,* July 10, 1979.

Fig. 19. Bill Day, *Detroit Free Press,* December 15, 1988.

Fig. 20. *Mad Magazine,* October 1982.

Arab-American literature,[1] drama coverage has been neglected. There are no published materials on Arab-American drama; the material presented here is new. Dr. Ala Fa'ik in "Issues of Identity: In Theater of Immigrant Community" traces the evolution of Arab drama in the United States and characterizes a number of representative plays. In the earliest phase Arab-Americans produced plays in their cultural clubs and organizations about the glories of Arab history. Before World War II the drama experience of most Arab-Americans was limited to viewing Egyptian movies. After the war large numbers of Arabs came from various Arab countries and created communities capable of sustaining Arabic language activities in religious observances, schooling, and the mass media. Theatrical performances also appeared, usually in the dialect of the local community. They dealt with issues of concern to the communities such as family, marriage, drugs, and working conditions, reflecting the change in traditional values as Arabs interacted with the values of this culture. Some plays were farces, aimed at entertaining the community, while others critically looked at life in this country. There were also musicals and children's productions, as well as some for a general audience, designed to present the frustrations and aspirations of the Arab community. Fa'ik discusses in some detail a play by Fareed Al-Oboudi, *Portrait of a Suspect,* which is about the ordeal undergone by a young Arab-American who is apprehended and interrogated in turn by authorities in the United States, Syria, and Israel. Based on research, the accounting of the interrogation techniques in each case is chillingly accurate. The young man's guilt is his identity—he is an Arab-American. Fa'ik concludes that "To be an Arab-American, say these plays, is to be both Arab and American and, for the time being at least, to be neither."

The marginalization of Arab-Americans is depicted by Ronald Stockton and Nabeel Abraham. Stereotypes are so insidiously common that we are often not aware that we are indulging in one. In "Ethnic Archetypes and the Arab Image" Dr. Stockton reports on

---

1. See, for example, Gregory Orfalea and Sharif Elmusa, eds., *Grape Leaves. A Century of Arab American Poetry* (University of Utah Press, 1988), short biographical sketches and English translations of a number of poems by twenty Arab-American poets; and Joseph Geha, *Through and Through. Toledo Stories* (Graywolf Press, 1990), a collection of short stories.

a study of several hundred cartoons from editorial pages and comics sections that depict Arabs in terms of pejorative stereotypes. He first shows how stereotypes of ethnic groups are generally of a common mold, one that designates a basic difference between the individual and all Others. Others are depicted as physically or mentally inferior. Stockton finds that stereotypes can be used over and over for any people group: many of the stereotypes of Arabs were earlier applied to Jews or Japanese. By depicting the Other as inferior in some significant way, stereotypes permit the stereotyper to feel superior and infallible and therefore to transgress with impunity against the victim. On a grander scale, stereotypes can justify major policy decisions; thus, by stereotyping Islam as barbaric and Muslims as depraved—stereotypes going back to the time of the Crusades—a people will not question its government's policies when, for example, it bombs a Qaddafi without just cause. Stockton emphasizes the dangerous nature of stereotyping, which permits both individuals and nations to commit injustice, or, since stereotypes inhibit one's seeking the full truth, even to commit egregious errors on a national scale.

Dr. Abraham deals with the vitally important topic of "Anti-Arab Racism and Violence in the United States." The curious thing about anti-Arab violence is that it is largely unreported in this country and generally ignored by the mass media and by governmental authorities. Dr. Abraham states that violence committed against Arab-Americans stems from three main sources: (1) ideologically motivated violence, such as that by the Jewish Defense League, a Jewish terrorist group that attacks "the enemies of Israel" and is the FBI's prime suspect in the murder of Alex Odeh; (2) anti-Arab xenophobia, which has nothing to do with the Arab-Israeli conflict but is based on perceived differences of race, culture, ethnicity, or religion; and (3) jingoist racism, a blend of knee-jerk patriotism and homegrown white racism toward the Other; it usually occurs during heightened international tensions (hijackings, hostage takings, or military conflict). Abraham also deals with the impact of the Gulf war on anti-Arab racism and violence, detailing the role of individuals, groups, and the federal government.

The present book is the product of a conference on the Arab-American Immigrant Experience mounted in 1990 by the Center for Middle Eastern and North African Studies of the University of Michigan. The immediate stimulus for the conference was an unpleasant incident that had occurred in a course at the university: A guest lecturer used most derogatory terms in referring to Arabs, stereo-typing them in an unjustified and tasteless manner in spite of the presence of Arab-American students in that course. In order to defuse the situation the center decided to present to the university community and to the community at large an up-to-date summary of the historical origins and present status of these Americans of Arab origin. While as individuals they have become prominent for their contribution in all walks of life in these United States, as a community they are one of the only ethnic groups that can still be stereotyped and maligned with impunity. It is our hope that this volume will help correct that situation.

I extend to Elizabeth "Betsy" Barlow our warmest thanks for her many contributions at every stage of the mounting of the conference on which this book is based and for her support in the production of this book.

"Coming to America": Dilemmas of Ethnic Groups since the 1880s

Éva Veronika Huseby-Darvas

"Coming to America": what kinds of expectations and aspirations, hopes and dreams, and yes, disappointments, pain, and struggles are behind such an event? What is it like being a new immigrant, a greenhorn, and then an ethnic? What kinds of dilemmas do immigrants and ethnics face? Here I will touch upon over a century of the immigrant experience and look a bit closer at the wave that scholars still refer to as the "new immigrants" although this term is no longer appropriate. I am referring to those millions who came from Eastern and Southern Europe approximately between the 1880s and World War I.

Why focus on the new immigrants? For one reason: because they were representative. Mutatis mutandis they were like so many others before and since them. Like the Irish[1] a few decades before (and so many other groups from all over the world since the arrival of the "new immigrants"), they were also pushed out of their homeland by changed conditions, either economic, political, or both. Then in the United States they also were met by xenophobia and suffered prejudice, discrimination, negative stereotyping, and ethnic slurs. Thus

---

1. Kerby Miller, *Emigrants and Exiles: Ireland and the Irish Exodus to North America* (New York: Oxford University Press, 1985).

they also were forced to put up their own struggle for survival both in their old world homeland and, at least during their first couple of decades, in their "land of choice," the new world. For these and other reasons I am convinced that the immigrant experience and ethnic dilemmas of that particular group are our still very vital legacy, and, as such, are our lesson for the present and very likely our paradigm for the future.

Surely there were differences in the treatment and accommodation of the different groups in the various periods, depending on a host of factors, but the differences were in degree.[2] I suggest that "coming to America" and becoming an immigrant here was most difficult in the past and remains to be that today. The same is the case with being "the new guy on the block," that is being the new ethnic group in this polyethnic setting. I am concerned about the frequently voiced yet mistaken notion that immigrants from Europe in general and from Eastern and Southern Europe in particular had in the past and have today a much easier, more effortless time instantly "making it" in the United States than do immigrants from other parts of the world. Recently, in early 1990 this was discussed on the otherwise valuable and informative PBS television program "New Immigrants: The Arab-American Experience." I would argue that this is not merely an erroneous notion that reduces an extremely complex reality, but that it is not a particularly useful approach to the study and understanding of the social history of U.S. immigration. Rather, confronting our legacy of "coming to America" and probing what we may learn from the experiences of yesteryear's immigrants make a significantly more fruitful approach, and, I contend, are decidedly more

---

2. It is impossible to even attempt to offer a selection from a huge body of scholarly literature on the topic. For a subjective selection, see, for example, Joseph Barton, *Peasants and Strangers: Italians, Romanians and Slovaks in an American City, 1890–1950* (Cambridge: Harvard University Press, 1974); Milton Gordon, *Assimilation in American Life: The Role of Race, Religion, and National Origin* (New York: Oxford University Press, 1964); John Bukowczyk, *And My Children Did not Know Me: A History of Polish Americans* (Bloomington: Indiana University Press, 1987); Stephan Thernstrom, ed., *Harvard Encyclopedia of American Ethnic Groups* (Cambridge: Harvard University Press, 1980); Ewa Morawska, *For Bread with Butter* (Cambridge, England: Cambridge University Press, 1985); William Thomas and Florian Znaniecki, *The Polish Peasant in Europe and America* (Chicago: University of Chicago Press, 1918–20); Virginia Yans-McLaughin, *Family and Community: Italian Immigrants in Buffalo 1880–1930* (Ithaca, New York: Cornell University Press, 1977).

in the spirit and aim of this conference in which I am happy and honored to participate.

Let us now turn to these "new immigrants" from Eastern and Southern Europe. Like others, Dinnerstein and Reimers show[3] a revealing demographic picture. The largest groups arriving were the Jews, Poles, and Italians. For that matter, during the five decades after 1880 the population of U.S. Jews increased tenfold, Poles thirtyfold, and Italians fortyfold. The great majority of these new immigrants came from rural areas of their homelands; most were peasants. But because of the changed economic, social, and demographic conditions here, most of the newcomers—unlike so many of the "old immigrants" who arrived from Northern and Western Europe earlier—became urban dwellers in the United States. In this and a number of other respects they were unlike their predecessors, and at the same time, regardless of how they were perceived by the host population, the newcomers were not all alike.

In fact, there were tremendous variations within these groups. For instance, the Italian immigrants came from a homeland where local identification was extraordinarily salient. People did not have national affiliation, but identified with their *paisanos,* those from their natal villages and regions. This was often the case with the other groups as well. In addition, many—particularly those from the Ottoman lands, Russia, and the Austro-Hungarian Empire—left multinational, multilingual empires behind. Frequently the people who came from these polyethnic and polyglot empires were members of minority groups in their homelands, so in the United States they became "twice-minority."

Without doubt, the new immigrants, who were so readily lumped together by immigration officials and so recklessly categorized by the host population, were unlike one another in customs and diets. They were also different from one another in the languages and dialects they spoke, the clothes they wore, the religions they practiced, the histories

---

3. Leonard Dinnerstein and David Reimers, *Ethnic Americans: A History of Immigration,* 3d ed. (New York: Harper and Row, 1988), chap. 3 and 4. This point, like some of the discussion in this chapter, was stimulated by George Colman's fine series "Culture, Community, Identity: An Ethnic Perspective," Wayne State University Ethnic Heritage Center.

they fabricated, and the social organizations they constructed. Briefly, they were unlike one another in the cultures, or in the systems of meaning and value they have woven for themselves.

Of course, there were similarities among the newcomers too. While a few of them fled from political persecution, the great majority of this particular wave left for economic reasons. As Prpic reminds us, they left in massive numbers, and they left behind economically depressed areas from where "the sole export was in human flesh—emigrants."[4] Still, their intentions to leave were often temporary. Like migrant laborers, these immigrants came with plans to return to their homeland. Andrew Vázsonyi remarks that

> when they arrived, [many immigrants] did not even think of settling down; they had simple and relatively short term plans. In one or two years they wanted to save enough money to enable them to buy a few acres of land and some horses, and cows when they returned to their native villages.[5]

Some worked a number of years, saved, lived under miserable conditions, and then returned to their homeland and remained there. According to rough estimates, 16 percent of immigrants from the period under examination belonged to this category.[6] However, before immigration restrictions were decreed, others engaged in circular migration. Actually, they moved somewhat like a pendulum between their natal villages and the United States, crossing the Atlantic Ocean five, six, seven, eight, or even more times. They worked a few years before returning home to spend their savings, and then over and over again they came back for more work (and more scrimping) to U.S. industry or mining. While for various reasons most immigrants did settle in the States, conceptualizing their stay as a transient one made

---

4. George J. Prpic, *South Slavic Immigration in America* (Boston: Twayne Publishers, 1978).

5. Andrew Vázsonyi, "The cicisbeo and the magnificent cockhold: Boardinghouse life and love in immigrant communities," *Journal of American Folklore* 91 (1978): 642–56.

6. See, for instance, Dinnerstein and Reimers, *Ethnic Americans*. I discuss the difficulties of those who returned to their natal Hungarian villages during the early part of this century, and the permanent stigma left by their U.S. experience. See Éva V. Huseby, "Community Cohesion and Identity Maintenance in Rural Hungary: Adaptations to Directed Social Change" (Ph.D. diss., University of Michigan, 1984).

a big difference in community formation, attitude, world view, and a host of other things that compounded their ethnic dilemma (for instance, neglecting to learn English because they intended to stay only a short time).

Let us not forget that in addition to seeking economic opportunities, the immigrants sought and believed in a social ideal. The United States was not only seen as a land of opportunity in the economic sphere, but also as the solace to troubles, the solution to problems, the answer to eternal questions. Indeed, most immigrants—old, new, or contemporary—believed (or wanted to believe) in the Constitution, in the marvelous notion that all people were created equal, and in the heady ideals of liberty and justice.

As Derek Wolcott, the poet of African and Dutch descent, contemplated recently on PBS, "the immigrants' dream is inviolable in America. . . . there is not another country in the history of the world where people want to go so much. Why do they? Because of the American ideal, the ideal of the Constitution, that all men are created equal." This very theme is present in the accounts of the scores of recent immigrants interviewed by Louis Mallè and shown in his fine film of the late 1980s ". . . and the pursuit of happiness." The theme recurs not only in the contemplation of contemporary poets, writers, and filmmakers, but also in the comments of the descendants of immigrants, and the autobiographical statements and scientific work of Franz Boas, the father of American anthropology.

While dedicating his play to his "Ma and Pa, and to the millions of [other] immigrants who enriched this country, flavored and nourished it," Jack LaZebnik, playwright and professor of writing and literature, pondered in 1989

> I look back with [wonder] at the courage of my father and mother when they came to America around the turn of the century; imagine, arriving after weeks in a crowded steerage of a coal-burning ship to pass through the confusion and turmoil of Ellis Island and then to find yourself in the Goldina Medina, the streets supposedly paved with gold, and to stand alone, unable to read the signs, to speak the language—from the village mud of Russia to New York and Detroit, skyscrapers and automobiles and the intensity of determined people. My mother did not know

how to ask for a glass of water. My father has never seen a banana before. . . . But they had fled, underground, from . . . the villages, from the pogroms . . . from ragged poverty. The raging desire of the immigrants in those years was for a better life, meaning freedom. Just to live in peace—at least that.[7]

Similar notions emerge from Franz Boas's account about why he left his homeland and came to the United States. As the father of American anthropology stated,

Why did I want to leave Germany in 1885 and come to America? Well, I wanted to get married. But there was much more behind it: the anti-Semitism during my university years, and the idea that America was politically an ideal country was the main motif.[8]

Thus Boas, like many millions of other immigrants, also believed in these ideals. Nevertheless, these lofty, noble notions and the realities of daily life and politics that the immigrants found were often in stark contradiction and conflict as they are today. For that matter, around 1910 the United States was seriously considering whether all the European emigrants should be allowed to enter. During that rabidly xenophobic period, Boas was trying to affect U.S. immigration policies with his scientific work. He was employed by a Senate-appointed commission that was to investigate which European populations were acceptable and which were less so. He used different instruments and measured various body parts of numerous immigrants and their American-born offspring. (As George Stocking points out, with this investigation he supplied the foundation for an important branch of physical anthropology that was to develop later.) In his report to the commission Boas stressed that

investigation of a large number of families shows that the makeup of man may be considerably influenced by social and geographic environment, rather than by race. . . . The old idea of absolute

7. Jack LaZebnik, excerpt from the dedication of his play, *Sam and Itkeh: A Story of Immigrants, of Love and Old Age, Life and Death* (1989).

8. George Stocking, Jr., *The Shaping of American Anthropology, 1883–1911: A Franz Boas Reader* (New York: Basic Books, 1974).

stability must be given up and along with it the belief in the hereditary superiority of some people over others . . .[9]

But Boas's objections and reasoning against the quota system and other restrictive measures in immigration policies were ignored. Yet as Stocking suggests,

"[Boas] introduced a new way of looking: he was the first one to minimize the effects of race and the validity of the race concept, and he believed that science can solve important social and political problems. But just how much actual impact did Boas have on American immigration policies, how successful was he in this reespect? Not very. Not until the triumph of Hitler and his Nazi racist philosophy was the Boasian perspective on race a bit more accepted officially, primarily, one suspects, because it then was more in accord with American domestic and foreign policies . . .[10]

The immigrants of the period faced not only poor working conditions, long hours, low wages, and industrial accidents, but also a generally antagonistic host society.[11] To get an idea of prevailing social attitudes we must briefly look at three prominent ideologies—Anglo-Saxon conformity, the melting pot, and cultural pluralism[12]—by which politicians and scholars attempted to define, analyze, and forecast the status and future of new immigrants in the social fabric.

Proponents of Anglo-Saxon conformity assumed an inherent superiority in the English language and in traditional Anglo-Saxon Protestant culture and institutions. They professed that all immigrants would inevitably shed their foreign ways and readily adopt the host society's values and lifestyle. Assimilation was the leitmotif in this ideology. It was presumed that in a progressive and linear process im-

---

9. Ibid.

10. Ibid.

11. Barton, *Peasants & Strangers.* Thernstrom, *Harvard Encyclopedia of American Ethnic Groups.*

12. For more detail and references for the following discussion, see my essay, entitled "Bevándorlók az Egyesült Államokban: kutatási irányok és eredmények az amerikai társadalomtudományokban" (Immigrants in the United States: research directions and achievements in American behavioral sciences) *Ethnográphia* 95, no. 1 (1984): 151–60.

migrants would assimilate into U.S. society. The result of the process would be the eventual disappearance of strange foreign customs, the enthusiastic adherence to Anglo-Saxon traditions; and total acceptance of the assimilated immigrants and their offspring by the host society.

Then, around the turn of this century the theme of the melting pot emerged, or, rather, *re-emerged*. Politicians, scholars, and writers began to perceive the United States as a sort of gigantic cauldron and predicted that, in time, the various immigrant groups would merge with one another and with members of the host society. The "prodigal harvest" of this biological, social, and cultural union was projected to be a strong, rich, and singular society: those who envisioned this hybrid genesis prognosticated a powerful, homogeneous new race.

As I have stressed, the melting pot theory *re-emerged* at around the turn of the century. It was first introduced by the French-born Jean de Crevecour who joyously reported as early as 1756 that "here in America individuals of all nations are melted into a new race of men, whose labor and posterity will one day cause great changes in the world."[13] This implied metaphor with all its industrial connotations became part of American English after 1908 when Israel Zangwill's play "The Melting Pot" began its sustained and triumphant run on Broadway. The central character in the play writes a symphony to represent a nation that is a crucible first for all groups to dissolve into and then in which a unique, superior stock is produced.

An extremely graphic enactment of the melting pot phenomenon was performed by Ford Motor Company workers and school children in Detroit during the early years of this century. The workers and children, clad first in their traditional national costumes and carrying their respective national flags, entered a huge cardboard cauldron on stage. After the pot was stirred, it crackled, sputtered, and bubbled over. Finally, "the new Americans" appeared, waving U.S. flags and singing "God Bless America." The workers were clothed in matching Ford plant uniforms, while the children were garbed in identical school clothes.[14]

---

13. Cited by anthropologists Howard Stein and Robert Hill, *The Ethnic Imperative* (University Park: Pennsylvania State University Press, 1977), 59.

14. These vivid images are depicted and examined in Michael Novak's controversial work *The Rise of the Unmeltable Ethnics: Politics and Culture in the Seventies* (New York: Macmillan, 1972), 139 ff.

Both of these pervasive ideologies—Anglo-Saxon conformity and the melting pot—must be seen in their historical and social context. Indeed, their images emerged, or were rekindled at a time of unprecedented social transformation, economic expansion, industrialization, and rapid urbanization in the United States. Clearly, there was a great demand and need for labor, which openend up the ports for millions of these Southern and Eastern Europeans, but—unlike the popular and still frequently cited myth has it, that American Society always welcomes the "homeless and storm-tossed huddled masses"—members of the core culture not only feared the millions of "strange foreigners" from Eastern and Southern Europe, but considered them racially, culturally, and intellectually inferior as well. These fears are reflected by a number of political measures and mirrored by the notions of Anglo conformity and the melting pot. In fact, the newcomers were rejected by the mainstream society. Both schools of thought were "scientific attempts" to alleviate the fear of foreigners, although there were differences between the two. The first, Anglo-Saxon conformity, emphasized the inevitability of total assimilation *into* the dominant and allegedly superior culture, while advocates of the melting pot theory stressed the immigrants' amalgamation *with* the host society. Thus inherent in both is the promise of the imminent disappearance of feared and hated "foreignness," the total elimination of cultural differences, and the hope for an "unmixed, pure, and superior" culture and society that were free of alien remnants.

Finally, during the second decade of the twentieth century Horace Kallen argued for cultural pluralism in his essay, "Democracy vs. the Melting Pot" while he described his vision of a multiracial, multicultural society in which discrimination, prejudice, and economic inequality were absent.[15]

While *melting pot* (and presumably all the phrase implies) appears to be a still frequently used, integral component of American English, Kallen's thesis has been the subject of considerable scholarly debate. In the 1960s Glazer and Moynihan categorically asserted that the "point about the Melting Pot is ... that it did not happen ... "[16]

15. In addition to Kallen's early work, see the essays by Novak "Pluralism: A humanistic perspective" and Michael Walzer "Pluralism: A political perspective," in Thernstrom, *American Ethnic Groups,* 772–81 and 781–87, respectively.
16. Nathan Glazer and Daniel Moynihan, *Beyond the Melting Pot: The Negroes, Puerto*

Since the late 1960s, instead of explicitly focusing on the imminent disappearance of differences among various immigrant and ethnic groups, politicians pay careful attention to cultural and other differences as they are busy courting the so-called ethnic vote. And scholars are concentrating on the maintenance of social boundaries and the perpetuation of cultural and linguistic variation; on the metamorphosis from immigrant to ethnic; on ethnic identities and the social and cultural consequences of long-term ethnic group persistence. At least in these circles, *melting pot* was replaced with new metaphors—salad bowl, stew, mosaic, and so on—that fit a cultural pluralistic model. At the same time, in some political and academic circles but not necessarily in the popular realms, the emphasis shifted from assimilation to acculturation. While both concepts deal with culture contact, assimilation implies total absorption of one culture into another (usually the dominant majority culture absorbs the dominated minority one), but acculturation suggests that one culture, selectively it is presumed, takes on chosen aspects of another culture while retaining its integrity. While the picture is considerably more complex than my brief and necessarily reduced discussion implies, and the cultural ideology regarding immigrants and immigration is still quite a distance from the social reality faced by today's immigrants and ethnics, in some respects we did come a long way since the "new immigrants."

Surely, related struggles with identity, culture, and marginality add to and confound the multilevelled dilemmas of ethnic groups. Identity, or the sense of self, is social and relational: our sense of who we are depends on and is the consequence of belonging to a society and participating in its culture. It is not at all surprising that an immigrant scholar, Erik Erikson, fathered the concept of identity in the social sciences and stressed its vital, strategic importance. He recognized in 1950 that

> we begin to conceptualize matters of identity at the very time in history when they become a problem. For we do so in a country

---

Ricans, Jews, Italians, and Irish of New York City (Cambridge: MIT and Harvard University Press, 1963). Also see W. H. Auden's "America is not a Melting Pot!" *New York Times Magazine,* March 18, 1972; and Novak, *Unmeltable Ethnics.*

which attempts to make a super identity out of all the identities imported by its constituent immigrants . . . [17]

From the moment of arrival in the United States immigrants combat identity-related confusion, starting with the perplexing problem of labeling and being labelled and continuing with the process of transformation from an immigrant to an ethnic to a member of an ethnic group in this complex, pluralistic society. Associated with the question of identity in the immigrant and ethnic experience are the problems of marginality and that of culture, that carefully constructed, shared web of meaning.

More specifically, what happened to the cultural concepts of those Southern and Eastern European peasants who left their traditional, familiar, rural-agrarian environment and entered a sphere that was modern, unfamiliar, and urban-industrial? What happened to their notions of time, ideas of place, continuity, belonging, love, parenthood, family? Certainly a key question of the ethnic group dilemma has to do with the cultural baggage immigrants bring with them. How do they maintain the appropriateness, relevance, and viability of cultural elements in the new environment? I am paraphrasing a student of American slavery when I ask: how do immigrants retain or reproduce a viable culture that continues to be meaningful to them in a world that labels their language, speech pattern, and accent odd, their food and smell weird, their clothes and the way they cover or do not cover their heads outlandish, their manner of walking and sitting grotesque, their greeting and gesticulating bizarre, their rituals, beliefs, and customs absurd? Here it is worthy to recall Margaret Mead's mocking remarks about an American identity. She commented that being an American means to refrain from foreign ways, foreign foods, foreign clothes, foreign accents, and so on.[18] In other words, how to retain a veritable culture in a world that detests and rejects the most salient elements of the very culture in question.

While it is obviously not a panacea, the construction, maintenance, and perpetuation of immigrant communities help in the

---

17. Erik Erikson, *Childhood and Society* (New York: Norton, 1950), 282.

18. Margaret Mead, "Ethnicity and Anthropology" in *Ethnic Identity: Cultural Continuity and Change,* ed. George DeVos and Lola Romanucci-Ross (Palo Alto: Mayfield, 1975), 173–97.

dilemma of being suspended between different worlds, between two cultures. Using selected elements of their cultural baggage, the immigrants created their distinctive cultures from which they derived their particular identities and they constructed immigrant and ethnic communities from which they validated and articulated these identities.[19]

At the beginning, particularly in the temporary phase that was migrant laborer-like, the immigrant community was frequently a simple construct, but with complex, multiple functions. For example, in 1901, as the widow of a bar's proprietor revealed,

> there was no center for the Hungarians of Delray. Our saloon was everything, all in one. . . . We did all kinds of business besides selling liquor. We made the place homelike and lots of single men ate at our saloon. We had a kind of a bank too. . . . The people brought us their money to deposit for them. We remitted money to Europe. . . . We sold steamship tickets and real estate. If the people wanted to have a meeting, they held it in the hall over our saloon. We conducted a sort of a general merchandise store right there in the saloon also.[20]

Then, with the growth and subsequent crystallization of a particular population, the ethnic community became increasingly more complex. There were mushrooming voluntary associations, churches, cultural centers, newspapers, radio programs, clubs, and ethnic enterprises. While in their structures and foci immigrant communities were quite unlike the natal village communities in the old country,[21] they

---

19. See Linda Dégh, "Survival and Revival of European Folk Cultures in America" in *Ethnologia Europaea* 2–3 (1968–69): 97–107.

20. Cited in Erdmann Beynon, "The Hungarians of Michigan" in *Occupational Adjustment of Hungarian Immigrants* (Ph.D. diss., University of Michigan, 1933), 12.

21. For a few selected examples of immigrant communities and their many functions see Dégh, "Folk Cultures"; Linda Dégh, "The ethnicity of Hungarian Americans" in *Congressus Internationalis Fenno Ugristarium* (Turku: Suomen Kielen Seura, 1980), 255–90; Linda Dégh, "Dial a Story, Dial an Audience: Two Women Narrators in an Urban Setting" in *Women's Folklore, Women's Culture,* ed. Jordan A. Rosan and Susan Kalchik (Philadelphia: University of Pennsylvania, 1985) 3–25; Éva V. Huseby-Darvas, "Immigrant Women as Agents of Continuity in the Hungarian-American Community of Delray" n.d., typescript; Éva V. Huseby-Darvas, "Migrating Inward and Out: Validating Life-Course Transitions through Oral Autobiography" in *Life History as Cultural Construction/Performance* (Budapest: The Ethnographic Institute of the Hungarian Academy of Sciences), 379–409; Éva V. Huseby-Darvas, "'Wednesday Hungarians' and Csiga-noodlemaking in Southeast Michigan" in *The Digest: A Review for the Interdisciplinary Study of the Uses of Food* ed. Yvonne Lockwood and William Lockwood, 9, no. 2: 4–8.

worked, and served a number of crucial functions. Indeed, by being instrumental in the social validation of a new ethnic identity and the articulation of ethnic culture they helped in diminishing the sense of alienation, marginalization and related ethnic dilemmas.

The Early Arab Immigrant Experience

Alixa Naff

Arabic-speaking people began emigrating from the Ottoman province of Syria, which included the administrative district of Mount Lebanon, to the United States in sufficient numbers to form communities in the last quarter of the nineteenth century. Like the millions who left their homes in Europe, they were drawn to the New World by the changing character of the United States in that period. While huge tracts of land remained to be cultivated in the West and Southwest, agrarian interests began to compete with burgeoning industrial interests in the East. Among other problems, both interests faced mounting labor shortages.

Even though their numbers were small relative to the large European groups, distinct Syrian communities were identifiable by the midnineties. In the next ten or fifteen years, these communities would proliferate throughout the nation—the result of pack peddling which became the immigrant occupation of most Syrians.

Arabic-speaking immigrants, now estimated at roughly 2 million, arrived in the United States in two major waves. The first, or pre–World War II wave, is distinguished from the second, or post–World War II wave, in a number of ways. The first wave overwhelmingly consisted of unsophisticated village farmers or artisans; they were relatively poor but not destitute and they were not well schooled, if at all. The initial aspirations of these pioneers who emigrated before about 1910 did not exceed the hope of earning as much money in as short a time as possible and returning home wealthier and prouder. The second wave had, and continues to have, a very large component of educated, bilingual, politicized, and nationalistic emigrants. Having originated in numerous Arab nations that gained their independence in the aftermath of World War II, members of this second wave identified themselves as Arabs. The United States they sought had filled its borders, experienced two world wars, and become the world's leading industrial, scientific, technological, and military power; thus, this second wave experienced a radically different immigration experience than their Syrian predecessors.

How many Syrians emigrated to the United States before World War II? How many were Christians and how many Muslims and Druze? From which strata of their society were they drawn? How many were skilled, how many were literate? All these questions have no reliable answers. Fragments of information provided by the immigrants themselves merely confound estimates in published sources and cast doubt on official data.

Immigration and census statistics are unreliable for several reasons. For example, before 1899, immigrants from the Eastern Mediterranean were recorded as arriving from "Turkey in Asia." Moreover, classification of immigrants by the Bureau of Immigration did not include religion or national identity. Emigrating, as the Syrians did, from a multinational empire where country of origin did not correspond with national identity and where the latter was as much determined by religion as by language and culture, Syrians were not distinguished from other Ottoman subjects.

However, in 1899, when immigration officials became aware that most of these Ottoman subjects were from Syria, they added a "Syrian" classification. This gave the Arabic-speaking immigrants a way of identifying themselves in a land teaming with immigrants from different ethnic origins. By World War I official statistics show that about 100,000 immigrated and by World War II, immigrants and their descendants numbered about 206,000.[1]

Lacking accurate data that would identify immigrants by faith, scholars estimate that 90 to 95 percent of the pre–World War II Syrian

---

1. For further details on the problems involved in the use of statistical data on Syrian immigrants, see Alixa Naff, *Becoming American: The Early Arab Immigrant Experience* (Carbondale, Ill.: Southern Illinois University Press, 1985), 107–17.

immigrants were Christians from Mount Lebanon. The rest were Muslims and Druze. The latter were so few that they hardly warranted passing mention in the literature on Syrians at the turn of the century.[2] Among them were a few thousand Palestinians.

In the United States most of these immigrants, including many Palestinians, called themselves and were referred to as Syrians until the independence of Syria and Lebanon after World War II. Rarely in their homeland would they have had to refer to themselves as Syrians; even more rarely as Arabs although they were proud of being Arab and of their Arab heritage. The Syrian and Arab references were cultural rather than nationalistic since there was no independent Syrian political entity to which nationalism could be tied. An incipient political component appeared in the identity of some Christians from Mount Lebanon after France established itself as the mandatory power over Ottoman Syria in 1920. Immigrants and their descendants debated whether to call themselves Syrian-American or Lebanese-American.

The most meaningful and reflexive identity factors which Syrians used among themselves were family name, religion, and place of origin—factors that were a source of factionalization and community fragmentation in the homeland as well as the new land. How the Syrians identified themselves in the United States, however, did not seem to interfere with their ability to assimilate.

Migration

Historians generally agree that in the late nineteenth century, Mount Lebanon was not a place to flee from. In the words of Albert H. Hourani, the period from 1861 to 1915 was "a period of increasing prosperity."[3] Philip K. Hitti, a native of Lebanon, noted that the people of Mount Lebanon "enjoyed a period of cultural flourish and economic prosperity and achieved a state of security and stability unattained by any Ottoman province, European or Asian. . . . It came

---

2. For example, Lucius Hopkins Miller, *Our Syrian Population: A Study of the Syrian Communities of Greater New York* (n.p., ca. 1904); Louise Seymour Houghton, "Syrians in the United States," pts. 1–3 *Survey* 26 (July, Aug., Sept. 1911), pt. 4, *Survey* 27 (Oct. 1911); and Philip K. Hitti, *Syrians in America* (New York: George Doran, 1924).

3. *Syria and Lebanon: A Political Essay* (London: Oxford University Press, 1954), 33.

to be acknowledged as the best governed, the most prosperous, peaceful and contented country in the Near East."[4] Moreover, it enjoyed a great deal of autonomy relative to its neighbors. If there were any push factors affecting Syrian emigration, they were more evident in the harsher political and economic conditions in Syria proper. Nevertheless, far fewer emigrants, even Christians, left Syrian villages and towns.

In fact, the immigrants were attracted to the United States by its accelerating urbanization and industrialization, which required a greater work force than was available in their country in the last quarter of the nineteenth century. Labor, therefore, was recruited from abroad by agents of industry, steamship lines, and even by the less populated western states and territories. As a result, millions of immigrants flooded to the country triggering a virulent anti-alien movement before and especially after World War I. In response, Congress passed a series of restrictive immigration laws culminating in the Johnson-Reed Act of 1924. Syrian immigration under this quota system was restricted to 100 annually until the repeal of the act in 1965.

The most reliable data on what triggered a mass migration of Syrians to the United States is the testimony of turn-of-the-century immigrants in interviews conducted in numerous communities in the United States and Canada.[5] Almost unanimously, they stated that they came on a two- or three-year sojourn to make money and return to the homeland, where most had left their families, lead better lives, and elevate their family status. They did not, they said, leave because of religious persecution or economic oppression. At that time, those who came in search of the lofty ideals of liberty and democracy were the rare exceptions.

Later, the pioneers would be joined by others. While making money continued to be the dominant attraction, some came because of personal problems at home or to escape military conscription or

---

4. *Lebanon in History* (New York: Macmillan, 1967), 447. See also A. Ruppin, "Syrien als Wirschaftsgebiet," in *The Economic History of the Middle East: 1800–1914* ed. Charles Issawi (Chicago: University of Chicago Press, 1966), 272; and Dominique Chevalier, "Western Development and Eastern Crisis," in *Beginnings of Modernization in the Middle East: The Nineteenth Century* ed. William R. Polk and Richard L. Chambers (Chicago: The University of Chicago Press, 1968), 220.

5. Conducted by Alixa Naff during a major research project on Arab-Americans, 1962 and 1980, under a grant from the National Endowment for the Humanities and included in the Arab-American Collection, Smithsonian Institution.

simply to join relatives. After World War I, they migrated because of the hardships, especially famine, which they had endured during the war.

The Immigrants

The way to the United States was opened by tradesmen and artisans who were encouraged to exhibit their wares at the Philadelphia Centennial Exposition in 1876 by the Ottoman Sultan, Abdul Hamid II, a trade-minded reform tyrant. Perhaps it was these trailblazers who returned to spread the word of easy wealth or "gold in the streets." Soon glowing letters from early adventurers describing undreamed-of wealth began to draw more immigrants. The exodus was further fueled by returning villagers in serge suits and shined leather shoes, sporting gold watch fobs. Faris N., after talking with visiting cousins and learning how much could be earned in trade, left with thirty-one men and two women in 1895. That same year Mike H. left his village with seventy-two friends and relatives. Similarly large groups left from other villages, inviting the comparison with a gold rush.

The pioneers were mainly young, single, and adventurous men. Some single women and some married men and women joined them. More often than not, the men, farmers and their sons, had to augment the family income by engaging in some kind of craft or trade. It was not uncommon for a family, who considered the costs of the voyage as an investment, to borrow money or to mortgage land to send a member or two to fulfill its dream of greater wealth and status.

In America

When villagers began to stream into the Syrian port cities of Beirut and Tripoli, there emerged a host of entrepreneurial and often unscrupulous agents to book steamship passage for the unsophisticated travelers who thought they were headed for New York or at least the United States. Many, instead, found themselves in Canada, South and Central America, the Caribbean, and even Australia. Many of them smuggled themselves across Mexican and Canadian borders, making it further difficult to generate accurate demographic data.

New York and the other ports of entry through which the Syrians entered the United States were merely gateways. Generally, they knew their specific destination and what they were going to do when they arrived there. They were going to pack-peddle merchandise from door to door in towns and cities and from farmhouse to farmhouse in the countryside. They pursued its get-rich-quick potential all over the United States. It was the major magnet that drew Syrian immigrants before about 1910. By that year, they had penetrated every state and territory of the country.[6] They covered the American continent in a network of peddling routes which radiated from a network of peddling settlements. Those few who eschewed peddling because they found it too difficult or too demeaning joined the labor force.

Settlements formed around a supplier—generally a veteran peddler who decided to settle down in a well-chosen location. He would then recruit peddlers from his village or from nearby villages. Kin drew kin and villager drew villager so that immigrants were able to group themselves by kinship, religion, sect, or place of origin as they had in the homeland. Subnetworks of settlements whose members were mainly from one village can be traced across more than one state. Immigrants of the Druze faith, an offshoot of Shia Islam, had one or two subnetworks of their own.

A peddling settlement was an open and fluid community. That is, peddlers came and went as their self-interest dictated. The supplier's settlement was the peddlers' home base and the supplier their acknowledged leader by virtue of their dependence on him. Yet no special title was attached to him; no abject obedience was demanded. He not only supplied merchandise to the peddler on credit, but guaranteed credit to uncapitalized recruits to induce them to come to him. He received their mail, banked their money, even frequently godfathered their children. He also served as liaison between them and the host community. The good relations between supplier and peddler were based on the canons of tradition and on mutual economic self-interest.

In the settlements the immigrants were taught the rudiments and tricks of the trade by friends and relatives. For example, they were taught the value of U.S. currency and how to address a woman who answered their knock. "Buy sumthin', Maam" was probably the first

---

6. *Reports of the Immigration Commission,* vol. 3, *Statistical Review of Immigration, 1820–1910* (Washington, D.C., 1911), table 27, "Destination of Immigrants Admitted to the United States, Fiscal Year 1899 to 1910, Inclusive, by Race of People," 269–92.

English sentence they learned. They also learned how to ask for a place to sleep and some food when they were in the countryside. In general, they initially learned how to survive with only a rudimentary knowledge of the language and customs of the country. Consequently, newcomers could start to earn a living almost on arrival. As a near replica of the village, peddlers would return to the settlements to revitalize their spirits after weeks or months on the road.

Immigrants were attracted to peddling because initially it required no capital, advanced training, or English-language skills. Moreover, it suited the Arabs' individualist nature and the immigrants' impermanence. Most important, it yielded quicker wealth than they had hoped for.

Peddling was the most fundamental factor in their assimilation for several reasons. It forced them to learn English quickly because learning English was critical to their success; and success, driven by the age-old native competition for family honor and status, was, in the final analysis, the engine that drove Syrians toward their goal in the United States. Peddling further enabled them to see the country and experience its way of life firsthand. It took them into U.S. homes and raised their aspirations. It spared them the uncertainty of finding factory work, standing in long job lines, and industrial layoffs. It spared them, too, a ghetto mentality. Finally, it provided opportunities for thousands of newcomers.

Peddlers were mobile department stores, even when they peddled on foot as most did at first. With well-packed suitcases, frequently one in each hand and one on their back, they carried almost anything a housebound urban housewife or isolated farmwife would need or desire. There were ready-made school clothes, men's work clothes, yard goods, linens, towelling, costume jewelry, and much more. There were also such special items as laces, doilies, crocheted tablecloths, embroidered bedspreads, and ribbon-decked dusting caps frequently made by the women in the peddler's family in a kind of settlement cottage industry.

In the notions case, which was the peddlers' primer and constant companion, were all the kinds of notions one would find at a Woolworth's notions counter plus icons, frames, rosaries, etc. If the peddlers' hands were full, the notions case dangled on his chest.

Some peddlers covered half a continent on foot and remained away from the settlment for months; others returned in a week or two, while usually, but not always, women and children remained closer to the settlement.

Peddling was a hazardous occupation. These villagers, accustomed as they were to hardships in their villages, never reckoned on what they would encounter on the road in the United States. Their hardships are preserved in a body of humorous anecdotes that glorify cunning and ingenuity, and which acted as a psychological safety valve for their fear, fatigue, and frustration when they told them to each other. Many of the anecdotes deal with the hardships of climate, lack of knowledge of the language, and the difficulties of finding lodging. They tell about frozen extremities, parched throats, relentless heat; of being mired in mud, robbed, beaten; of killings and being lost; and of being chased by farmers with guns and dogs. "How do you tell a dog to go away if it doesn't understand Arabic?" complained an informant. One peddler, articulating the consensus, said that he "endured a lot" but enjoyed this country and he was "free to make money."

Peddlers did indeed make money. As a whole, they averaged $1,000 annually when the U.S. labor force was averaging about $650 annually. High earnings and unrelenting frugality allowed them to send remittances home, pay debts, and buy fares to bring other family members to the United States. They contributed to U.S. commerce by expanding the market of small industry products to the most remote areas of the country.

By about 1910, peddling declined as an immigrant occupation. Immigrants had outgrown it, and its services to U.S. consumers were replaced by proliferating department stores and mail-order houses such as Montgomery Ward and Sears Roebuck.

Becoming "American"

When immigrants decided to settle down and make the United States their permanent home, they adhered to the cherished cultural ideal of being in business for one's self. They turned to family businesses in which the whole family participated, even the young. Usually, the home and the store were a staircase or a door apart. Dry goods and grocery stores were most popular, but businesses ran the gamut from banking and wholesaling and manufacturing to movie houses, pool rooms, confectionery stores, and dry cleaning. With little or no experience in most of these endeavors, failure was common but not daunting. They simply kept trying until they succeeded.

Many immigrants who arrived in the period of peddling's obsolescence and afterward in the 1920s entered the labor force. They were attracted by industry's payment of five dollars for an eight-hour day, which was initiated during the war by the Ford Motor Company and adopted by other manufacturers. This innovation coincided with the influx of Syrian Muslims. Yet many of the men who worked on assembly lines also opened stores which were operated by their women relatives and children.

The Americanization process advanced most rapidly after World War I. Settlements, generally located in ethnically mixed low-income neighborhoods, ultimately matured into stable communities as immigrants bought homes and acquired middle-class symbols such as home appliances and cars. In general, they followed the middle-class path up the economic and social ladder. Moreover, they adopted the respective regional social attitudes, tastes, and accents and became New Englanders, Southerners, Midwesterners, etc.

The ethnic institutions which they established—churches, an Arabic-language press, and voluntary associations—not unexpectedly reflected the traditional identity factors and perpetuated the traditional community fragmentation. The first churches were of the Eastern-rite faiths. Most prominent among them were the Maronite, Melkite, and Eastern Orthodox. There was also a Syrian Protestant church. These were built in the early 1890s in New York City which was the Syrian mother colony and the cultural and economic center. Churches increased slowly and unevenly across the country in the next half century. Nevertheless, vast areas were, and remain, unserved. Syrians in these areas, therefore, attended "American" churches, that is, Roman Catholic and Protestant. This accounts, in large part, for the relatively high percentage of mixed marriages before and after World War I. Syrian identity in these households, even more so in those of their descendants, was consequently diluted.

The accelerating assimilation of Syrians reduced attendance at all Eastern-rite churches. In order to arrest the defection, to reach the nonspeaking offspring, and to perpetuate the unity of the subgroup, the leaders acknowledged the inevitable. Liturgies were anglicized and shortened, chants were westernized, and choirs replaced cantors.

Americanization of the Maronite and Melkite churches had begun very early because, as affiliates of the Roman Catholic church, they came under the administrative authority of the church in the United States. Consequently, Maronite and Melkite churches served by their own clergy spread very slowly until their independence from Roman Catholic authority after World War II.

On the other hand, the Eastern Orthodox church turned for guidance in the United States to the Russian Orthodox archdiocese. The latter, in turn, ordained the first Syrian bishop in the United States. A year after his ordination in 1904, he established a cathedral in Brooklyn. Under his leadership, Orthodox churches increased and many adherents returned to their native faith.

Only in four Muslim communities were mosques known to have been built before World War II. Yet Muslims fulfilled their spiritual obligations without fear of perdition. For Muslims, any uncontaminated place at home or work could be a place to pray. Both Muslims and Druze immigrants could compensate for lack of consecrated religious institutions by gathering for prayer, reading from holy books, discussing religion, or celebrating religious festivals.

The traditional identity factors prevailed in the Arabic-language press and in the formation of clubs and societies. It was in the United States that Syrians learned to organize around a common purpose or cause. They developed such a propensity for it that at any given time, the number of organizations was out of proportion to the number of Syrians in the United States. Most, of course, were short-lived.

Family, religious, and village social clubs proliferated in part to counter the rate of mixed marriages and to maintain the continuity of the subgroup. If these clubs had a central and common theme, it was the underlying one of group solidarity mainly through in-group marriage. They tended, therefore, to be exclusivist. Attempts by the U.S.-born Syrians to change this divisive custom succeeded only after World War II.

Homeland politics played little or no part in the formation of clubs until the French mandatory rule replaced the defunct Ottoman Empire in the former Syrian province in 1920. It was not so much that political clubs multiplied at any noticeably high rate as that the social clubs became embroiled in an identity controversy. France triggered the controversy by granting increased autonomy to the Lebanese, favoring Christian (and particularly Maronite) domination, and laying the foundation for the modern independent state of Lebanon by expanding its territory from Syrian lands, including major port cities. With kin pitted against kin and friend against friend, clubs hotly debated whether to call themselves Syrian- or Lebanese-American. Maronites formed Phoenician clubs in an effort to tie themselves historically to that ancient civilization and to distance themselves and Lebanon from Arab Syria and from Muslims whose larger population threatened Maronite domination.

An active and highly competitive Arabic-language press was centered in New York City. The impetus for its development was provided by the immigration of a few intellectuals who were graduates, for the most part, of religious and secular schools of higher education in the cities of Syria. It was coincidental and fortuitous that in New York the publishers of newspapers and journals, many of whom had had little or no prior journalistic training or experience, came together with émigré Arab writers and poets in a symbiotic relationship to form an immigrant intelligentsia.

The Syrian penchant for publishing matched their penchant for organizing clubs and societies. Dailies, weeklies, and monthlies appeared and disappeared regularly between 1892 and 1930. Yet the press was influential and contributed significantly to the Americanization process. From its inception it explained the U.S. social, economic, and political life to its eager readers, albeit in fairly simple and idealized terms. It tied success to becoming "American", and encouraged and taught good citizenship. In addition, it kept immigrants informed about events in the homeland. Many Syrian immigrants became informed, for the first time, about the society, politics, history, literature, and culture of Arabs in general and Syrians in particular. Never before had these predominantly village centered, poorly schooled readers learned so much about their heritage even though it was filtered through sectarian biases. Having befriended the intellectuals, Syrian publishers from the start used the pages of their publications to launch, test, and advance the early literary output of a school of modern Arabic literature in the United States which was to revolutionize age-old Arabic literary forms.

Only three of several influential newspapers survived into the post–World War II period. *Al-Hoda,* published six years after *Kawkab Amrika,* the first Arabic-language newspaper, appeared in 1898 and spoke for the Maronite community. *Meraat al-Gharb,* the voice of the Syrian Orthodox and of anti-Ottoman Arab nationalists, was launched in 1899 to oppose what its publisher considered to be the political and religious biases of *Al-Hoda. Al-Bayan,* not published until 1911, spoke for the Druze and Muslim community although it was started by a Druze.

To its own detriment, the Arabic press, for all its complaints against fragmentation of the community, succeeded, in effect, in exacerbating the divisions. Moreover, by establishing itself on a sectarian basis, its respective publications did not address themselves objectively to the interests of the broad readership, thus limiting that readership.

The appearance in 1926 of *The Syrian World,* a monthly opinion and literary journal in English, signified the publisher's recognition of the end of an era as well as a crisis in the use of Arabic. It was aimed at the U.S.-born generation which could not read Arabic, the generation that the publisher, Salloum Mokarzel, called the Syrian-American generation. The immigration quota act limited the entry of Arabic readers and speakers at the same time that the accelerated Americanization process was eroding the use of Arabic. English increasingly replaced the native language in the homes and at the social functions of immigrants and those of their married children. Attempts by community leaders to teach Arabic to their offspring who were products of U.S. schools and ardent consumers of such innovations as moving pictures and radio programs were defeated by the pace of assimilation. The usefulness of Arabic publications, therefore, declined, as did their numbers.

The impact of the Americanization process was most evident in the family and most significantly in the role of women. Women gained greater self-confidence and a sense of independence as they assumed responsibilities traditionally performed by the patriarch of the household. Their increased participation in the economic welfare of the family as well as in more disciplinary and decision-making responsibilities led to the gradual eroding of traditional social restrictions on women—mainly in the Christian community.

Rapid Americanization did not, however, prevent parents from inculcating their children with an important and, it seems, ineradicable set of traditional values. Most notably among them were strong family units, upholding the family honor, improving its status, and adhering to the family's religious beliefs. These core values drove the

Syrians to achieve their primary goal in the U.S. and gave rise to
corollary values which proved to be compatible with the most cherished U.S. values: self-denial, thrift, initiative, perseverance, individualist attitudes, and a strong work ethic.

In their eagerness to succeed, the immigrant generation neglected
to preserve their cultural heritage. Much of what that generation
knew of their heritage was, in any case, centered on village life and
its mythology. About the great Arab-Islamic contributions to world
civilization the majority of the immigrants knew little, and what they
did know was selective and refracted through traditional biases.

This village view of Arab culture left immigrant children poorly
informed about their deeper historical roots. They knew little of the
kind of events that in other nations produced national heroes and
kindled ethnic and national pride. The void, therefore, was filled from
the well of American myth and history. As a further consequence,
the American-born and American-raised generations showed scant
interest in or knowledge of their ethnic origins. References to Arab
or Syrian culture were as remote as their parents' homeland. If the
political events in the post–World War II Arab World had not reactivated Arab immigration and provoked the descendants of the first
wave into an Arab identity, they might have assimilated themselves
out of existence.

Arab-Americans and the Political Process

Michael W. Suleiman

In this chapter, I will attempt to delineate the political identity of Arab-Americans from the time of their arrival in the United States over a century ago until the present. The term "political identity" refers to the views, attitudes, orientations, and affiliations of Arab-Americans as these related to the political process on all levels, whether local, regional, national, or international. The term "Arab-Americans" refers to the Arabic-speaking groups and individuals who emigrated to the United States and have settled in this country. Especially in the early period of their immigration to the United States, these people were referred to, and referred to themselves, as Syrians or Syrian-Lebanese.[1] More recently, they have been identified, and have identified themselves, as Arab-Americans. The use of terms like "Syrians," "Syrian-Lebanese," "Arabs," or "Arab-Americans" does not imply that these people constituted or that they now constitute a cohesive community. Indeed, the purpose of the chapter is to trace the development (or the setbacks) in the search for identity and a sense of community among the diverse elements of the group. However, these terms, as well as the word "community," will be used

---

1. However, there never was one specific name that was used exclusively and invariably to describe these Arabic-speaking Americans. It was not unusual for them to be called Arabs or "Arabians." See, for instance, "Arabian Colony," *Detroit Journal,* July 21, 1897, 3.

merely as shorthand references to the Arabic-speaking group, but with a definite effort at proper identification.

Knowledge of the political orientations and activities of the early Arab immigrants to the United States is sketchy at best, and incomplete or inaccurate much of the time. Conventional wisdom, based on oral interviews, secondary sources, and some personal accounts, presents a picture of a quiescent community that is either uninterested in politics or fearful of the consequences of a potential challenge to constituted authority—even in the free and democratic atmosphere of the U.S. arena. That picture is not completely accurate. However, a detailed accounting of the political activities of early Arab-Americans will be done in a later study. For now, a few tentative remarks will be offered based on a quick, though fairly extensive, review of primary sources.

1. From the 1870s to World War I, Arabs in the United States thought of themselves as in, but not part of, U.S. society and body politic.

2. Up to World War I, Arab immigrants in the United States were an itinerant, sojourner-type group whose members' primary concern was financial betterment, especially the quick accumulation of wealth for the purpose of assuring a comfortable life and high social status in the old country. Consequently, their involvement in U.S. society, other than in the workplace, was consciously and deliberately minimal, if not practically nonexistent. They called themselves *al-Nizaleh* (i.e., travelers or guests), or "Syrians" or "Ottomans"— all such terms indicating a temporary U.S. presence and/or noncitizen affiliation.

3. Up to World War I, politics among Arab-Americans reflected and emulated the politics of the original homeland in both substance and style. In other words, by and large, members of the group thought of themselves *and* acted not so much as citizens of the United States but rather as subjects of the Ottoman authorities in control of their homelands, the only difference being that they were temporarily away from that homeland.[2] While this was in and of itself a major difference, its full implications dawned on them only gradually and somewhat tentatively.[3] Furthermore, this startling awakening and the

---

2. As *Al-Hoda* wrote addressing its fellow "Syrians": "You remain settlers in a foreign land. Remember that you are Ottomans." May 23, 1899, 20.

3. A very good example of an attempt to educate the Arab-American community on

realization that they were, at the very least, not completely under the control of their former sovereigns began to substantially alter their relationship with the Ottoman authorities.

As is usually the case, however, the reaction of these pioneer Arab settlers was neither united nor uniform. It also varied over time. Thus, *Kawkab America,* the first Arabic-language newspaper established in the United States in 1892 to cater to the needs of the community, declared in its very first issue its unequivocal support for the Ottoman sultan whose exemplary virtues it enumerated at length and for whose good health and long life it earnestly prayed.[4] This was tremendous praise, indeed, especially coming from the Arbeely brothers, Najib and Ibrahim, whose family allegedly fled Syria to be spared the calumny and unbearable terror of the "terrible Turk."[5] Almost all other newspapers established after that had to define in one way or another their attitude toward (if not their relationship with) the Ottoman authorities. In a very real sense, they felt this to be mandatory if only because their readers, regardless of whether or not they had acquired U.S. citizenship, still thought of themselves as Syrians who were temporarily away from home, i.e., only temporarily away from their Ottoman rulers. Furthermore, they had to worry about potential reprisals against their relatives still in Syria— and against their own person if they ventured back for a visit.[6] Additionally, the Ottoman rulers had a large economic carrot stick which they could and did use to entice loyalty or punish opposition. Indeed, economic gain was the accusation used most often by the editors and publishers of the Arabic-language newspapers in the United States in their attempt to denigrate their opponents, or, by denying their own interest in economic gain, these same editors and publishers were able to assert their "Syrian" patriotism.

---

the values of freedom (including freedom of speech) in the United States, as opposed to tyranny under the Ottomans, may be found in an article entitled "What We Call a Crime, They Call a Virtue," *Al-Ayam,* March 29, 1900, 4–5.

   4. In fact, the Arbeely brothers had intended to begin publishing *Kawkab America* on "the birthday of our Great Sultan," but delays in the arrival of the Arabic printing press frustrated their plans. *Kawkab America,* April 15, 1892, 1, Arabic section. However, the Arbeelys went on to heap praise upon the Ottoman ruler: "Among all the Sultans who have sat upon the throne of the Ottoman Empire, none has achieved greater success in raising the Ottoman people to a higher position among the nations of the Earth, than the present 'Great Prince of the Faithful' Abdul-Hamid." Ibid., 1, English section.

   5. *New York Times,* Aug. 23, 1878, 8.

   6. *Al-Hoda,* May 23, 1899, 20.

While *Kawkab America* was pro-Ottoman at least initially (as no record of the newspaper is available after 1896), *Al-Ayam* was clearly and openly the most vehement opponent of the Ottoman authorities, a role it later shared with *Al-Mushir.* In its articles, signed and unsigned, its news reporting and its editorials, *Al-Ayam* hit hard against the cruelty, oppression, corruption, and overall villainy of the Ottoman rulers, both in Istanbul and in the Syrian provinces, especially Mount Lebanon. Furthermore, it called for rebellion and encouraged movements and individuals who were working for the overthrow of the Turkish tyrants. It also tirelessly reminded its readers of the fruits of freedom and urged them to exercise their rights in the United States to call for freedom and democracy in their original homeland. Other newspapers, including *Al-Hoda* and *Meraat-ul-Gharb,* fell in between the above two extremes of total support or extreme opposition and rejection of the Ottoman rulers.

The Arabic newspapers, as well as the books published by their printing presses, did not so much mold as *reflect* the attitudes and opinions of the Arabs in the United States. In other words, Arabic-speaking groups and individuals in the United States had multiple identities. Under such circumstances, many, if not most, merely allowed convenience and opportunity to dictate their actions, whether for or against the Ottomans. However, most of the time they kept their opinions to themselves for fear of unpleasant repercussions. In any case, either because their most salient convictions were sectarian or because they found in sectarianism an acceptable alternative to the dangers of open and clear political affiliations, most Arabs in the United States let their religious sects and their press speak for them.[7]

4. Up to World War I, Arabs in the United States found themselves in an anomalous and unenviable position. If European-Americans paid any attention to them at all, they considered them with a variety of pity, disdain, or total rejection. They were considered an inconvenience at best and a threat to the purity of the white race and U.S. moral and public order at worst.[8] Under such circumstances,

---

7. For a comment on the press and sectarianism, see "Our Newspapers," *Al-Hoda,* March 29, 1898, 4–6.

8. See, for instance, Edward Corsi, *In the Shadow of Liberty* (New York: Macmillan,

how did the *nizaleh* react? Again, there was no unanimity of response. Since the group's main objective, however, was survival under reasonable conditions, disagreements arose over how best to achieve this minimal objective.

One approach, which was dominant in the earlier period, was to go about one's business of making money with as little interaction as possible with European-Americans, in order to avoid any potentially embarrassing or threatening situations. In other words, members of the group were repeatedly reminded that they were guests in a foreign land and that they should be well-behaved in order not to irritate their hosts. In practice, this meant that they were to be law-abiding, to live a good moral life, to avoid having their women peddlers staying away from home overnight (since this activity almost invariably resulted in malicious gossip and was a source of shame and embarrassment for the community as a whole), to avoid overcharging or begging when they engaged in trade, and not to allow their communal fights to become violent, public, or such as to require police intervention. In sum, most of the injunctions were negative: "Don't do this; don't do that."

However, consciously or subconsciously, a more assimilationist approach began to gain favor and became the dominant orientation by World War I. The push for assimilation was neither elaborate nor ideological. It was merely a suggestion that Arabs should no longer feel like, or be, outsiders in the United States. Proponents of this approach suggested that the nizaleh should make a positive contribution to the United States in order to show gratitude for reaping the benefits of being in this country. Specifically, the Arab settlers were urged to volunteer in the U.S. armed forces to fight in Cuba (and later in the Philippines) in the Spanish-American war. Some even advocated the establishment of a Syrian regiment for this purpose.[9] By World War I, members of the Arab nizaleh showed their loyalty and commitment to the United States by joining the armed

---

1935), 265–66. On the question of racism toward foreigners, including those from the Arab region, see Paul W. McBride, *Culture Clash: Immigrants and Reformers, 1880–1920* (Saratoga, Calif.: R&E Research Associates, 1975).

9. See the various articles in the Arabic press, especially in *Al-Ayam* and especially by Gabriel E. Ward who also repeated these views in his book, *The Syrian Soldier in Three Wars* (New York: Syrian-American Press, 1919). In Arabic.

forces in very large numbers, estimated at about 7 percent of the whole community—and they were (and are) very proud of that achievement.[10]

5. Up to World War I, the main political activity of the Arab group was intersectarian and intracommunal. In other words, the competition was focused on a display of loyalty, pride, and glorification of one's sect, often combined with derision and vilification of leaders of other sects, particularly those sects viewed as large or strong enough to threaten the primacy of one's own sect. This competition manifested itself in different ways, depending on the circumstances. Thus, particularly in the early period, financial support of one's church constituted a major element of satisfaction and pride for community leaders. Another source of satisfaction was to compete with others in one's church by hosting visiting sect leaders, and to combine this with an ostentatious display of wealth and spending. In other words, the respect and support heaped upon religious leaders were not merely religious or sectarian but also—and sometimes more importantly—political. Thus, among the early Arab immigrants, sect was a substitute for and an embodiment of the community, country, *and* nation—and religious figures also doubled as community symbols and leaders of the nation. Not unlike politics in Mount Lebanon and later in the Republic of Lebanon, each sect was often divided into two main factions that vied for supremacy in that sect, and each sect competed and fought for a somewhat ill defined position of supremacy among all "Syrian" sects. Somewhat reminiscent of early Arabian tribes where each major tribe's poet glorified his own group and vilified all other competitors, the newspapers and printing presses of the early Arab immigrants imitated the role of tribal poets. Therefore, it was important that since *Kawkab America* was owned by a Greek Orthodox, *Al-Hoda* had to be established to cater to Maronites. Despite the best efforts of mediators and peacemakers, intra- and intersectarian competition could not be contained or controlled and resulted in factional fights, sometimes conducted with fists, knives, and even firearms.[11]

---

10. Ibid.; also see Philip K. Hitti, *The Syrians in America* (New York: George H. Doran, 1924), 102. In addition, see the very strong plea by Amin Rihani urging his fellow Arabs to join the U.S. forces in World War I, "To the Syrians in the Military," republished in *Sourakia,* March 5, 1990, 20–21.

11. Intersectarian squabbling was almost continuously reflected on the pages of the

6. World War I affected the Arab settlers in the United States in many ways. Thus, for all practical purposes, it cut off the group from its people in their homeland, and, consequently, intensified its members' sense of separation and isolation—and enhanced its sense of solidarity as a community. Furthermore, as is usual on such occasions, the U.S. media emphasized nationalism, patriotism, and military service in preparing the public for the United States' participation in the war in Europe—a war that was also fought against the hated Ottoman regime. These two elements greatly strengthened the assimilationist trend—a trend already much reinforced by the U.S.-born children of these Arab immigrants.

The separation from the old homeland became almost complete with the introduction of very restrictive immigration quota systems in the United States in the 1920s, which practically put an end to large numbers of new arrivals from "Syria," and established the size of the community.

After World War I, the Arabs in the United States became truly an Arab-*American* community, i.e., they realized that, much as many of them desired to go back, there was no "going home again." This does not mean that this decision was unanimously accepted or that it was accepted with equanimity. It does mean that serious thought was given to the idea of the United States becoming their permanent home—and what that entailed for them and their children.[12] In the area of politics the following activities and modifications were implemented or began to manifest themselves.

1. Factional conflicts (both intra- and intersectarian) became fewer in number and much less intense.

2. Calls for unity among the different elements of the community were heeded more often. They were no longer the empty slogans resorted to in the past, when in reality they signalled the start of a divisive campaign whose sponsors used that tactic in order to exonerate themselves and blame the disunity on the opposition. This is

---

various Arab-American newspapers. In late summer, 1905, conflict within the Arab community in New York City became somewhat violent and quite public. See some of the accounts in the *New York Daily Tribune,* especially the one appearing on Aug. 28, 1905, 5.

12. Perhaps reflective of this Americanization, Salloum Mokarzel established an English-language journal, the *Syrian World,* in 1926, a journal that devoted much coverage to the issue of permanent settlement in the United States—and all the challenges and problems this entailed.

the period when the various Syrian-Lebanese clubs formed regional (Southern, Eastern, etc.) federations and a national federation.[13]

3. A strong identification with the United States as the adopted homeland was accompanied by a tentative but tangible process of U.S. politicization. This began with voting, party membership, and some public or political service on the local and state levels. Also, different parts of the country witnessed the rise of Syrian Republican and Syrian Democratic clubs. As the Arab immigrants increased their involvement in U.S. politics, they also lessened their competition and conflict over leadership within the Arab community. Thus, the arena for political competition changed as the Arab community became part of the U.S. body politic.

4. Factionalism became simultaneously more *and* less particularistic with the development of a campaign to change the name of the community, its clubs and societies, its churches and its politics from "Syrian" to "Lebanese". With the establishment of the Republic of Lebanon in 1926, the various sects and factions were urged to unite and to use the correct identity, i.e., Lebanese instead of Syrian.[14] However, to many the move was Maronite oriented and it threatened to remove from the now well established "Syrian" community all those members whose places of origin fell outside the borders of the new Lebanon.

5. In the matter of style (as opposed to substance), there was also a gradual but clear change—and for the better. Thus, in the very early period there was almost a complete absence of politics as a process in that there was hardly any room for compromise or a search for what is possible (rather than presenting a visionary ideal). Therefore, conflicts quickly transformed themselves into absolute and total splits between any two factions. It followed also that members of one group saw themselves as having a monopoly on truth whereas the opposition represented total error and falsehood. Obviously, the leadership was viewed as either the epitome of goodness or the height

---

13. The *Syrian Voice,* published in the 1930s, considered itself the official organ of the various Federations. See its February, 1937 issue, 4.

14. By far the most vocal proponent of this notion was N. A. Mokarzel who championed the cause of Lebanon and Lebanonization in his newspaper, *Al-Hoda,* and in speeches throughout the United States and other parts of the *mahjar.* Perhaps responding to this kind of pressure, the *Syrian Voice* changed its name to the *Syrian and Lebanonite Voice* in the late 1930s.

of evil. Under such circumstances, the language used to describe one's group or the opposition was often extreme, biased, inflamed, derogatory, and uncivilized.[15] By the 1930s, however, the conflicts became fewer, somewhat less personal (though not entirely so), and the language was less offensive or at least it was offensive less often.

6. As the Arab community assimilated and Americanized, it began to work for an improved image of itself and its people in the old homeland. More effort was spent on campaigns to inform U.S. citizens, as well as the Arab community, about Arabs and the rich Arab heritage. In the political arena, there were also numerous, and, on occasion, serious efforts to get the United States to support foreign policy positions advocated by the Arab community, most particularly in regard to Palestine.[16]

Post–World War II Orientations

By World War II, the Arab-American community had pretty much assimilated and stabilized. In fact, in some respects, especially in the Arabic-language and ethnic church area, the Arab community's integration in U.S. society was nearly total, and witnessed a major weakening or near extinction of Arab ethnicity.[17] Concomitantly, other than the concern and attendant informational activity about Palestine, the political identity of the Arab community was for all intents and purposes wholly American, i.e., not even hyphenated Arab-American.

Several factors intervened, however, and caused a substantive and major reversal in the above situation. First, the dismemberment of Palestine and the creation of the state of Israel resulted in the

---

15. In particular, see the attacks on the Arbeelys in *Al-Ayam* throughout 1899.

16. The establishment of the Institute of Arab American Affairs in New York City in 1945 reflected the Arab community's concern about the fate of Palestine and represented the concerted effort of the community's members to do something constructive about defending the Palestine cause and informing the nation about the issue. The Institute "temporarily" suspended its operation in January, 1950. See *Arab American Affairs Bulletin* 5, no. 7 (Jan. 15, 1950).

17. Discussion and debate concerning the use or nonuse of the Arabic language in the United States may be found in the various issues of the *Syrian World*. The U.S. impact on the Arab ethnic church is discussed in Philip M. Kayal and Joseph M. Kayal, *The Syrian-Lebanese in America: A Study in Religion and Assimilation* (Boston: Twayne Publishers, 1975).

displacement of hundreds of thousands of Palestinian Arabs now categorized as refugees, some of whom at least were ready to seek an alternative, even if only temporary, homeland in order to escape their miserable existence and improve the lot of their families. Eventually, therefore, a substantial number of Palestinians from both the Arab diaspora as well as Israel found their way to the United States.

Second, the turmoil which the Arab region experienced as a result of the struggle for independence, the postindependence instability, the regional wars and internal conflicts, as well as the major social and economic gyrations produced a new group of highly educated but disgruntled professionals and intellectuals ready and willing to seek a new and better life anywhere. Many of them had already experienced such a good life in the United States when they came to complete their higher education. Thus, when the United States changed and liberalized its immigration laws, the above groups took advantage of these opportunities and emigrated here.[18]

The new Arab immigrants were markedly different from the earlier arrivals. Thus, a large majority of the Arabs who came to the United States in the 1950s and 1960s were either university students (many of whom stayed and became citizens) or members of the educated elite in their countries of origin. They also came as *immigrants,* consciously seeking to start new lives in this country. They were frustrated and dismayed by the instability and the lack of opportunities for advancement back home. At the same time, however, they were most dedicated to the vision of a better life for their homeland and for their people and/or the Arab nation in general. It took them a while, however, before they built up the courage to work in the U.S. political arena for the advancement of causes they championed. The courage and the urgency for action were joined as a result of the 1967 war and the consequent Arab military disaster.

The 1967 Arab-Israeli war, initiated by a surprise and devastating Israeli air strike which crippled and almost immediately defeated the Arab forces, marked a watershed and had a major impact on the Arab-American community. By then, the third generation of the early Arab immigrants had started to awaken to their own identity—and

---

18. Aspects of the Arab brain drain, including immigration of Arab professionals to the United States, may be found in A. B. Zahlan, ed., *The Arab Brain Drain* (London: Ithaca Press, 1981).

to see that identity not as "Syrian" in the old sense of the term but rather as Arab. Thus, elements of this third generation combined with the new and politically sophisticated immigrants to work for their ethnic community and the causes of their people in the old homelands. The result was the establishment of the Association of Arab-American University Graduates (AAUG) in late 1967. The AAUG was the first post–World War II national, credible, nonsectarian organization seeking to represent different elements of the Arab-American community and to advance an Arab (as opposed to regional or country) orientation. It is important to emphasize, however, that U.S. hostility to Arabs and the concept of Arabism was so extreme and so widespread among both policymakers and the general public that the AAUG considered it practically useless to attempt to have an impact on the political process or public policy. In other words, both the Republican and Democratic parties were almost completely and solidly one-sided in their support of Israel as well as their hostility to Arabs—even though the United States had huge economic and military assets in the region and was on the friendliest terms with most leaders and countries of the Arab world. As a single issue organization advocating different and opposing views, the AAUG sought support from or identified with other individuals and groups in a similar position. Among these were a few politicians like Senator William Fulbright and others who were brave enough to voice criticism of U.S. policy in the Middle East, other minority or disenfranchised groups in U.S. society, as well as the intellectuals who began to criticize the regime and its policies.[19]

AAUG's first and major priority, therefore, was to begin the long, tentative, and difficult process of providing accurate information about the Arab world and Arabs in the United States, and to try to distribute this literature to the public at large, wherever access was possible. Furthermore, it sought to educate the Arab countries and people about the true nature of the problems facing the region, and to educate Arab intellectuals and political leaders about U.S. policies and the U.S. political process. While the AAUG sought mainly to inform and educate, it also performed other tasks, if only because

---

19. For an account detailing the suffering of some of the individuals and groups at the hands of the Israeli lobby, see Paul Findley, *They Dare to Speak Out* (Westport, Conn.: Lawrence Hill, 1985).

no other organizations existed to perform them. Among the tasks to which the AAUG devoted some small amounts of time and effort were: political lobbying, attacks against defamation of and discrimination against Arabs and Arab-Americans, and activism among Arab-Americans in order to get them to participate in politics. These ancillary tasks of AAUG were later championed by newer organizations. Thus, the National Association of Arab-Americans (NAAA) was formed in 1972 to act as a political lobby in order to defend and advance Arab-American interests and causes. In 1980, in response to the continuing slanders and attacks against Arabs and Arab-Americans, the American-Arab Anti-Discrimination Committee (ADC) was established, and quickly drew widespread support from the varied elements of the Arab community. Then, in 1985, the Arab-American Institute was formed, primarily to encourage Arab-Americans to become more participant and active in the U.S. political arena.

Arab-American Political Identity Today

In order to delineate and assess the political identity of Arab-Americans today, a list of about four hundred politically active Arab-Americans was compiled from a variety of sources.[20] Out of a total of 394 questionnaires mailed out, 161 usable responses were returned.[21] It should be clearly noted that the majority of politically

---

20. For the purposes of the survey, the term *politically active* refers to individuals who participated in the following political activities: local, city, county, state, or federal volunteer group activity; and elected or appointed office at any government level, i.e., local, city, county, district, state, or federal. Numerous sources were consulted before compiling the list. Among the most fruitful were Arab-American magazines and newspapers as well as *Who's Who in America* (Chicago, Ill.: Marquis Who's Who, 1989); *Who's Who in Government* (Chicago, Ill.: Marquis Who's Who, 1977); and *Biographical Directory of the American Congress 1774–1971* (Washington, D.C.: U.S. Government Printing Office, 1971). The most useful and comprehensive listing for Arab-Americans currently active in politics is at the Arab American Institute (AAI). I am grateful to AAI for providing me with many names and addresses.

21. Of the 394 questionnaires mailed out, 23 turned out to be duplicates, 23 were returned because of incorrect addresses, 2 addressees were deceased, and 3 were non-Arab spouses of Arab-Americans. The rate of return, then, is 161 out of 343 or 47 percent— a much better response than I anticipated. My concern was that many would be afraid to participate in such a survey, suspecting that their views might be publicly announced and that they would suffer harassment or other penalty as a consequence.

active Arab-Americans today are the product of the post–World War II era both in sentiment, sophistication, and style, as will be seen below.

About half of the respondents (55 percent) are fifty years of age or younger, and the rest (45 percent) are over fifty. The large majority are male (83 percent), married (76 percent), and belong to a Christian church (83 percent). Of the 27 Muslims in the sample, fully two-thirds (18) are Sunni. Among the Christians, the Catholic groups (Roman Catholic 25 percent, Maronite 18 percent, Melkite 14 percent) predominate (58 percent), and the Greek/Syrian Orthodox constitute 29 percent, i.e., the largest single sect. The members are extremely well educated, with less than 7 percent having merely an elementary or secondary education. Forty-two percent are college graduates and an impressive 51 percent have postgraduate degrees, primarily M.D.'s and Ph.D.'s (35 percent).[22] A majority of the members in the group (53 percent) are employed in professions, 26 percent are entrepreneurs, and 14 percent are in some government post.[23] Seventy-three percent were born in the United States to immigrants from the Arab world, and 27 percent were born in an Arab country and emigrated to the United States. Without exception, the respondents are thus first or second generation Americans. Of those who are married, only 40 percent have spouses of Arab background. Also, other than those born in the Arab world, respondents and their spouses speak, read, and write little or no Arabic.

Over the past six or seven years, there has been a major increase in political activity among Arab-Americans, perhaps energized by the presidential candidacy of Rev. Jesse Jackson. After all, for the first time in American politics, a major presidential candidate articulated the feelings and concerns of Arab-Americans—and many within the community were ready, willing, and able to respond. The times were right, compromises were already made, and, for the first time, Palestine was a legitimate and viable issue in U.S. politics. Thus, almost one half (44 percent) of the sample had either never participated in politics before the 1988 election year or had done only volunteer work. A large portion of these entered the political process in the

---

22. This is even more impressive if we consider that only 21 percent of their fathers and 11 percent of their mothers had a college education.

23. 7 percent are retired or in nonprofessional occupations.

late 1980s either to run for office, to accept appointments to major state or federal committees, or to become delegates to political party conventions.

Table 1 presents the political party affiliation of the respondents and their parents. It is clear that among politically active Arab-Americans today, a clear majority of respondents (58 percent) favor the Democratic party, whereas only about one-third (32 percent) are Republicans, and a surprisingly small number (9 percent) are basically unaffiliated with a political party. This is in clear contrast with the political orientations of their parents who are somewhat equally divided among Democrats (39 percent), unaffiliated (37 percent), and Republicans (24 percent). A cautionary note is in order here. It should be stated that at least some of the increase in Democratic party affiliation among Arab-Americans could be attributed to the presidential candidacy of Rev. Jesse Jackson who was practically the only prominent U.S. politician to address the Palestine question in terms that Arab-Americans might find acceptable. The consequence was a definite increase in Arab-American political activity, especially in Democratic party participation and affiliation. However, it is too early to tell whether or not this situation will prove to be more permanent.

Table 1 also clearly shows a substantial increase in membership for both Republicans and Democrats, but especially for Democrats. However, the main finding here is that there is a very large (28 percent) increase in affiliation with the two main parties. This signifies a move toward establishment politics, and a substantial movement in the direction of greater assimilation and integration of the Arab community in U.S. society. More specifically, it means a definite enhancement of the sense of political efficacy among Arab-Americans, i.e., they now feel that some of their most salient concerns can be addressed by the political system.

Arab-American activists tend to be ethnically oriented. Thus, only one-third (34 percent) of the respondents grew up discussing "mostly domestic U.S. politics," whereas two-thirds discussed both Arab community and U.S. politics (47 percent) or mostly Arab politics (19 percent). As for their personal identity, the ethnic connection is predominant. Thus, only 10 or about 6 percent of the respondents eschewed the hyphenated designation to stress that they are Americans of Arab (i.e., Lebanese, Syrian, etc.) origin. On the other hand, 39

TABLE 1.　Party Affiliation of Arab-American Activists and Their Parents

Political Party	Respondents		Parents	
	Number	Percentage	Number	Percentage
Democrats	94	58	62	39
Republicans	52	32	39	24
Other, N.A.	15	9	60	37
Total	161	99	161	100

percent called themselves Arab-Americans, 25 percent stated that they were Lebanese-Americans, and 12 percent Palestinian-Americans.[24]

Ethnic concerns were *not* the motivation for most (56 percent) of these activists in running for political office. In fact, ethnic issues were a definite motivating factor for only 23 percent of the respondents.[25] However, the Arab-Americans' ethnic background appears to be more of a liability (37 percent) than an asset (23 percent) in the run for political office.[26] It is, therefore, somewhat surprising that some one-third (34 percent) of the respondents claim to emphasize ethnic issues in their campaigns.[27] Furthermore, almost half the respondents (48 percent) claim that their opponents do *not* emphasize the ethnicity of Arab-American candidates.[28] In addition, almost two-thirds (60 percent) of the respondents claim to definitely seek the support of their ethnic group. About the same number (62 percent) strongly advocate organizing their ethnic community for political purposes. This is, in good part, based on their assessment that Arabs in the United States definitely (70 percent) or perhaps (24 percent) constitute an ethnic community. They also overwhelmingly (89 percent) believe that "Arab-Americans are not as [politically] active as they should be."[29]

24. About 7 percent stated that they were Syrian-Americans. Also, 11 percent were different varieties of Arab-Americans, with an additional country (Syria, Palestine, Egypt, etc.) designation. The remaining 6 percent either did not respond or were not clear in their response.

25. An additional 21 percent stated that their run for political office was related to their ethnicity "to some extent."

26. 40 percent claimed that their ethnic background was "neutral" i.e., was neither an asset nor a liability in running for political office.

27. An additional 40 percent claimed that they do so on occasion. Their response was "Not necessarily. It depends." 26 percent avoided ethnic issues completely.

28. 23 percent stated "Not necessarily. It depends." Only 28 percent claimed that the opponents emphasized the Arab ethnicity of Arab-American candidates.

29. 11 percent stated that the political activity of Arab-Americans is "just right", i.e.,

On the question of U.S. attitudes toward Arabs and Arab-Americans, the survey respondents clearly feel (70 percent) that U.S. citizens are biased against both Arabs and Arab-Americans. Only a tiny 4 percent believe that there is a bias in favor of Arabs.[30] The U.S. media in particular (television, movies, press, etc.) are overwhelmingly judged (87 percent) to be guilty of presenting a negative image of Arabs and Arab-Americans.[31]

Table 2 shows that Arab-American activists find that fiction (51 percent) and the movies (43 percent) are the least objective and most negative in their treatment of Arabs and Arab-Americans. On the other hand, of the five instruments of U.S. media, the respondents rate newspapers and magazines as relatively more objective and positive (37 percent), followed by radio (25 percent).

However, while Arab-Americans feel that U.S. citizens and the media are biased against them, they do not see that bias translates automatically into discrimination. Thus, only 20 percent of the respondents feel that U.S. citizens "definitely discriminate . . . against Arab-Americans in jobs, business, etc." Fifty-one percent are not sure, though they think there might be some discrimination.[32]

There is one area, however, where bias and discrimination are definitely combined. Thus, a very large number of the respondents (69 percent) believe that there is a "definite attempt to *exclude* Arab-Americans from political participation and election" (44 percent) or that "perhaps" there is such an attempt (25 percent).[33] Zionists, pro-Zionists, and pro-Israeli groups are the ones clearly identified (81 percent) as working to exclude Arab-Americans from participation in the political process. The consequence is often (53 percent) the

---

not too much and not too little. Not a single respondent believed that Arab-Americans are "too active."

30. 19 percent answered that Americans are "neutral or balanced" in their attitudes toward Arabs. 7 percent answered "Don't know."

31. Less than three percent (2.6 percent) stated that U.S. media presented a "generally positive image." About 6 percent thought the media were neutral or balanced and 4 percent did not know. Similar results on this issue (and others) were obtained from another survey which the ADC conducted about the same time (1989). See Baha Abu-Laban, *Social and Political Attitudes of Arab-Americans* (Washington, D.C.: ADC Research Institute, 1990), 20.

32. 29 percent stated that U.S. citizens "definitely do not discriminate" against Arabs and Arab-Americans.

33. About one-third (31 percent) stated that they did not believe there was an attempt to exclude Arab-Americans from the political process.

TABLE 2. Arab-American Activists' Ranking of U.S. Media Coverage of Arabs and Arab-Americans

Ranking	U.S. Media				
	Newspapers and Magazines	Radio	Television	Movies	Fiction
1	37%	25%	18%	4%	6%
2	23	35	16	6	13
3	23	25	28	9	10
4	8	10	17	39	21
5	9	5	21	43	51

Note: 1 = most objective, 5 = least objective

dissemination of hostile propaganda, specifically highlighting, attacking, and denigrating the Arab-American candidate's ethnic background. In the experience of those answering the survey, the outcome of such hostile propaganda was either the loss of campaign support (21 percent) or the loss of the campaign itself (23 percent).[34]

Under such difficult circumstances, where do politically active Arab-Americans go for help, and are the major Arab-American organizations able and willing to provide assistance? Table 3 presents the reactions of activist Arab-Americans to four national Arab-American organizations on the scene today, concerning their effectiveness in two specific areas, namely improving the image of Arabs in the United States and providing assistance to Arab-Americans running for political office. It is clear that a significantly large number of the respondents find these organizations to be ineffective in their handling (or absence thereof) of these two issues. Thus, from about one-third (32 percent) to almost one-half (48 percent) refused to rank any of these organizations on the issue of image improvement. As for political assistance, the situation is worse, since between 62 percent and 88 percent did not bother to assign a ranking for one or another of these organizations. The conclusion one draws, therefore, is that these organizations are viewed as of little or no help in political campaigns.

Where rankings were assigned, the respondents rated the ADC

---

34. On the other hand, 32 percent stated that there was no impact at all, and 25 percent claimed that they *gained* additional support as a result of hostile propaganda based on ethnic attack.

TABLE 3.   Arab-American Activists' Ranking of the Major Arab-American Organizations on the Basis of Their Perceived Contributions to (1) Improving the Arab Image and (2) Providing Political Assistance

	Arab-American Organization			
Ranking	AAUG	NAAA	ADC	AAI
	Image Improvement			
1	3%	16%	32%	24%
2	7	17	20	19
3	19	19	7	14
4	24	14	9	6
No role	3	1	2	1
N.A.	45	34	30	35
	Political Assistance			
1	1%	7%	3%	33%
2	0	10	12	3
3	1	4	7	0
4	11	1	3	3
No role	24	23	24	23
N.A.	64	55	52	39

Note: 1 = most helpful, 4 = least helpful

as the most effective (32 percent) in improving the Arab image, followed by AAI (24 percent), NAAA (16 percent), and AAUG (3 percent). On the issue of providing political assistance to candidates, the respondents rated AAI as by far the most helpful (33 percent), followed by NAAA (7 percent), ADC (3 percent), and AAUG (1 percent).

Recent Trends

The age spread among the respondents (ranging from 20 to over 60) makes it possible for us to compare the older and newer communities as represented by their politically active members. Thus, the survey data show that there has been a definite shift in the political affiliation of activists from a somewhat equal division between Democrats and Republicans among the earlier immigrants (here represented by those respondents 51 years or older) to a definite preference (about 70 percent) for the Democratic party among the newer immigrants (here represented by those respondents 50 years or younger).

The post–World War II community has been more politically

oriented and motivated, especially among the more recent arrivals. This is indicated by the fact that the younger respondents were somewhat more likely than the older respondents to have had political discussions at home while growing up. Also, the data show that the younger the Arab-American activists the more they tend to be ethnically oriented. Thus, whereas almost half (46 percent) of those over 60 years of age grew up in homes where political discussions were "mostly about domestic U.S. politics," this percentage decreases steadily among younger activists and we find that, among the 21 to 40-year-old activists, only 23 percent grew up discussing mostly U.S. politics. Instead, almost two-thirds (59 percent) grew up in homes where a "mixture of domestic and Arab community politics" was discussed.

Table 4 shows that there has been a major shift in attitudes among political activists. Thus, there is a much larger number of younger Arab-Americans entering the political process specifically because of ethnic concerns, i.e., they feel the need to either defend their community and its causes or else enhance its position in U.S. society, or both. This is in major contrast with members of the older community where ethnic concerns have been only a very minor part of the motivation to become politically active. The differences on this issue are statistically significant, i.e., they are not by chance.

It is also worthy of note that the younger group is more than twice as likely (about 50 percent) as their older colleagues (about 20 percent) to feel and state an ethnic Arab background is a liability or at least more of a liability than an asset. Furthermore, despite or perhaps exactly because of this situation and the need to face the issue of discrimination openly in order to defeat it, the younger activists are a lot more likely to emphasize their ethnic background when running for political office, as table 5 clearly shows.[35]

Clear and statistically significant differences are found on three other issues concerning the opinions and attitudes of Arab-American activists on the question of ethnicity. Thus, younger Arab-Americans active in politics are generally twice as likely (about 38 percent) as their older colleagues (about 18 percent) to feel that their opponents

---

35. The breakdown for those answering "yes, definitely," and those responding "yes, somewhat" is as follows: 24.3 percent vs. 24.3 percent for those aged twenty to forty; 37.5 percent vs. 9.4 percent for those forty-one to fifty; 16.7 percent vs. 8.3 percent for those fifty-one to sixty; 7.7 percent vs. 3.8 percent for those over sixty years of age.

TABLE 4.   Ethnic Concerns as a Motivation for Political Activity

Age	Number	Ethnic Concerns a Motivation?		
		Definitely	To Some Extent	Not at All
20 to 40	37	37.8%	37.8%	24.3%
41 to 50	34	38.2	11.8	50.0
51 to 60	34	8.8	14.7	76.5
Over 60	28	0.0	17.9	82.1

Note: $X^2 = 36.54$, sig. $= 0.001$, $C = 0.464$

TABLE 5.   Ethnic Emphasis in Political Activity of Arab-Americans

Age	Number	Respondents Emphasize Ethnicity?		
		Yes, Yes Somewhat	Not Necessarily	Not at All
20 to 40	37	48.6%	40.5%	10.8%
41 to 50	32	46.9	40.6	12.5
51 to 60	36	25.0	33.3	41.7
Over 60	26	11.5	46.2	42.3

Note: $X^2 = 20.78$, sig. $= 0.01$, $C = 0.37$

specifically emphasize or highlight these activists' Arab background, in order to discredit them and/or reduce their public support (see table 6).[36]

As if in response to the above, the younger Arab-American activists are clearly and openly turning to their ethnic community for support—much more so than their older colleagues ever did or do. This is particularly the case for those most emphatic ("yes, definitely") in their response to the question "Do you invite the support of your own ethnic group (Arab, Lebanese, Palestinian, etc.) in your campaign for political office?" as table 7 shows.[37]

Finally, it follows that the younger activists, therefore, would be much more likely than their older colleagues to believe that Arab-Americans are definitely an ethnic community and that they should

36. The breakdown for those answering "yes, definitely," and those responding "yes, somewhat" is as follows: 15.2 percent vs. 21.2 percent for those aged twenty to forty; 28.6 percent vs. 14.3 percent for those forty-one to fifty; 9.1 percent vs 9.1 percent for those fifty-one to sixty; and 12.0 percent vs. 4.0 percent for those over sixty years of age.

37. The breakdown for the other categories at various age periods is as follows: twenty to forty years: 15.2 percent yes, somewhat; 6.1 percent not necessarily; and 0 percent not at all; forty-one to fifty years: 9.7 percent, 12.9 percent, and 3.2 percent respectively; fifty-one to sixty years: 25.0 percent, 21.9 percent, and 6.3 percent respectively; and over sixty: 16.0 percent, 24.0 percent, and 20.0 percent respectively.

TABLE 6.   Opinions of Arab-American Activists as to Whether Their
Opponents Emphasize Candidates' Arab-American Ethnicity

		Opponents Emphasize Arab-American Ethnicity?		
Age	Number	Yes, Yes Somewhat	Not Necessarily	Not at All
20 to 40	33	36.4%	42.4%	21.2%
41 to 50	28	42.9	17.9	39.3
51 to 60	33	18.2	18.2	63.6
Over 60	25	16.0	12.0	72.0

Note: $X^2 = 22.61$, sig. $= 0.001$, $C = 0.4$

TABLE 7.   Views of Arab-American Activists on Seeking Support of Their
Ethnic Community

		Invite Support of Their Community?	
Age	Number	Yes, Definitely	Yes Somewhat/ Not Necessarily/Not at All
20 to 40	33	78.8%	21.2%
41 to 50	31	74.2	25.8
51 to 60	32	46.9	53.1
Over 60	25	40.0	60.0

Note: $X^2 = 13.99$, sig. $= 0.01$, $C = 0.32$

organize themselves *as a community* and put up candidates for political office, as indicated in tables 8[38] and 9.

Continuing the same pattern, older Arab-American activists are
less likely than their younger colleagues to feel that U.S. citizens
discriminate against Arabs and Arab-Americans, less likely to feel
that they themselves experience hostile propaganda, and less likely
to feel that there is a concerted effort to exclude Arab-Americans
from political participation and election (see tables 10, 11, 12).

It is furthermore just as important to point out the areas where
both older and younger Arab-American activists are in general agreement. Thus, both agree (or at least the differences in orientation are
not statistically significant) that U.S. citizens are generally biased
against Arabs and Arab-Americans, that the Arab image in the U.S.
media is quite negative, and that, while there is an attempt to exclude

---

38. The breakdown for those answering "perhaps, not sure" and those responding
"definitely not" is as follows: 12.8 percent vs. 2.1 percent for those aged twenty to forty;
17.5 percent vs. 5.0 percent for those forty-one to fifty; 25.6 percent vs. 10.3 percent for
those fifty-one to sixty; and 45.2 percent vs. 9.7 percent for those over sixty years of age.

TABLE 8. Views of Arab-American Activists as to Whether Americans of Arab Descent Constitute an Ethnic Community

| Age | Number | Do Arabs in the United States Constitute an Ethnic Community? | |
		Yes, Definitely	Not Sure/No
20 to 40	47	85.1%	14.9%
41 to 50	40	77.5	22.5
51 to 60	39	64.1	35.9
Over 60	31	45.2	54.8

Note: $X^2 = 15.95$, sig. $= 0.01$, $C = 0.3$

TABLE 9. Views of Arab-American Activists Concerning the Need to Organize Politically as a Community

| Age | Number | Should Arab-Americans Organize as a Community? | | |
		Yes	Perhaps	No
20 to 40	44	81.8%	13.6%	4.5%
41 to 50	38	65.8	21.1	13.2
51 to 60	37	51.4	32.4	16.2
Over 60	33	39.4	27.3	33.3

Note: $X^2 = 19.90$, sig. $= 0.01$, $C = 0.34$

TABLE 10. Do Arab-American Activists Believe U.S. Citizens Discriminate against Arab-Americans?

Age	Number	Yes	Perhaps	No
20 to 40	46	32.6%	50.0%	17.4%
41 to 50	40	25.0	50.0	25.0
51 to 60	35	8.6	51.4	40.0
Over 60	30	6.7	53.3	40.0

Note: $X^2 = 14.26$, sig. $= 0.05$, $C = 0.29$

TABLE 11. Experience of Hostile Propaganda by Arab-American Activists because of Their Ethnicity?

| Age | Number | Experienced Hostile Propaganda? | | |
		Yes	Perhaps	No
20 to 40	35	48.6%	20.0%	31.4%
41 to 50	29	48.3	20.7	31.0
51 to 60	30	20.0	16.7	63.3
Over 60	25	24.0	12.0	64.0

Note: $X^2 = 13.31$, sig. $= 0.05$, $C = 0.32$

TABLE 12. Do Arab-American Activists Believe There Is Concerted Effort to Exclude Them from Political Participation?

Age	Number	Yes	Perhaps	No
20 to 40	47	59.6%	25.5%	14.9%
41 to 50	40	45.0	20.0	35.0
51 to 60	39	28.2	30.8	41.0
Over 60	32	34.4	25.0	40.6

Note: $X^2 = 12.69$, sig. $= 0.05$, $C = 0.27$

Arab-Americans from the political process, those working for this objective are the Zionist, pro-Zionist, and pro-Israeli groups. Another surprising area of agreement concerns the respondents' personal identity, namely Arab-American.

Summary and Conclusions

Arabs began to come to the United States in relatively large numbers late in the nineteenth century. They came essentially in two waves, the first ending around World War I, and the second beginning after World War II. There are some definite differences in the political orientations and identity of the two groups. These differences were detailed and discussed in the text. A few of these basic differences may be highlighted here.

1. The earlier community was generally less educated, rather naive and politically passive. Its members came specifically to make money and return home. They were rather afraid of any political activity—and, in any case, U.S. politics did not concern them since they thought of themselves as outsiders and temporary guests. The emphasis was on obeying laws and avoiding trouble. The picture changed somewhat, but not radically, after their assimilation and permanent settlement in the United States. They came with no notion, let alone any strong sense, of nationalism. In very real terms, their sect was their nation. Their politics was also often the politics of sectarianism—factional and generally uncivic. Once integrated into U.S. society, their politics was not generally the politics of ethnicity, but that of "Americanism." They thought of themselves as Americans of Syrian, Lebanese, or Arab descent.

The more recent arrivals were generally very well educated, quite sophisticated, and politically active. They had a strong sense of political efficacy. They also had a strong commitment to democracy and were anxious to participate actively in the political process. As democrats, they did not fear but practiced criticism of unacceptable policies and leaders. They fought for what they believed, even when the political establishment held strongly opposing views. Their political identity was shaped by a strong commitment to justice and fair play, an acceptance of the values of democracy and a concern that U.S. democratic practices were being manipulated for specific and selfish ends, especially on the Palestinian issue. They came mostly accepting the "Arab" orientation and nationality. As they integrated into U.S. society, they came to view themselves as Arab-Americans—and were (and are) proud of it.

2. The Arab community in the United States today is basically a composite of the recent arrivals and the third or fourth generation members of the earlier arrivals. As such, the differences between the two are not as striking as those sketched above. Their differences stem primarily from the fact that the older or earlier community has been well-integrated in U.S. society, and, so far as those of its members who are active in politics are concerned, the emphasis is not on their ethnicity but on their Americanism. On the other hand, the more recent arrivals feel themselves to be an ethnic community—and one that suffers exactly because it is so identified by others and because Arabs and Arab-Americans are subjected to negative and hostile propaganda. The response of these younger political activists, therefore, is to face the issue head on, declare their pride in their heritage, urge the community to organize on an ethnic basis, and fight any bias, discrimination, or attempts at exclusion from the political process. Bias, discrimination, and attempts at exclusion from politics, especially by Zionist groups in the United States, are beginning to unite the older and younger Arab-American activists, as they see the need for a unified effort to overcome the hurdles in the way of complete integration, and to advance the interests of their community as well as U.S. democracy.

Maintaining the Faith of the Fathers: Dilemmas of Religious Identity in the Christian and Muslim Arab-American Communities

Yvonne Yazbeck Haddad

The Arab-American community in the United States is made up of a variety of peoples who came or whose ancestors came during the last 120 years from the Arab world, a geographic area divided by the colonial powers in the postwar period into what today constitutes twenty-one nations, currently members of the League of Arab States.[1] For the purpose of this chapter, the term Arab-American will be used to describe immigrants from the countries of Southwest Asia as well as North Africa who have made their way to the United States since the late 1870s. Even this designation is problematic since the meaning of "Arab" can be and has been redefined in a variety of ways.[2]

What complicates the study of the maintenance of the faith

---

1. The members of the Arab League include Algeria, Bahrain, Egypt, Iraq, Jordan, Kuwait, Lebanon, Libya, Mauritania, Morocco, Oman, Palestine, Saudi Arabia, Somalia, Syria, Tunisia, Sudan, United Arab Emirates, Qatar, Yemen (formed in 1990 by the union with Democratic Yemen), and Djibouti.

2. As more nation states joined the Arab League, countries that had not previously been considered Arab such as Djibuti and Somalia took on that identification. This study will not deal with immigrants from these two nations.

is not only the variety of the peoples often referred to as "Arab-Americans," the majority of whom (about two-thirds) are foreign-born, but also the variety of changes that have impacted their lives during this century and the ways in which those changes have affected their sense of identity.[3]

Arabs have come to the United States for the same reasons as other immigrants have come from other parts of the world; seeking refuge and safety from political upheaval, religious strife, and economic hardship. Many of the early Arab pioneers came to work, save as much money as they could, and return home. They remained highly involved in the fate of their homelands and followed events there closely. A number of them were eager for the Arab world to be free of Ottoman domination, and were devastated by the treachery of the colonial powers in refusing to grant Arab countries their freedom after the overthrow of the Ottoman yoke during World War I. While a few opted to return and try to find employment in the new colonial bureaucracies, many decided to remain in the United States. It is after World War I that we see the first real evidence of a desire to establish roots in this country and the serious development of religious and cultural institutions (churches and mosques; clubs and fraternities).

Initially they arrived as migrant labor from Lebanon and Syria[4] in the 1870s and from Yemen[5] from the 1960s to the 1980s. They came as refugees from Syrian territory occupied by Turkey in 1939, from Iraq because of Ottoman massacres, from Palestine when they were expelled by the Israelis in 1948 and 1967, and from Lebanon to escape the ravages of civil war since 1975 and when they were displaced by the Israeli invasion of 1982.[6] Some took advantage of

---

3. The early Christian immigrants do not appear to have been identified as Arab until the middle of the century. Philip K. Hitti, writing in 1924, pleaded for recognition of the immigrants as Syrians, a people with a particular history and a unique civilization. *The Syrians in America* (New York: George H. Doran, 1924).

4. Alixa Naff, "Arabs," in *Harvard Encyclopedia of American Ethnic Groups* ed. Stephan Thernstom (Cambridge: Harvard University Press, 1980), 128–36.

5. Mary Bisharat, "Yemeni Migrant Workers in California," in *Arabs in America: Myths and Realities* ed. Baha Abu Laban and Faith T. Zeadey (Wilmette, Ill.: The Medina University Press International, 1975); Nabeel Abraham, "Detroit's Yemeni Workers," *MERIP Reports* 57, (1977): 3–9.

6. Lafi Ibrahim Jaafari, "Migration of Palestinian Arab and Jordanian Students and Professionals to the United States" (Ph.D. diss., Iowa State University of Science and Technology, 1971).

immigration laws in the 1950s and 1960s and came to the United States for a better life, higher education, advanced technical training, specialized work opportunities, or ideological fulfillment.[7] Thus the community consists of those who suffer from traumatic experiences that have had a formative or transformative impact on their lives and their consciousness as well as those who are more comfortable with the life they left behind.[8]

Of the immigrants who came to the United States up to the 1950s, about 90 percent were Christian while the others were Sunni, Shia, and Druze Muslims. By the middle of the century the constituency of the group began to reverse, and eventually some 90 percent of the immigrants from the Arab world were Muslim. In the last decade there has been a rise in the number of Christians emigrating as a variety of Christian groups have become convinced that there are very limited economic opportunities for their children in their home countries as well as a substantial number of Shiites displaced by Israeli incursions into southern Lebanon.

The Arab world in this century has been captured by a number of different ideologies, all of which were efforts to create a bond among people that would transcend their religious and ethnic differences. Earlier in the century the rise of Arab nationalism focussed on Arabs as a collectivity of people who share a proud heritage of a great civilization that flourished for several centuries in the area and whose hegemony spread from the Atlantic to China. Arab identity was therefore proudly assumed by various ethnic and religious minorities in different countries. For persons who were struggling against foreign domination, whether Ottoman or Western, to be Arab was to be distinct from those increasingly perceived as outsiders who were oppressing the local inhabitants. The designation Arab was also associated with speaking Arabic and with savoring its literary and artistic heritage; it involved a process of identification as well as a commitment to strive to concretize a new vision for a flourishing future of the Arab nation.

In the 1950s Arab socialism became dominant, taking hold of

---

7. Saad Eddin Mohamed Ibrahim, "Interaction, Perception and Attitudes of Arab Students Toward Americans," *Sociology and Social Research,* 55 (1970): 29–46.

8. Yvonne Yazbeck Haddad, "The Muslim Experience in the United States," *The Link* 12, 4 (Sept.–Oct. 1979); idem., "Muslims in America," in *Islam: The Religious and Political Life of a Community,* ed. Marjorie Kelly (New York: Praeger Press, 1984).

the imagination of many people as a means of bringing strength through unity based on social and economic justice with total disregard for the traditional divisions within the Arab community. Arab nationalist ideology encrusted with socialist ideas was posited as a way of forging an identity to supersede all religious, ethnic, tribal, and national differences in the Arab world. All peoples living in the area were seen to share a common bond which did not distinguish between Christian and Muslim, Druze or Sunni, Mutawalli (Shiite) or Alawi, Orthodox or Catholic.

The 1967 Arab-Israeli war undermined both nationalism and socialism. This led directly to the rise of religious revivalism, particularly in Egypt where both the Coptic Christians and the Muslims began to articulate reality from a religious perspective. The 1970s brought sectarian strife to Lebanon, which was fueled by local grievances that went ignored by Lebanese governments, ignited by the residuals of the Arab-Israeli conflict and the festering issue of the Palestinian situation, and perpetuated and financed by various local and international interests. The perception of Maronite collusion with Israel gnawed at the core of Arab nationalism, raising fears that Muslims could not trust Christians to be faithful to Arab interests. Arab nationalism also suffered as a consequence of the oil boycott which saw the transfer of economic power to the Gulf countries and the reduction of Arab professionals to mercenaries employed by the various Gulf countries as guest workers to help develop and maintain their economies. Except for rare occasions, they were not allowed to become citizens.

The influences of all these varying and often conflicting ideologies, including fluctuations in the perception of the role of religion in forging identity, were transported by new waves of immigration and new students coming to the United States. They made a significant impact on the Arab-American community at a time when Arab consciousness and identity were being encouraged as a means of bringing the disparate communities together on the U.S. scene. The Arab community thus is and has been for the past several decades subject to a great variety of influences and interpretations of what it means to be Arab, and includes in its constituency several U.S.-born generations who are highly assimilated to Western culture and whose connections to the Arab world are slight.

The meaning of Arab-American has fluctuated dramatically in

the last ten years or so, and has led to some confusing and even seemingly contradictory sets of definitions. It is possible to find two members of the same family, for example, one of whom would identify him or herself as Arab while the other would dissociate violently from such an identity. Some of the Lebanese Maronites who appropriated the Arab-American identity in the 1960s discarded it by the 1970s and instead began to affirm their Phoenician roots when they perceived that the survival of the Maronite community in Lebanon was at stake. Parallel to that is the tendency among Copts recently arrived from Egypt who identify with Pharaonic roots, rejecting their role as Arabs because being Arab is equated with being Muslim. This perception seems to be in agreement with the current Muslim Brotherhood understanding that only Muslims are Arabs, and poses a perplexing problem for a generation of Arab Christians who continue to identify themselves as Arabs.

"The Faith of the Fathers"

For Christians, Muslims, and Jews from the Middle East, one's religious affiliation determines one's identity. A person is born, grows up, and dies in a specific religious community. Religious (and sectarian) affiliation is predicated essentially by accident of birth, and church commitment for Christians is developed by tradition. One's doctrinal persuasions are part of his or her identity and integral to his or her welfare.

The millet[9] system devised by the Ottomans to govern their domain divided all subjects into Muslim and non-Muslim groups. The Muslim majority population was seen as subject to the Islamic sharia, while the various Christian minority groups were recognized under the jurisdictional bodies that exercised autonomy in ordering the lives of their adherents in the millets and solving community problems. Thus the millet system actually sustained Christian communal life that was governed by the church and led by clergy whose leadership was approved by the Ottoman Sultan. These communities became

---

9. The millet system appears to be based on the precedent of organization of subjects in the Byzantine Empire with Islamic overtones developed under the Umayyad and Abbasid dynasties.

increasingly insular, with group allegiance and survival dependent on mutual corporate responsibility.[10]

Within the millet system education was left in the hands of the respective religious authorities, as a result of which Christians and Muslims received not only separate but basically different kinds of education. In each case the goal of the educational process was to inculcate the faith of the fathers into the children. The Ottomans recognized not only religious but also national, ethnic, and linguistic differences within the respective communities. Thus religious groups were allowed to use their distinctive languages—Greek, Aramaic, or Syriac—in the performance of the liturgy and in the education of their children.

The Christian immigrants from the Arab world are the remnants of the apostolic churches that have survived in the area. Over the centuries their numbers have decreased as a consequence of persecution, emigration, conversion to Islam, or major massacres. Some of the leaders of these churches even call themselves "the crucified church" in reference to the Mongol hordes from the East and the crusading Christians from the West who massacred countless Eastern Christians because they were not under papal jurisdiction. All Eastern churches trace their roots to apostolic times: the Antiochian churches were founded by St. Paul, the Assyrian by St. Thomas, and the Coptic by St. Mark. These historical realities are very powerful in the thinking of Middle Eastern Christians. Thus in places like Jordan, Syria, Iraq, and Israel, to affirm that one belongs to any of the Eastern churches—Syriac, Chaldean, Maronite, Byzantine, Melkite, or Protestant—may be less a statement of faith than of a political and/or ethnic affiliation based on centuries of experience or persecution as well as on the vestiges of the sociopolitical structure of the Ottoman Empire.

The problem of transplanting the Eastern churches into a North American context has been complicated by the ethnic and sectarian divisions that plague the Middle Eastern churches as well as the hostility and prejudice harbored for them by the Western churches. The differences date to the early church councils, the most divisive of which was the Council of Chalcedon in 451 A.D. which affirmed Christ's full humanity as well as his complete divinity. The non-

---

10. Aziz S. Atiya, *A History of Eastern Christianity* (London: Methuen, 1968).

Chalcedonian churches are currently represented by the Monophysites who believe that Christ's divinity superseded his humanity (the Coptic Church of Egypt,[11] the Armenian Gregorian church, and the Syrian Orthodox church), and the Nestorians who believe that Christ's humanity superseded his divinity.[12]

The Eastern Chalcedonian churches include the Antiochian Orthodox church[13] and the churches that were created as a consequence of Roman Catholic educational and missionary activities among the Eastern churches by Franciscans, Salesians, Dominicans, Jesuits, Christian Brothers, White Fathers, Little Sisters of Jesus, Sisters of Zion, and Sisters of the Sacred Heart. Along with the Latin church[14] (Roman Catholic) a variety of Uniate churches arose:[15] the Maronite[16]

---

11. Gabriel Abdelsayed, "The Coptic Americans: A Current African Contribution," in *The New Jersey Ethnic Experience,* ed. Barbara Cunningham (Union, N.J.: Wise and Co., 1977); O. H. E. KHS-Burmester, *The Egyptian Coptic Church* (Cairo: French Institute of Oriental Archeology, 1967).

12. "Christians in the Arab East: An Informal Introduction," *The Link,* 6, 5 (Nov./Dec. 1973), 1–12; S. Colbi, *Christianity in the Holy Land, Past and Present* (Tel Aviv: Am Hassefer, 1969); Paul Fries and Trian Nersoyan, *Christ in East and West* (Macon, Ga.: Mercer University Press, 1987).

13. Robert M. Haddad, *Syrian Christians in Muslim Society* (Princeton: Princeton University Press, 1970); W. F. Adeney, *The Greek and Eastern Churches* (Clifton, N.J.: Reference Book Publishers, 1965); Gregory Abboud, "History of the Syrian Orthodox Archdiocese of North America," *The Word,* Nov./Jan., 1965–66; Alexander Doumouras, "Greek Orthodox Communities in America Before World War I," *St. Vladimir's Seminary Quarterly,* vol 2, 172–92.

14. The Roman Catholic church is of recent history in the Middle East. Most of its members are converts from Eastern churches while a few were European expatriates. It is referred to locally as the Latin church because of the use of Latin in the liturgy. John Allhoff, "Analysis of the Role of St. Raymond's Maronite Church as an Agent in the Assimilation of Lebanese Families in St. Louis" (Master's thesis, University of Mississippi, 1969).

15. The Uniate churches split from the Eastern churches as a consequence of Catholic missionary activity among the congregations of the latter. They came under the jurisdiction of the pope but were allowed to maintain their traditions of married priesthood, provision of wine for laity in the mass, practice of baptism by immersion, and use of traditional languages (Greek, Syriac, Aramaic) and liturgies in their services. D. Attwater, *Churches in Communion with Rome,* vol. 1 of *Christian Churches of the East* (New York: Bruce, 1961–62).

16. The traditions of this church go back to the teachings of St. Maron in the fifth century. He advocated a monothelite (one will) doctrine of the nature of Christ as an attempt at compromise between the Chalcedonian and non-Chalcedonian churches, both branches of which considered his teachings as heretical. May Ahdab Yehya, "The Lebanese Maronites: Patterns of Continuity and Change," *Arabs in the New World: Studies on Arab-American Communities,* ed. Sameer Y. Abraham and Nabeel Abraham (Detroit: Wayne State University Center for Urban Studies, 1983).

church which established relations with Rome in 1180 and gained full status in 1736, the Melkite church (also known as Greek Catholic),[17] the Syrian Catholics (also known as Jacobites),[18] the Coptic Catholics,[19] and the Chaldean Catholics[20] (table 1).

Other Chalcedonian churches that were formed out of the Eastern churches were the Protestant congregations that were the product of Congregational and Presbyterian educational and missionary proselytizing activities in Syria, Lebanon, Iraq, and Egypt; the Anglicans (Episcopalians) who established the Evangelical Episcopal church in Palestine, Jordan, and Egypt; the Lutherans whose primary activities were centered in Palestine and Lebanon; and the Baptists who worked in Lebanon, Palestine, and Jordan. More recent missionary activity is represented by the Seventh Day Adventists, Pentecostals, the Church of God, and Jehovah's Witnesses.

Protestant missionary activity was allowed in the Middle East as a concession to the British in gratitude for the military aid they gave to the Sultan in 1839. The initial object of the missionaries was to convert the Muslims, but once they found their efforts unsuccessful they turned their attention to members of the Eastern churches in the hope of evangelizing them to become the agents of Muslim conversion. Their activities expanded after World War I under colonial tutelage. The curricula used in the missionary schools (both Catholic and Protestant) replicated educational systems in Italy, Russia, Britain, France, and the United States, with a daily dose of religious instruction. The aim was not only to win religious converts, but to westernize students in the process. The Christian message they preached was imbued with the deep conviction of the superiority not only of western Christianity but also of the enlightenment and the western sociopolitical order which they sought to bring about in the world. While Catholic and Protestant missionaries served as agents of cultural change, it is questionable whether or not they consciously

---

17. They split from the Byzantine church and accepted the authority of the pope in 1724. Maximos Hakim, "On the Melkites in the United States," *Melkite Digest* 4, 3 (June/July 1968).

18. They split from the Syrian church and came under papal jurisdiction in 1783.

19. They split from the Coptic church and came under the jurisdiction of the pope in 1895.

20. The split came in 1830 and they gained full status as a Uniate church in 1854. Mary C. Sengstock, *The Chaldean Americans: Changing Conceptions of Ethnic Identity* (New York: Center for Migration Studies, 1982).

TABLE 1.   Eastern Churches

Church	Christology	Rite	Liturgy
Antiochian Orthodox	Chalcedonian	Byzantine	St. James of Jerusalem
Coptic Orthodox	Monophysite	Alexandrian	St. Mark
Syrian Orthodox	Monophysite	Antiochian	St. James, the less
Maronite	Monothelite	Antiochian	St. James, the less
Chaldean	Monophysite	Chaldean	St. Thomas
Assyrian	Monophysite	Antiochian	St. James, the less
Melkite	Chalcedonian	Byzantine	St. James of Jerusalem

understood Christianity to be a means of transforming culture. What is clear is that they were as repulsed by the unfamiliar rituals of Eastern Christianity, whose differences they judged as basically heathen, as they were intolerant of cultural practices and norms that differed from their own. They sought to change everything from the role of women to medical practices to codes of dress and personal conduct, with the result that Christianization and westernization became virtually synonymous.

In the process, Western missionaries created a host of new churches whose congregations were taken out of the already beleaguered Eastern churches. This continued until the 1950s when most Arab nations gained their independence, and in an attempt to forge a cohesive national unity and limit foreign intervention in education they banned mainline Christian missionaries from propagating their teachings in various parts of the Arab world.

Several of the Middle Eastern churches have successfully transplanted their ecclesiastical jurisdiction to immigrant congregations in the United States (table 2). While this may parallel patterns of other ethnic and national churches that have set up shop in North America, the success of the Eastern churches in most cases has been enhanced by two factors. One is the long-standing and prevalent racist attitude of U.S. and western churches toward the churches of the East and the people from the Arab world, which has slowed down the assimilation of Arab Christians into western congregations. The other is the heritage of tenacity, perseverance, and struggle for survival that these churches have developed over the centuries in response to a history of suffering, vilification, and persecution.

Among the early immigrants were the Syrian Orthodox. Most

TABLE 2.   Eastern Churches in the United States

Church Judicatory	Parishes	Members	Recognized North American
Antiochian Orthodox	150	280,000	1975 archdiocese of North America
Coptic Orthodox	50	185,000	(under Egyptian jurisdiction)
Syrian Orthodox	28	30,000	1958 patriarchate, 1968 archdiocese
Maronite	43	51,700	1966 exarchate, 1972 St. Maron's diocese
Chaldean	10	45,000	1982 exarchate of Detroit
Assyrian	24	80,000	NA
Melkite	36	25,150	1966 exarchate
Protestant	100	1,000	United Arabic church ministry

settled in Rhode Island, Detroit, and Quebec. The first Syrian Orthodox priest ordained for service in the United States was the Most Reverend Hanna Koorie in 1907. The community was augmented by fresh immigrants after World War I who were seeking refuge from Ottoman persecution. In 1952, Archbishop Mar Athanasius Yeshue Samuel was appointed Patriarch Vicar in the United States and Canada and in 1957 he was proclaimed Archbishop of the Archdiocese of the United States and Canada. Recent immigrants arrived from Palestine after the 1948 and 1967 wars and most recently have come from Iraq and Syria. The cathedral for the diocese was constructed in Hackensack, New Jersey in 1958. The church now serves some 30,000 parishioners in its twenty-eight churches spread throughout the United States.

The Melkite Greek Catholic Eparchy follows the Byzantine rite. The first Melkite community was founded in 1893 in Chicago while the first church was built in Lawrence, Massachusetts in the early part of the century. Other churches were constructed between 1910 and 1930. The Roman Catholic bishops strongly opposed the transplantation of these churches to North America but finally in 1966 an exarch was appointed. There are thirty-four parishes and mission centers in the United States with an estimated membership of 25,150.

Also among the early arrivals in the United States were the Maronites. The first U.S. bishop was appointed in 1966, and the St. Maron diocese was created in 1972. There are now forty-three Maronite churches serving 51,700 parishioners in this country. The Chaldeans, who are mainly from Iraq with a small minority from Syria, first came to the United States at the turn of the century. A larger group arrived after World War I. For many decades they were under the jurisdiction of the Catholic bishops; in 1982 Father Ibrahim Ibrahim was elected as the first Exarch of the Chaldean church (based in Detroit) in North America. They now have ten parishes with 45,000 members.

It is worth noting that the Uniate churches did not establish independent judicatories until the 1960s because the international hierarchy of the church kept them from having control of their own affairs. It is only when papal policy changed in the 1960s that there was a consequent change in the attitude of the Catholic bishops. When a group in Hartford, Connecticut invited a Maronite priest to celebrate the traditional mass in the 1970s, for example, the local priest at first told them to use the basement of the church but then changed his mind and would not allow them to hold the service at all. They had to use a Protestant chapel.

Orthodox immigrants were first served by the Russian Orthodox church which established its Syro-Arab Mission in 1892. The first Arab bishop was elected in 1904. For several decades, the parishes were divided between those administered by the Russian See and those who were under the jurisdiction of the patriarch in Damascus. In 1975, after a great deal of discussion, the Antiochian Orthodox churches were united under the leadership of the latter. Currently the Diocese has 280,000 parishioners in 150 churches.

Coptic Christians were later arrivals; it was not until the 1960s and particularly between 1967 and 1969 that they came in any significant numbers. Since then they have arrived in a fairly steady stream. The first two churches were established in New Jersey and California. Today they have fifty churches with 185,000 members. The Coptic Evangelical church in Egypt, which is the only Eastern church that has a recent history of missionary outreach, has been concerned about the severe drain of Christians from the East to the West. They have even begun a ministry to Coptic evangelical immigrant groups in North America. At present five of the functioning Coptic congregations are served by the Egyptian church.

The United Arabic Church Ministry (Protestant) was founded in 1979 to organize, advise, and plan for the purposes of unifying the spiritual efforts of Arabic-speaking people. The organization is an "independent, interdenominational, nonsectarian and God-honoring, Christ-centered mission," comprised of persons who like to refer to themselves as "born-againers."

There are an estimated one hundred Arabic-speaking evangelical congregations in the United States, the numbers fluctuating depending on the presence of new immigrants. Of these, five congregations are an outreach of the Coptic Evangelical church in Egypt as an extension of its mission, thirty congregations have Presbyterian leanings, while the rest are supported by the Southern Baptist Convention. The majority of people in the congregations are from Egypt, with substantial groups from Iraq, Syria, Lebanon, Jordan, and Palestine. "We function as feeder churches to the American churches," said Rev. Hamarneh of the Arabic Baptist church in Washington, D.C. "When our parishioners are ready, or when they intermarry with Americans, they move into the American churches. We function as a missionary outreach with a support from the Southern Baptist Convention" (interview with the author, June 1989). What is interesting about these congregations is that many of their constituent members are not Baptist prior to their arrival in the United States, but represent a variety of Eastern churches (Coptic, Orthodox, Catholic, Protestant), with imported evangelical leadership from the Arab world. They have a large number of older people, some of whom are not fluent in English, as well as many young people. Special efforts are made to get the young people to meet each other so that they will socialize and marry within the group and thus be protected from the temptations of the dominant culture.

The Protestants, whether Episcopalians from Jordan and Palestine or Presbyterians from Syria and Lebanon, usually had become fluent in English while still in the Middle East and had worshipped in Western churches known locally as the English church in Palestine and Jordan and the American church in Syria and Lebanon. They had been socialized in their schools by the missionaries who were good agents of westernization, and they expected to transfer their church affiliation to the corresponding churches in the United States. However, this happened only in a few cases. Both the Presbyterian and Episcopal churches in the United States have been very conscious of social class and ethnic background, and over the years adopted an increasingly liberal theological stance. The missionaries they had commissioned to labor overseas, however, were advocates of the more evangelical and fundamentalist trends in the church. Thus the immigrant Protestants from the Arab world found themselves unwelcome in these churches. In the early part of the century, two Arabic-speaking Presbyterian congregations were formed to accommodate the immigrants, one in Brooklyn, New York, and the other in Pittsburgh, Pennsylvania.

The influx of Palestinian and Jordanian Episcopalians and Lutherans after the 1948 and 1967 expulsions by Israel, of the Evangelical (Presbyterian) Copts from Egypt since the 1970s, of Lebanese Presbyterians from Syria and Lebanon since 1975, and of Evangelical and Episcopal Iranians since 1979 has led to the establishment of a number of ethnic churches. Again, this is not because the congregations lack facility in English or are new initiates in the faith; rather, it is because they are considered to be too evangelical for the mainline churches that have spawned them and to be unmeltable in the class structure of these churches. The Presbyterians have lately initiated efforts to form Arabic-language congregations and appointed Amal Halaby as coordinator. To date, churches in ten cities have opted to join as members and another five have become affiliated.

While there is a strong element of racism in this practice that is generally excused as the desire of the immigrants to socialize with their own, it is also evident that some of the Arab clergy, imported from Lebanon and Egypt to shepherd these congregations, have tapped into the social distinctions of the group. Charging racism on the part of the U.S. church as responsible for these language mission churches, they nonetheless justify them as a means of keeping the immigrant community protected from the breakdown of the Christian moral and ethical structure evident in the mainline denominations. As one Egyptian minister put it, "Frankly, these American Presbyterians are not Christian. They are promiscuous, they believe in divorce, practice serial polygamy, welcome unwed mothers, and consider ordaining homosexual clergy in the church. This is unacceptable" (interview with the author, March 1989).

The first Arab Muslim immigrant wave came about a decade after the Christians.[21] They, too, came mainly from impoverished villages of Mt. Lebanon. They were Sunni, Shia, Alawis, and Druze, all of whom used to be governed by the same Islamic laws of the Ottoman Empire. While the sultan by the end of the nineteenth

---

21. Abdo A. Elkholy, *The Arab Moslems in the USA: Religion and Assimilation* (New Haven, Conn.: College and University Press, 1966); Yvonne Yazbeck Haddad and Adair Lummis, *Islamic Values in the United States* (New York: Oxford University Press, 1987); Yvonne Yazbeck Haddad, *The Muslims of America* (New York: Oxford University Press, 1991).

century had recognized several patriarchates representing the various Christian groups in the empire, all Muslims, regardless of sectarian affiliation, were treated as subjects of the state under the jurisdiction of the Sheikh al-Islam.

The early immigrants had no interest in institutions. Mostly single men who lived in rooming houses, they remained on the periphery of U.S. society. By the turn of the century those who had settled and married began to organize prayer meetings in such disparate places as Brooklyn, New York, and Ross, North Dakota. By the 1930s increasing numbers of their relatives were arriving in this country, and as their settlements began to spread several mosques were built (in Dearborn, Michigan, Cedar Rapids, Iowa, Quincy, Massachusetts, and Michigan City, Indiana). By 1952 these mosques had formed an umbrella organization, the Federation of Islamic Associations (FIA), in the hope of providing community solidarity and opportunities for Muslims to meet across the country. Most of the mosques were Arab in constituency, with a few Tartars, Albanians, and Turks.

The influx of Muslim students in the 1950s and early 1960s who opted to settle in the United States had very little influence on the mosque movement. The majority of these students were modernized secularists who were not interested in the organized religious institutions. Their concerns lay in participating in U.S. civic and professional organizations. Studies show that two-thirds of them married U.S. citizens, a fact that may have speeded their participation in the Americanization process.

The 1970s saw a profound change in the Muslim community in the United States. First the death of Elijah Muhammad in 1975 brought his son Warith Deen Muhammad to the leadership of the Nation of Islam. He immediately discredited his father's teachings and moved the convert African-American community into Sunni Islam.[22] This move served to double the number of Muslims in this country, but it also challenged the "Arab" nature of Islam in North America. Also complicating the picture was the emigration of large numbers of non-Arab Muslims (Pakistanis, Indians, West Indians, etc.) who were taking advantage of the new immigration law that

---

22. For the content of his speech see Wallace Deen Muhammad, *As the Light Shineth From the East* (Chicago: WDM Publishing Co., 1980).

allowed Asian entry into the United States. The Muslim Student Association (MSA), with its particular interpretation of Islam, was also experiencing significant growth. Its members had been turned off by the Americanization that had taken place in the Arab mosques. They established the MSA in 1963 as an alternative umbrella organization with a mandate to propagate true Islam. Finally, with the dramatic growth of the number of Muslims also emigrating from an Arab world disenchanted with nationalist and socialist ideologies and experimenting with Islamist doctrines, the FIA was relegated to a very marginal role. The number of mosques involved in its activities never exceeded twenty-seven at any one time, while the overall number of mosques and Islamic centers that have been established by 1990 has been estimated at about a thousand.

It is clear that Islam has flourished in the United States despite the difficulties often cited such as the unavailability of properly slaughtered (*halal*) meat and of food untainted by pork, lack of time away from work to perform the prayers, insufficient areas in which to do ablutions and prayers, and the unwillingness of employers to reduce work schedules so that Muslims can endure the rigors of fasting. Also of concern is the difficulty of maintaining Islamic law, which is believed to be a divine mandate for a wholesome society, in the U.S. context. Conflict has to be resolved in U.S. courts that make no allowances for Islamic precedent or practice.

The MSA not only dwarfed the FIA, it also absorbed a large number of Arab Muslims who shared the Islamic interpretation they professed. This interpretation understands Arab nationalism as anti-Islamic since it advocates allegiance to something other than the brotherhood of Islam and urges its members to eschew cooperation with worldly organizations that do not share its worldview.[23] It was only after the formation of the Islamic Society of North America (ISNA) in 1982 as an umbrella organization interested in Muslim life in the United States that we see a shift from self-imposed alienation from U.S. culture to tentative experiments at political participation. This transformation came about as the original founders of the MSA began to mature, and their U.S.-born and U.S.-raised children who

---

23. For details see Yvonne Yazbeck Haddad, "Nationalism and Islamic Tendencies in Contemporary Arab-American Communities," in *Arab Nationalism: and the Future Arab World,* ed. Hani Faris (Belmont, Mass.: AAUG Press, 1987).

had little to do with the home countries from which their parents emigrated began to live their lives as Americans and as Muslims.

Muslim leaders from overseas have contributed to the dilemma of Muslims in the United States, especially concerning the adjustment to local conditions and participation in local issues. The moderate leadership of the Muslim Brotherhood has differed with that of the Pakistani-Indian Jamaati Islami, the latter strongly advocating isolationism and the former representing several perspectives. Jamaati representatives Abu al-A'la al-Mawdudi and Abu al-Hassan al-Nadawi travelled across the United States urging the membership of the mosques not to trust Christians and Jews, but to form strong bonds to withstand their hatred and envy.[24] In the 1960s Muhammad al-Ghazzali, the popular Egyptian leader from the Muslim Brotherhood, opened his remarks at the annual convention of the MSA in Chicago with the following words: "I bring you greetings from the abode of peace, you who dwell in the abode of war . . ." Two other Arab leaders, however, have provided a somewhat different message. Rashid al-Ghannoushi of Tunisia told the students that they live in a free country that has given them the right to speak up and propagate their faith, and urged them to cooperate in matters of mutual interest. Hassan Turabi, head of the Muslim Brotherhood of the Sudan, has been a frequent lecturer at Islamic conventions and has written urging the need to free Muslims on the local level to fashion their own community in the context of their own reality, free from the judgment of some fanatics who insist that they must replicate a universal tradition.[25]

The mosques of the United States as well as the ethnic churches are learning how to adjust to U.S. realities. In the Hartford mosque, for example, Qur'anic verses translated and chanted in English are played on a tape recorder prior to the noon prayer. The role of the Imam in many mosques has been altered so that his function begins to resemble that of a Christian clergyman. In addition to his traditional role of leading the prayers, the Imam is now expected to provide counseling as well as to act as spokesman for the community. In a few cases Imams have been called upon to participate in ecumenical

---

24. See for example Syed Abdul Hassan Ali Nadvi, *Muslims in the West: The Message and Mission* (London: The Islamic Foundation, 1983), 111–14.

25. Hasan al-Turabi, "Awlawiyyat al-Tayyar al-Islami Lithallath 'Uqud Qadimat," in *Al-Insan* 1/2 (Aug. 1990), 12.

gatherings and in attempts at Christian-Muslim-Jewish dialogue. Mosques themselves have acquired functions similar to those of ethnic churches in the Arab world. They serve as centers for community bonding and social integration. Like churches they often hold bake sales to raise money and potluck suppers as social occasions for their members. Events in these mosques have made it possible for families to socialize with each other, whereas at other mosques strict segregation of the sexes is maintained and each group eats in a different room.

It is clear that there is a need for a critical mass of people who are willing to invest time, energy, and funds in order for the mosque organization to flourish, and for it to become a viable institution that can serve the needs of the Muslim communities just as churches and synagogues serve Christians and Jews. The majority of Muslims, however, are not involved in organized religion. Interest in attending the mosque appears to relate directly to a concern that children receive a religious upbringing, to specific events, or to anxieties during times of stress. For example, there was a sharp increase in the number of Muslims attending the mosque around the time that Ayatollah Khomeini came to power. This interest appeared to have receded by 1983 as many became disenchanted with the regime. The next peak in attendance came during the Rushdie Affair (estimated at up to 50 percent). Both practicing and secular Muslims were appalled at U.S. misunderstanding of the issues at stake and hurt by what appeared to be deliberate misrepresentation of the religion of Islam by the media; and many began regular attendance at the mosque to ensure that living in the West would not turn their children into apostates rejecting the faith of the fathers and mocking its most sacred tenets, as seems to have happened with Salman Rushdie.

Some cosmetic changes are taking place in both churches and mosques. In the Chaldean church, for example, it is possible to be baptised by the pouring of water rather than by immersion. At some weddings a musical solo with organ accompaniment has been allowed. The segregation by sex into separate areas, as practiced in the Chaldean churches of Iraq and the Coptic churches in Egypt, is slowly being modified.[26] In the Orthodox services English translations of

---

26. Mary C. Sengstock, *The Chaldean Americans* (Staten Island, N.Y.: Center for Migration Studies, 1982), 79, 89.

prayers were available as early as 1917 and a shorter liturgy was introduced in 1920 with the mass in English, sometimes set to Western music. In some cases choirs were substituted for cantors.[27] There are also some innovations in the mosque services. Women are attending in greater numbers, although with the influx of the new immigrants there are increased pressures for segregation, and with the coming of new leaders committed to Islamic revival, women are strongly urged to cover themselves while in the mosque.

Both Christian and Muslim Arab immigrants continue to experience varying degrees of cultural stress in the U.S. context. They worry about sending their children to the public schools.[28] They are turned off by dating practices and what they perceive as a pornographic, hedonistic, drug-addicted society. In general they fear that the fabric of U.S. society and its moral and ethical underpinnings are being undermined and eroded, and in differing ways they rely on their own communities to provide the structures in which to relate socially as individuals and as families, and in which they can feel comfortable raising their children.

Enhancing the maintenance of the faith is the phenomenon of conversion on the part of other Americans to the religions of the Arabs. The converts affirm immigrant identity by a reinforcement of the understanding that their faith and traditions are superior to those of the host culture. Membership in the group therefore becomes a mark of distinction affirmed by those who are willing to reject traditional western religion. Acceptance by the dominant society now moves to a deeper level in which one does not have to renounce one's own culture but can actually share it.

While a great number of these conversions are a consequence of intermarriages, there are a number that are the result of a choice of conscience. These conversions provide the churches and the mosques with new personnel who have instinctive knowledge of the American way. Converts have contributed invaluable services to the maintenance

---

27. Alixa Naff, *Becoming American: The Early Arab Immigrant Experience* (Carbondale: Southern Illinois University Press, 1985), 293–305.

28. Early Muslim immigrants sent their children to Christian Sunday schools and daily vacation bible schools so that they would receive a proper moral education. Even today some Muslim parents opt to have their children educated in Baptist and Catholic schools where moral upbringing is emphasized rather than have them attend the public school system.

of the faith by organizing Sunday schools and other educational as well as cultural activities. They are often more enthusiastic about the faith than regular members, which serves both to invigorate the group and also to impede the processes of change.

Arab-Americans: The Birth of a Hyphenated Ethnicity

The 1967 Arab-Israeli war, with its onesided press coverage, the general U.S. public support of Israeli aggression, and the apparent deliberate effort by the United States government to prolong the United Nations debate for the ceasefire in the area until Israel had achieved its objectives, shocked the Arab community in the United States and gave birth to the Arab-American identity.[29]

It is clear that the word Arab has meant different things to different Arab groups in this country. Earlier generations and their descendants have understood it as a means of national and ethnic identification, functioning in the same way that relationships with countries of origin have functioned for other immigrants. The term Arab connoted something more to recent arrivals, suggesting the common heritage of a powerful community with a common language and experience, and of a great civilization that had once ruled much of the world. By the 1960s a number of things were taking place in the U.S. context that encouraged the rethinking of ethnic identity. The Black Power movement in this country had opened the way for various minority groups to consider both their commonalities with and their distinctions from prevalent U.S. society. It was with the advent of the Arab-Israeli war in 1967, however, that new meaning came to be attached to the term Arab-American. The specific experiences of Arabs in the United States became the subject of study and analysis by a number of Arab intellectuals. The realities of

---

29. Elaine C. Hagopian and Ann Paden, *The Arab-Americans: Studies in Assimilation* (Wilmette, Ill.: Medina University Press International, 1969); Philip M. Kayal and Joseph M. Kayal, *The Syrian-Lebanese in America: A Study in Religion and Assimilation* (Boston: Twayne Publishers, 1975); Barbara Aswad, *Arabic Speaking Communities in American Cities* (Staten Island, N.Y.: Center for Migration Studies, 1974); Sameer Y. Abraham and Nabeel Abraham, *Arabs in the New World: Studies on Arab-American Communities* (Detroit: Wayne State University, 1983); Eric J. Hooglund, *Crossing the Waters: Arabic-Speaking Immigrants to the United States before 1940* (Washington, D.C.: Smithsonian Institution Press, 1987); Gregory Orfalea, *Before the Flames: A Quest for the History of Arab Americans* (Austin: University of Texas Press, 1988).

prejudice that were fostered by the sentiments engendered during and after the war were confronted directly, and Arabs were forced both to articulate and to defend their right to be considered full U.S. citizens.

As their self-definition became clearer and Arab-Americans consciously chose to affirm their common identity, several things happened. On the one hand, as this identification was forged it took on a visibility that made it more easily the target of prejudice and hatred. On the other hand, Arab-Americans found security in being able to confront other Americans' anti-Arab feelings through belonging to a group and having an identity in which they could feel a common sense of pride. The very designation Arab-American provided common ground as well as a common bond that made their national, religious, and cultural differences seem anachronistic in the modern world. Together they affirmed their allegiance to this country and to its ideals, and pressed for constitutional guarantees of freedom of speech and assembly and for more equitable U.S. foreign policies in regard to the Palestinian issue.[30]

As U.S. Jews became more specifically identified with Zionist interests after 1967, Arab-Americans reaffirmed their own commonalities. Seeing the political effectiveness of the Jewish community in garnering support for the expansionist policies of the Israeli government, Arab-Americans solidified their efforts to become more politicized and to form their own blocs in the hope of influencing the direction of U.S. foreign policy and correcting inaccurate information about them, their culture, their history, and their faiths. This was the period of the formation of various national organizations, the titles of which reflect concern for Arab-American interests. Among these were the National Association of Arab Americans (NAAA),[31] whose purpose is to support the involvement of Arabs in political action through political, social, cultural, and educational activities; the Association of Arab-American University Graduates, Inc. (AAUG);

---

30. For a discussion of the influence of U.S. foreign policy on Christians in the Middle East and on Muslims in the United States, see the author's "The Anguish of Christians in the Middle East and American Foreign Policy," *American-Arab Affairs* 26 (Fall 1988): 56–74; and "American Foreign Policy in the Middle East and Its Impact on the Identity of Arab Muslims in the United States," in *The Muslims of America* ed. Yvonne Yazbeck Haddad (New York: Oxford University Press, 1991).

31. Nabeel A. Khoury, "The Arab Lobby: Problems and Prospects," *The Middle East Journal,* 41, 3 (Summer, 1987).

The American-Arab Anti-Discrimination Committee (ADC), working specifically to counter prejudice against Arabs and Arab-Americans; and The American Arab Association (AMARA), successor to the Eastern States Federation (ESF).

All of these organizations provided a new forum of understanding for Arab-Americans as well as a common ground for activity. They helped bring together the U.S.-born as well as those more recently arrived who identified with Arab nationalism. They appealed to a sense of shared history and a common destiny in the United States. They transcended religious and sectarian differences as their membership included concerned people from all faith communities: Sunni, Shia, Druze, Orthodox, Melkite, Catholic, and Protestant.

Just as the 1967 war brought Arabic-speaking people together into organizations seeking to balance U.S. foreign policy in the Middle East, Israel's intervention in Lebanon and its subsequent invasion of the country provided a test for their survival. For among their constituents were Maronites with special ties to the Phalangists for whom they lobbied for support from the U.S. government. On the other hand, the Druze felt that a U.S. government tilt toward the Maronite-Israeli view would decimate their fellow religionists in Lebanon.

The American Lebanese League (ALL) was formed as a lobby group to advocate Maronite interests. Its platform was anti-Palestinian, supporting a strong U.S. policy against Syria and the Palestine Liberation Organization. The struggle in Lebanon also brought about the formation of the American Druze Political Action Committee (ADPAC), concerned with balancing what was perceived as U.S. government leanings toward the Maronites. Its political activity ceased with the end of the civil war in Lebanon.

By 1984 there were American Druze Societies in West Virginia, California, Virginia, New York, New Jersey, Connecticut, Massachusetts, Texas, and Georgia. For a study of the community, see Yvonne Yazbeck Haddad and Jane Idleman Smith, *Mission to America: Five Islamic Sectarian Communities in North America* (Gainesville: University Press of Florida, 1993), pp. 23–48.

The 1980s also saw a rise in Muslim interest in the political arena. Several Islamic political action committees were formed in the hope of impacting the U.S. political process (United Muslims of America, ISLAM PAC, and IMPAC). (These political action committees included a large number of Asian Muslims who were also disenchanted by U.S. foreign policy in the Middle East.) What is interesting about the individuals involved in these groups is that a decade earlier their concern had been for political change in their home countries and the establishment of Islamic governments. It was not until the 1980s that recent Muslim immigrants began to feel at home in the United States and gingerly began to experiment with political processes in this country. While some of the other Arab organizations enjoyed the participation of Arab-Americans who had attempted to influence government policies, these Muslim immigrants were new to this kind of organizational activity.

The Arab-American community at times feels pressures for control from outside groups who begin to see that with the proper kinds of funding, Arabs in the United States can serve as a lobby for these groups' national interests in the same way that the Jewish community functions as a lobby for Israeli interests. In a few cases diplomats from Arab countries have funded various U.S. organizations. For example, during the early 1980s, the Iraqi government appears to have gained influence over the bureaucrats of the FIA whose journal was used to support Saddam Hussein and vilify Ayatollah Khomeini during the Iran-Iraq war. The struggle between the Iraqi Ba'th regime and the Saudis led the organization to sue the Muslim World League over property rights of mosques in the United States. Consequently, a wariness of accountability of any sort to any non-American sources has developed. Arab-Americans are also concerned that affiliation with outside groups will lead to a division within their community as different governments begin to use the ethnic organizations as an extension of their public relations endeavors in the United States.

The presence of Arab expatriates (students, businessmen, tourists, relatives, and diplomats as well as those who settle and find employment) and their involvement in the Arab-American community has had an impact on what might be called the process of Americanization of members of that community. Increased modernization in the Arab world and the growth of an affluent class that can afford to travel has provided a continuous flow of new people who bring with them information about the latest developments in their home countries. The students of the 1960s sought to provide a coherent reality to Arab-American identity, and to help articulate its focus and worldview. Those of the 1970s and especially the 1980s have tried to offer an Islamic vision that basically rejects Arab identity as a return to tribalism. With little initial appreciation and knowledge of the U.S. scene, they affirm perceptions, ideals and visions that have been developed overseas.

Conclusion

While there is no consensus among Muslims about the Islamic role of a minority population in what is experienced as a predominantly Christian society, there is the hope that the United States will live up to its professed values of separation of church and state, and that those who talk about the United States as a nation based on Judeo-Christian values will not advocate a religious grounding that would rule out Muslims. That a few political leaders have expressed interest in the day when presidents and members of congress will talk about an America that is Christian, Jewish, and Muslim is taken as a hopeful sign. President Reagan's welcome of the pope in Florida in the name of religious Americans in the churches, synagogues, and mosques, and the comments by Presidential candidate Michael Dukakis in his address at the Democratic Convention about Americans who are Christians, Jews, and Muslims, were interpreted by some in the Muslim community as well as those outside to mean that the Muslims of this country have finally gained recognition.

For Christians from the Arab world, the struggle for acceptance as part of the mosaic of U.S. religious life was achieved in some sense in the 1960s when the communities were reorganized as separate judicatories. The Antiochian church is an active member of the National Council of Churches of Christ in the United States. It also has close ties to Russian, Greek, and Albanian Orthodox churches in North America. Its seminaries have graduated priests for its parishes including, among others, several Irish converts. Its larger constituency promises survival. The Uniate churches, on the other hand, continue to experience the pressure to Latinize. Many of the children of Uniate church families have joined Roman Catholic parishes. Given the small number of members of these churches, and the fact that they seem to function as feeder churches for Roman Catholicism, it will be interesting to see whether or not the Uniate churches will be able to survive in U.S. society if and when there is a cessation in the flow of Arab Christian immigration.

Regardless of the survival of religious particularity, the Arab

Christian community in North America appears to be on its way to full social and political assimilation. Its sons and daughters have been elected to office not because of ethnic bloc voting but rather because they have become assimilated into U.S. life.[32] Integration of Muslims is also taking place, but it seems to be more difficult because of the long-standing U.S. distrust of Islam which has only been exacerbated by recent events in the Middle East and U.S. involvement there. The growing perception among Muslim revivalists is that the United States is a Christian country that fears and dislikes Islam, illustrated by the cycle of anti-Islamic incidents—sometimes violent—that are a consequence of events in the Arab world and the spread of disinformation about Islam in this country.

The Arab-American community as a whole, both Christian and Muslim, will continue to change both in constituency and in its forms of self-identification in the years to come. It will be influenced by waves of immigration and by the ideologies and commitments those new immigrants bring with them. It will be affected by the level of U.S. tolerance, or intolerance, that it experiences and the necessary formulation of its own responses to those feelings. And it will be affected by the assimilative process at work in the United States by which members of ethnic groups are transformed, whether or not they are ready, into Americans.

---

32. This includes such politicians as Congressmen Mitchell and Rahall, Congresswoman Oaker, Senators Aburezk and Abdnor and Governors Sununu and Atiyeh. President Clinton has appointed the first Arab-American, Donna Shalala, to a cabinet post.

Palestinian Women in American Society: The Interaction of Social Class, Culture, and Politics

Louise Cainkar

Research on the lives of female Arab immigrants in the United States is sorely lacking. Most studies of Arab immigrants have focussed on the lives and social and economic patterns of male members of these communities, although this focus usually went unstated (Cainkar 1988). The literature on Arab immigrants is not unique on this score. Milton Gordon's *Assimilation in American Life: The Role of Race, Religion and National Origins* (1964) continues to be one of the most important theoretical works on immigrant adjustment, yet it is based almost exclusively on studies of male immigrants. This state of the literature is particularly disheartening in light of the fact that since 1930 women have dominated immigration to the United States (Houston, Kramer, and Barrett 1984). Indeed, the literature on immigrant communities, assimilation, and identity stresses the importance of primary groups and the ethnic community in reproducing ethnic culture, yet frequently omits the main actors in this reproductive work: women. The growth in studies of women and women as immigrants in the 1970s and 1980s has so far led to few changes in the main body of literature on immigrants. "Male bias has continued to persist," according to Mirjana Morokvasic, editor of *International*

Migration Review's special issue on *Women in Migration* (Morokvasic 1984). Unfortunately, this statement remains largely true in 1991.

This essay is part of a larger study of Palestinian immigrants in the United States which examined the relationships between gender, class, ethnicity, sociopolitical context, and the Palestinian immigrant experience. Gender was found to be a critical variable, determining patterns of daily life among Palestinian immigrants at least as much as class and ethnicity (Cainkar 1988). The daily lives of immigrant Palestinian women, the ways they interacted with the host society, and their level of public political involvement were clearly different from those of immigrant Palestinian men. And while it has been shown in studies of Arab immigrants in the United States that the sociopolitical context negatively affects Arab assimilation into U.S. culture and society,[1] I found that, at least among Palestinians, women bear more of the antiassimilation burden than men. That is, the strong ethos shared by Palestinian men and women in the United States "to keep Palestine alive" by maintaining a strong attachment to their native culture, perceived to be facing possible extinction, places more antiassimilation pressures on Palestinian women than on Palestinian men.

Ethnicity and gender are powerful determinants of the parameters of the daily lives of immigrants, but their effects are not uniform. After providing a general profile of Palestinian women immigrants in the United States, this essay looks at the effect of socioeconomic status on their lives, especially as it interacts with ethnicity. The profile, data, and conclusions are drawn primarily from my research on Palestinians and Palestinian Muslim women, both immigrant and U.S.-born children of immigrants, which was formally conducted between 1982 and 1986. Since then I have continued to conduct follow-up interviews in order to assess any changes that may have occurred over time. Formal data collection combined historical research, field work (participant and observation) in the community, and 150 fo-

---

1. Glaser noted in "The Dynamics of Ethnic Identification" that the process of assimilation is hindered by "experiences in America which make those who participate in them feel less than full Americans." Studies of Arab immigrants have shown that political events in the homeland (Zaghel 1977), U.S. policy toward Palestine (Elkholy 1966), political alienation and cultural differences (Kasees 1970), and a perception of living in forced exile (Stockton 1985) worked against the assimilation of Arab immigrants to U.S. culture and society.

cussed and 42 in-depth life history interviews with Palestinian Muslim women between the ages of nineteen and forty (born between 1942 and 1963). All of the interviews were conducted in English[2] and in the Chicago area. Single and married women were equally represented in the sample, as were women from different social classes. However, in order to produce a representative sample of the Chicago community (which reflects patterns evident in the United States as a whole), I sampled more heavily among persons from the Jerusalem/Ramallah area of Palestine, who greatly outnumber Palestinians from other regions. The Palestinian community in Chicago is estimated to be one of the four largest in the United States. It has numerous organizations and is characterized by class, educational, and ideological differences. It provides a balanced portrait of Palestinians in the United States since it is not skewed to overrepresent any one social class, regional, or occupational grouping of Palestinian immigrants to the United States. The discussion in this essay is confined to immigrant Palestinian women, to the exclusion of the U.S.-born and raised.[3]

Commonalities

Palestinian women generally emigrate to the United States as the wives, daughters, or sisters of Palestinian men. Relatively few emigrate autonomously. This is not true for Palestinian men, who com-

---

2. The necessity of conducting interviews in English put some bias into the sample, but how much is not clear. Among non-English-speaking Palestinian women, the majority are older women who would not have been interviewed anyhow because of age limitations on the sample. Women within the age group I studied tend to speak some English once living in the United States, but when they begin to do so varies according to their educational background, their access to U.S. citizens and whether they take a course here in English. English is taught in Palestinian schools beginning in late elementary school, although most Palestinians claim it is not sufficient training for living in an English-speaking country. Palestinian women who have had some college education in Palestine or another Arab country are better equipped in English. Most likely the sample is biased to exclude very recent immigrants (less than one year) and women who have absolutely no contact with Americans and who did not take a course in English while in the United States. My own estimation from extensive contact with the community is that this number is fairly small in the age group I studied.
3. The differences between immigrant Palestinian women and the U.S.-born and raised daughters of Palestinian immigrants are too large to be addressed here. See Cainkar 1988, 1991.

monly emigrate autonomously for study or work, or to precede a family emigration. This pattern is not unique to Palestinians or Arabs. In fact, it is the most common pattern of immigration to the United States and reflects a near universal social relation of gender in patriarchally structured societies.[4] The attachment of female immigrants to families, a patriarchal practice, allows the family to continue exercising traditional patriarchal notions about women after immigration. This results in a different kind of immigration experience for women from that experienced by autonomous men, or men in general. It means that women may not be free to determine on their own how they will interact with their new host society. It also means that the roles women held in their families are likely to be carried over to their new environment, no matter how different this environment may be. In a community like the Palestinian, where maintaining traditional culture is politically extremely important due to statelessness, occupation, and diaspora and because this work of course must primarily be done in the home or in the confines of the community, women are under more pressure than men to be traditional and maintain traditional roles. Consequently, gender and politics interact to place a double burden of tradition keeping on Palestinian women.

Palestinian women immigrants, despite differences among them, share certain other characteristics. On the level of political values, it is difficult to find a Palestinian woman in the United States who is not deeply concerned over the stateless political status of the Palestinian people, along with the military violence and land confiscations occurring in Palestinian areas under Israeli occupation. Since the majority of Palestinian immigrants now in the United States come from the West Bank and have lived under such occupation, this is not surprising (Cainkar 1988). In addition, the vast majority of Palestinian women in the United States say they plan to return to Palestine if a Palestinian state is created. Whether this would in fact occur is a matter for speculation; but as long as return is not possible, as is presently the case, this stated goal significantly affects the Palestinian experience in the United States.

The sociological concept of the stranger was defined by Simmel (1921, 402) to describe persons with such an orientation: "the person who comes today and stays tomorrow . . . the potential wanderer."

---

4. See Cainkar 1988 for a detailed discussion of gender and immigration patterns.

Bonacich (1973, 584) used the concept of sojourners to describe immigrants who do not plan to settle permanently and who keep alive an unusual attachment to the homeland and desire to return to it. Studies have shown that such immigrants tend to sustain a high degree of internal solidarity in their country of exile and shun lasting relationships with members of the host society. They strive to maintain strong ethnic ties "for these will persist in the future toward which the sojourner points" (ibid., 586). The future toward which the sojourner points is the homeland, thus social patterns incompatible with homeland culture should not be adopted. Sojourners also tend to occupy certain economic positions in the host society, that of middlemen between producer and consumer. That is, they tend to make a living in retail and wholesale goods and services. These attributes of strangers and sojourners quite neatly describe Palestinian immigrants in the United States.

On the level of social values, the majority of immigrant Palestinian women in the United States believe that certain values considered traditional in Western society form the backbone of their culture and deserve the highest respect. These include the primacy of the extended family, collective responsibility for kin, hospitality, respect for status superiors, and control of women's sexuality. Palestinians are not alone in subscribing to these values; they are currently found among other subcommunities in the United States, most often among immigrant communities from the so-called Third World.

Differences

These values shared among Palestinian women immigrants in the United States are nonetheless *interpreted* differently by different subgroups within the community, which are largely determined by differences in social class. Gordon's (1964) concept of ethclass is useful in explaining why within an ethnic group characterized by a high degree of internal solidarity and shared values there exist diversities in behavioral patterns and interpretations of values. Within ethnic groups, persons have two types of identification that operate simultaneously: historical identification—a sense of peoplehood shared with other group members—and participational identification—a sense of primary identification with an ethnic group with whom one shares values and behavioral patterns. Primary relationships are normally confined to persons who share both these identifications, persons of the same ethclass, since values and behavior tend to be related both by class and ethnicity. To be viewed by other Palestinians as ethnically appropriate, or properly Palestinian, it is important for Palestinian women to conform to the value interpretations and behaviors considered appropriate in their particular ethclass, or reference group. The opinions of other Palestinians are less important than these, for these are the ones that define them as members of the group, or, conversely, as ostracized persons.

Since Palestinian immigrants in the United States do not all belong to the same social class, the way they lead their lives is no more the same than the way lower-, middle-, and upper-class Americans— or Palestinians in Palestine of different social classes—lead their lives. Palestinians in the United States are clustered in the middle and lower classes. For the sake of analysis they can be divided into two major groupings: those in the middle and upper-middle class and those in the lower-middle and upper-lower class.[5] Each of these two groups shares certain demographic and historical characteristics which are key to both their class position and their interpretations of Palestinian values and culture in the United States. I found that urban versus rural origin does not predict class status or behavior patterns in the United States because most Palestinians here originate from villages, nor does year of immigration, education level, or age at immigration; but family immigration history and socioeconomic status in Palestine have great predictive value (Cainkar 1988).

Middle-Class Chain Immigrants

Background

The majority of Palestinians in the U.S. middle and upper-middle class are from families in which at least one member immigrated to the United States before 1967, in the 1950s or early 1960s, or even more likely, between 1900 and 1920. Over the span of these years, the initially poor male immigrant of peasant background climbed up the socioeconomic ladder in the United States, shifting occupationally

---

5. See Cainkar 1988 for a detailed discussion of the economic profile of Palestinians in the United States.

from street peddler and small merchant to stable business owner or skilled semiprofessional service worker. This type of socioeconomic mobility is fairly typical of most immigrants in the United States. By the time the large wave of post–1967 Palestinian immigrants came to the United States, these Palestinians, who began to bring wives over and establish families after 1949, were faring well economically. Pressure to remain Palestinian while in the United States was less strong in the community prior to 1967 than after, when the last remaining parts of Palestine fell under Israeli military rule, and the de-Arabization of all of Palestine was in process. Until that time, the part of Palestine from which the majority of these immigrants came (the West Bank) still existed under Arab (Jordanian) rule. This group of early (pre-1967) Palestinian immigrants saw themselves as economic migrants and approached adaptation to U.S. society with reservations similar to other immigrants. Muslim Palestinians, the focus of this chapter, faced a largely Christian culture which hindered their adaptation to U.S. society, but, based on studies of earlier Palestinian communities in the United States and interviews conducted with pre–1967 Palestinian immigrants, the religious difference hindered adaptation far less than did the effect of the total loss of Palestine in 1967.[6]

Family members that later joined these initial immigrants received rapid economic benefit from the resources, business experience, and networks their predecessors had established. Newcomers in these family chains did not have to endure the struggle to gain solid economic footing in the United States like the initial early immigrants. Whether they came before or after 1967, relatives of the early immigrants moved quickly, economically speaking, into middle-class U.S. society.

Patterns of adaptation to U.S. society were already established by their predecessors. While preserving Palestinian culture and behaving in ways compatible with Islam were important values, so was adopting some of what were perceived as the better aspects of U.S. middle-class culture. For young Palestinian women in this social class, whether they immigrated before or after 1967, being a Palestinian in the United States meant taking the best of both cultures.

This somewhat tolerant attitude of Palestinian immigrants to-

---

6. See, e.g., al-Tahir 1952 and Cainkar 1988.

ward Western culture was not initiated upon immigration. Studies of Palestinian villages which had large numbers of immigrants in the West prior to 1967 have shown that families living on remittances from the West were perceived by other villagers as adopting Western values and rejecting traditional lifestyles (Lutfiyya 1966: Escribano and el-Joubeh 1981). For this, they were the subject of some scorn in the village. Remittance incomes from the Americas (North, Central, and South) allowed peasants to make leaps in status that altered traditional feudal relations. Families that had for years lived on the income generated by a small piece of land invested their remittance income in more land, buildings, new homes, and education for their sons. During the times of British and Jordanian rule over the West Bank, these young men were no longer farmers but small businesspersons, clerks in the civilian government, and school teachers. These families challenged both the traditional social structure of the village and traditional values at the same time. Thousands of Palestinians who had been living on remittances from the United States began emigrating to the United States each year following the Israeli occupation of the West Bank. These Palestinians were, by the time they left their homeland, members of the new, semiwesternized Palestinian middle class in occupied Palestine. Their values and lifestyles did not clash as much with the U.S. society they moved into as did those of the large wave of Palestinian peasants who came to the United States after 1967.

Values

Palestinian women in this subgroup who came with or to join their husbands or fathers moved into an entrenched network of relatives in the United States and fairly rapidly into the U.S. middle class, where they acclimated well to many U.S. middle-class values. Now they live in white, middle-class suburban neighborhoods, which daily expose them to and reinforce middle-class values. Their homes, their families, education of their children, and the acquisition of comfort-providing or labor-saving material goods are values they share with their non-Palestinian neighbors. While both Palestinian men and women support the traditional Palestinian cultural notion that women should dress and behave modestly, their clothing is Western and fashionable and simply excludes shorts, short skirts, and sleeveless tops. Upon entry to their homes, the visible signs of Palestinian identity emerge. Palestinian women decorate their homes with Palestinian artifacts—such as maps, embroidery, and pottery. While these Palestinian women believe that support, closeness, and solidarity among the extended family are important, they also value family privacy. Traditional Arab hospitality is seemingly reproduced without thought by Palestinian women, but these women often forgo the preparation of time-consuming Palestinian foods for more quickly prepared U.S. items.

These women want their children to speak Arabic, but find their efforts have been only fairly successful. One reason for this is that English is spoken frequently at home by both parents and relatives, from whom the children must learn Arabic. Some relatives have been in the United States for a considerable period of time and have adopted English as their primary language. In addition, a majority of these middle-class Palestinian women work by choice outside the home. Their jobs generally require speaking English, interacting with Americans, and dressing in a Western professional manner. They tend to be employed in semiskilled white-collar or service work, such as real estate, insurance, travel, or in small retail shops. For these jobs, many women have attended special training and certification classes. In spite of their wish that their children speak fluent Arabic, children of this social class tend to reach adulthood understanding only some of the language and unable to read and write it.

Despite their class position, immigrant Palestinian women over thirty in this group, especially those who immigrated before 1980, tend not to be highly educated. Depending upon when they left Palestine, they generally have from a sixth grade to a high school education. Unmarried women who immigrate to the United States and who do not marry soon after they arrive are the ones most able to obtain a university education. University education was not available in Palestine prior to 1980. Once married, it is difficult for a woman to manage college studies, especially since cultural expectations are that she begin a family soon after marriage. Palestinians place strong value on college education, viewing it as a moveable asset, and these women want both their sons and daughters to have one. Its value for their daughters is not only educational; these women feel their daughters will find better husbands and be able to care for themselves and their families if they are educated, especially if it is economically necessary that at some point they work outside the home.

Sexual Mores and Marriage Patterns

Concern over the behavior of women in the family—in public, with respect to unrelated males, and sexually—is one area of traditional culture that has witnessed a degree of bending among this Palestinian subgroup but nonetheless remains markedly distinct from white U.S. middle-class culture. Palestinian women are generally not allowed to date, although exceptions may be made in some middle-class families if the woman is of marriageable age, the man is an Arab Muslim, and marriage is a potential outcome. Marriage of a Palestinian Muslim woman to a non-Arab, especially a non-Muslim Arab, is highly frowned upon by the entire Palestinian community, regardless of social class. Coming from a tradition of arranged marriages, most often between cousins, this subgroup has liberalized the traditional rules by allowing a woman to select the Arab Muslim man she wishes to marry and spend some time getting to know him before marriage. Whether this period of getting to know a man can occur only after formal engagement varies by family, but if it is before engagement it should be supervised or at least out of the sight of other community members. A Palestinian woman seen in public with an unrelated man, or behaving in an unsubdued manner around unrelated men, is subject to community gossip and will be labeled as a woman with loose morals. Marriage within the community then becomes difficult. Palestinian women should be virgins when they marry; their parents expect this as do most of their potential spouses.

None of these rules apply to Palestinian men. They are allowed to date European-Americans, spend nights out of the home, even live with U.S. women they are not married to. And while most Palestinian families would prefer their sons to marry another Palestinian Muslim, marriages outside the ethnic group are accepted. They are in fact frequent in this social class among both immigrant men and U.S.-born and raised men, which makes it more difficult for middle-class Palestinian women to find a suitable Palestinian mate. Marriage outside the ethnic group by men but not women reduces the number of available men for Palestinian women. It is not uncommon to find single Palestinian women in their forties in this subgroup. Some women end up turning to the traditional family network for marriage, harkening back to the old days they so sought to avoid.

Basic social interaction between unrelated men and women, whether at someone's home, community events, work, or school, has nonetheless lost the dangerous sexual and moral connotations it once had for these Palestinians. Weddings, parties, and family gatherings are not separated by gender as they traditionally were. It is understood that men and women can socially interact without expressing or inviting sexual interest; and, more importantly, such behavior on the part of women is not condemned by their reference group as long as the setting is business or in a group and in public. Such social interactions are disapproved of if public displays of affection or physical contact between a man and a woman occur, or if a woman consumes alcohol and becomes excessively loud. If a Palestinian man engages in these behaviors with a non-Arab woman, however, different rules all together apply.

Immigrant Palestinian women in this subgroup generally feel that dating and premarital sex are negative aspects of U.S. culture that lead to social disrespect for women and many other social ills that are not evident in Palestine: broken families, single mothers, high divorce rates, and homeless women. Their approach to adjusting to U.S. life by taking the best of both cultures allows for some liberalization of traditional rules on female behavior but leaves other parts intact. As for what language spoken in the home, dress codes, and the fruits of hospitality, Palestinian ways are meshed with U.S., but more so for men than women. This was the approach adopted by their Palestinian predecessors, their reference group, and was normal for an immigrant population that had fared well economically in the United States and had a choice about whether to return to their homeland or not.

Since the 1967 Israeli military occupation of the West Bank and Gaza, when the option of returning to Palestine has become practically impossible, Palestinians in the United States realize that preserving their culture in diaspora is critically important to their survival as a people. A community-wide ethos has emerged encouraging as few adaptations to U.S. society as possible. This group of Palestinians, however, especially the women, while agreeing in theory with the political importance of such a goal, are not about to turn back after so many accommodations have already been made. Their identity as Palestinian-Americans has become entrenched, but they note that they cannot consider themselves full Americans as long as U.S. policy prevents the possibility of their return and encourages the destruction of their homeland. They remain determined to pass this hyphenated identity on to their children and will in all likelihood be somewhat successful as long as they feel they are in the United States by force, not by choice.

From Peasant to Petit Merchant

Background

The Palestinian women just described contrast sharply with the tens of thousands of Palestinian women who emigrated to the United States after 1967 and especially after 1975; they are also primarily from West Bank villages with few family ties to the West, and had been surviving on local means of support. Normally, their income came from farming small landholdings or from laboring in Israel, a labor market that opened to Palestinians after 1967 and became necessary for survival in light of continued Israeli confiscations of Palestinian land. Although the Jerusalem, Ramallah, and Bethlehem areas of Palestine had always been the source of most Palestinian immigrants to the United States, the Israeli concentration on land confiscations in these areas in the 1970s and 1980s created an even greater emigrant push. Palestinians from other parts of Palestine, especially men, also began leaving at this time in larger numbers than before, but it was the Palestinians from these central West Bank areas who were most likely to emigrate to the United States rather than seek jobs in Kuwait, Jordan, or other Arab countries (Migdal 1980). These Palestinians uprooted themselves from traditional peasant life in the 1970s and 1980s and came to the United States to escape political and economic oppression.

Their migration to the United States normally began with a male who either had a relative here or entered the country to study. Unlike the chain immigrants described above, this group of immigrants had not been living on incomes supplemented by remittances nor did they walk into an already entrenched network of middle-class relatives living in the United States. The men could get help finding work from other members of the Palestinian community, but normally started at the bottom, for example as underpaid clerks in Palestinian grocery stores. In time, with about $5000 saved, they could join with another Palestinian to purchase a small business, such as the infrastructure and stock of a grocery store or fast-food stand. Military occupation made life fairly intolerable and often dangerous in Palestine, so these Palestinians chose within a few years of their arrival to bring their families or new wives to the United States despite their limited incomes.

These Palestinians occupy the lower-middle and upper-lower class in the United States, which places them in about the same position they were in in Palestine. They brought with them the customs and values of the Palestinian peasantry, at a time when the ethos of keeping Palestinian culture alive (post–1967 occupation) had gained considerable strength as a political mandate among Palestinians in the United States. The ethos reinforces the propriety of remaining Palestinian against all odds in the United States and members of this subgroup subscribe to this viewpoint not only theoretically but also in their daily patterns of behavior. Traditionalism has become a badge of honor. It is measured, by both Palestinian men and women in this subgroup, more by the behavior of women than men.

Palestinian women in this group survive economically on the income their husbands or fathers make while employed either in factories, or more likely, as self-employed owners or renters of small businesses in poor, minority neighborhoods. Family income is not high, and especially in the case of merchants, the male head of the household works long hours and is gone at least twelve hours a day, six days a week. Sunday work hours are cut short to afford time with family and for social visits. Women bear full responsibility for child care, housework, and food preparation and these tasks consume most of their waking hours. They prepare time-consuming Palestinian dishes nearly every day, and in their spare moments they pickle olives and eggplants and make homemade yogurt and cheese.

In general, only men work outside the home and interact extensively with U.S. society. Unlike the middle-class families who live in white suburbs, these families tend to settle in urban neighborhoods near other Palestinians like themselves. Often they form a buffer community between whites and African-Americans. The community of Palestinians in which they settle shares their values and perspectives and actively reinforces the maintenance of conservative ideas and modes of behavior. Palestinian women are in charge of recreating a Palestinian home and cultural milieu in the United States and are evaluated by other members of their subcommunity on how well they do it.

Values

Everything about these women's homes is reminiscent of life in Palestine: the furniture arrangements, the wall decorations, the types of food cooked and served, the way guests are treated—and at times separated by gender—and the language, which is Arabic. Children are spoken to in Arabic and frequently begin school in the United States knowing only the English they hear on television. They continue to speak Arabic at home, even as their public lives become more centered around the English language. Parents often send their children back to the village in the summer to immerse them in Palestinian language and culture. By adulthood their Arabic is quite good, although they are not able to read and write it without formal schooling.

Married women tend to have from four to seven children and reside in apartments or small houses with two or three bedrooms. Few women work outside the home because it is interpreted by community members as a sign that the male wage earner cannot adequately support his family. Women only leave their homes to visit other women, to shop or to attend school, and usually only after consulting with an appropriate family male. A woman frequently out of the home without good reason is talked about by other women and men. If this happens, another woman in the community will speak to her about her behavior, warning her before the gossip gets out of hand. Once it does, she will be reprimanded by her husband, father, or mother for soiling the family's reputation.

Like the middle-class Palestinian women described above, these women tend to have from a sixth grade to a high school education. In all likelihood, even if they had stayed in Palestine, they would not have been sent to college by their parents. They nonetheless believe that a college education is important for both their sons and daughters. Whether their daughters will gain this education is another story.

Due to concerns over women's sexuality and virginity, members of this subgroup tend to want their daughters married shortly after high school. This is not necessarily the case in the Middle East; it is related to fears generated by the greater sexual freedoms women have in U.S. society and the preponderance of premarital sex. Many women marry with the agreement of their spouse that they can finish college, but find that childcare and housework make it difficult to actually accomplish this. Since it is assumed that the extended family will care for a woman if she loses her spouse, a wife gains social insurance if not her education.

Sexual Mores and Marital Patterns

While in public these women are careful not to engage in extended conversation with unrelated men and not to behave in a way that would call attention to themselves—by talking loudly or laughing in an obvious manner. Private social visits are limited to women only; if men are present, women should be accompanied by their fathers, brothers, or husbands and even then will likely be separated into rooms by gender. In mixed company of relatives and married couples, women should maintain proper decorum and not be outspoken. To be aggressive around like-aged women and children is perfectly acceptable and normal; to be aggressive to older women is disrespectful and to do so around men reveals a lack of self-control. This invites sexual innuendo, as a woman repeatedly lacking self-control is seen to be sexually untrustworthy.

Dating by single women is absolutely forbidden, as is attending parties and community events where men are present without family supervision. The imperative of an arranged marriage to a cousin (in the manner of the parents' marriage) is waning in this subgroup, but a marriage offer—which must be from an Arab Muslim, preferably Palestinian—is usually made first to the family, and only after family approval does the daughter have the opportunity to meet and speak with the suitor. She must normally make her decision about marriage after just a few supervised meetings with the man. Only after engagement, which in Muslim tradition is actually the signing of a binding marriage contract, can the couple go out with each other alone.

Single Palestinian men in this group are not subject to these constraints. They are free to date American women, engage in pre-marital sex with them, and marry them. This double standard is also true for middle-class Palestinians, but the amount of leeway and trust granted women of that class means that their every move is not scrutinized for possible violations, nor would they risk total social isolation if caught. Palestinian women from the lower socioeconomic strata would be severely punished for such behavior, which might take the form of "house arrest," or being returned to relatives in the Middle East and socially ostracized. In a milieu where socializing is confined to family and local women, and women are chosen for marriage based partly on their reputation, social ostracism is a heavy price to pay.

Marriage outside the ethnic group is less common among men in this class than in the middle class, but problems remain that reduce the number of male suitors for Palestinian women seeking marriage in this subgroup. Men frequently marry Palestinian women (often relatives) from Palestine or Jordan in keeping with family tradition. These women are seen by this group of Palestinian men as "more Palestinian" than the women who have lived in the United States and thus more likely to treat them in the privileged way their mothers did. For the same reason, Palestinian men in the Middle East of this socioeconomic background are less likely to favor marrying a woman who has lived in the United States, unless they are seeking to emigrate. This provides another reason for the earlier marriage of women in this group—the younger and less educated they are, the more appealing and educationally equivalent they will be to their potential pool of suitors.

These Palestinian women say they are not in the United States to stay and therefore seek to maintain the behavioral patterns that were normative in their social group when they left Palestine. They quite openly admit that this is more difficult in the United States than in Palestine and results in significant losses in freedom for them. In Palestine, where the basic values are shared by all and where women do not fear rape or assault on the street, women's freedom of movement is far less constricted than it is in the United States, where fear of attack provides a rationale for others to keep women's autonomous social movements in check. Of course, their assumption that social patterns in Palestine have remained static in their absence is untrue, but it is nonetheless the only Palestinian reality known to them. Even if some women would like to abandon a few of the more restrictive features of the culture, especially as they play out in the context of the United States, the community of eyes ensures proper behavior so that individual attempts to stretch the boundaries risk social isolation. Straying from tradition is viewed as something akin to revolt. These Palestinians identify themselves as Palestinians in the United States, rather than Palestinian-Americans. Only upward social mobility and their children's generation will bring about acceptance of a hyphenated identity. But like the other Palestinians discussed above, acceptance of a full U.S. identity is a matter of future generations and the political status of Palestine.

When the Two Meet

These two types of Palestinian women are readily distinguishable from each other at community *hafles* (parties) or events. While the middle-class, semiacclimated Palestinian woman will normally be wearing Western clothes, the conservative Palestinian woman will be wearing the traditional Palestinian dress, and many of them will have their hair covered. I found during my extensive interviews with Palestinian women that each group disagrees with the other as to how to live as Palestinians in the United States. While one group criticizes the other as being too Western and not real Palestinians, the other says that the conservative, traditional women are leading lives that are backward and oppressive. Although both types of women may be from a village in Palestine, may have married a relative in an arranged marriage, and may not have more than a high school education, their lives are clearly very different. While middle-class Palestinian women see the United States for all the opportunities it affords them, lower-middle and lower-class Palestinian women see it as merely a place to live for a while, devoid of the land, family, customs, foods, and community life that gave their lives meaning in Palestine. These women have little in common with each other aside from their ethnic background, continued respect for certain cultural values, and their political commitment to Palestine, which requires that they maintain their Palestinian identity and avoid full assimilation.

Beginnings of a New Immigration

This portrait of Palestinian women covers the vast majority of adult immigrant Palestinian women in the United States. Additionally, since the late 1970s there has been an increasing number of Palestinian women immigrants who came from different parts of Palestine or came after marrying Palestinian men who entered the United States for different reasons than those discussed above. These men initially came to the United States only to study and had planned to leave once finished. But they decided, usually on the basis of job opportunities and the declining job market in the Gulf states, to stay. Unlike the others who emigrated from the Jerusalem, Ramallah, and Bethlehem areas of Palestine, these Palestinians originated from the Nablus, Jenin, and Tulkarm areas in the north of Palestine, or were refugees from the parts of Palestine that became the State of Israel and who resettled in the West Bank, Gaza, Jordan, or Kuwait.

These women may fall into either subcategory mentioned above, depending on their family income. Some of them are well-educated while others have a high school education. But they all share a feeling of great loneliness. Torn away from their family and friends and not sharing bonds of kin or community of origin with other Palestinians in the United States, the social and emotional deprivations they endure make adjustment to life in the United States very difficult. While many of these women said they thought marriage to a man living in the United States would be exciting, they soon discovered that this was not the case.

Political Life

Despite differences, Palestinian women share a deep concern for the fate of their people in Palestine and other Arab countries and feel strongly that a Palestinian state must be established. Prominent in any discussion with them is mention that Palestinians are stateless people, that they have few freedoms in their own country, that their land is being stolen, their way of life controlled and destroyed, and that most have no right to return to their country. Every Palestinian woman I spoke with emphasized the tragedy of the Palestinian people and how it has affected her life and split apart her family. Each also spoke of the general hostility or lack of concern U.S. citizens show about this situation. My conversations with Palestinian women affirm what Edward Said noted in his book *After the Last Sky* (1986): While there is not a singular Palestinian experience due to the various and scattered fates of the Palestinian people, Palestinians do in fact form one community, "if at heart a community built on suffering and exile." The ethos of exile prominent among Palestinians in the United States developed out of this communal experience. It means not forgetting that one is a Palestinian. For Palestinian women, it means not only maintaining a strong Palestinian ethnic identity, but raising children to be Palestinian.

Palestinian political activities and the ethos of exile merge together in different ways for Palestinian women. Beyond raising their children as Palestinians and maintaining respect for certain traditional Arab values, middle-class Palestinian women are more likely than other Palestinian women to be politically active publicly, normally through Palestinian or Arab-American organizations. Observation of such organizations shows this to be the case. This is why studies of Palestinian immigrants or Palestinian women that focus on accessible and visible participants in organized groups are skewed toward the patterns of the middle-class, semiacclimated Palestinians.

Traditional Palestinian women, from the lower social classes, have tended to shun public political life because they, their husbands, or fathers believe that such activities are not appropriate for Palestinian women. Within the communities in which they live, politically active married women are frowned upon because it is assumed they must be neglecting their families; and single women who have that much time should be married, they say. Public politics is seen as a man's activity. On the other hand, these Palestinian women believe that their daily lives are an active expression of the Palestinian political ethos of exile: keeping Palestine alive. Through their daily work of maintaining a Palestinian home, preparing arduous Palestinian meals, speaking Arabic and teaching it to their children, and focusing their lives on the maintenance and fulfillment of traditional Palestinian values, they are keeping alive what occupation and exile are destroying. Others talk politics, they live them. Within broadly based Palestinian community organizations their way of life is respected, even when it is not adopted by everyone.

Conclusion

While social class certainly does not explain everything about the lives of Palestinian women in the United States, I have found it the best way to characterize the diversity of lifestyle patterns existing within the larger community. All of the women I studied were Muslims. Most of them defined Islam as a way of life. Few attended the mosque or felt it necessary to do so; few prayed at home. Still, different persons interpreted Islamic injunctions differently, especially as they relate to women. They were sometimes used to justify limiting a woman's movements, but more often culture was used as the rationale. While I note recently an increase in the number of fundamentalist Muslims in the United States, they still remain a minority among Palestinians.

In conclusion, there is no typical Palestinian woman in the United States. Those who wish to highlight the fact that Palestinians have adapted well to the United States focus on one part of the community, while those who wish to show that they are a traditional people who have changed little since they left their Arab villages focus on another sector. In fact, both of these realities exist at the same time and both groups of people insist that their identity as Palestinians lies at the core of the alienation they feel in the United States. The Intifada and the Gulf war only served to reinforce this feeling.

BIBLIOGRAPHY

al-Tahir, Abdul Jalil. 1952. *The Arab Community in the Chicago Area: A Comparative Study of the Christian-Syrians and the Muslim Palestinians.* Ph.D. diss., University of Chicago.

Bonacich, Edna. 1973. "A Theory of Middleman Minorities." *American Sociological Review* 38 (October): 583–94.

Cainkar, Louise. 1988. "Palestinian Women in the United States: Coping with Tradition, Change and Alienation." Ph.D. diss., Northwestern University.

———. 1991. "Palestinian-American Muslim Women: Living on the Margins of Two Worlds." In *Muslim Families in North America,* Earle H. Waugh, Sharon McIrvin Abu-Laban, and Regula Qureshi, eds., (Edmonton: University of Alberta Press).

Elkholy, Abdo A. 1966. *The Arab Moslems in the U.S.* New Haven, Conn.: College and University Press.

Escribano, M., and N. el-Joubeh. 1981. "Migration and Change in a West Bank Village." *Journal of Palestine Studies* 11, no. 1 (Autumn).

Glaser, Daniel. 1958. "Dynamics of Ethnic Identification." *American Psychological Review* 23 (1): 33.

Gordon, Milton. 1964. *Assimilation in American Life: The Role of Race, Religion and National Origins.* New York: Oxford University Press.

Houston, Marion F., Roger G. Kramer, and Joan Mackin Barrett. 1984. "Female

Predominance of Immigration to the United States since 1930: A First Look." *International Migration Review* 18: 908–63.

Kasees, Assad. 1970. *The People of Ramallah: A People of Christian Arab Heritage*. Ph.D. diss., Florida State University.

Kayal, Philip M., and Joseph Kayal. 1975. *The Syrian Lebanese in America*. Boston: Twayne Publications.

Lutfiyya, Abdulla. 1966. *Baytin*. The Hague: Mouton and Co.

Migdal, Joel. 1980. *Palestinian Society and Politics*. Princeton, N.J.: Princeton University Press.

Mills, C. Wright. 1959. *The Sociological Imagination*. New York: Oxford University Press.

Morokvasic, Mirjana. 1984. "Birds of Passage are also Women . . ." *International Migration Review.* 18: 886–907.

Said, Edward. 1986. *After the Last Sky: Palestinian Lives*. Pantheon: New York.

Simmel, Georg. 1908. *Soziologie,* Leipsig: Dunche and Humblot, translated as "The Sociological Significance of the 'Stranger,'" in Robert E. Park and Ernest W. Burgess, *Introduction to the Science of Sociology,* Chicago: University of Chicago Press, 1924, 322–27.

Stockton, Ronald. 1985. "A Survey of Palestinians in Detroit." *Psychological Reports* 120–30.

Zaghel, Ali. 1977. *Changing Patterns of Identification Among Arab Americans: The Palestinian Ramallites*. Ph.D. diss., Northwestern University.

Issues of Identity: In Theater of Immigrant Community

Ala Fa'ik

Theater Development of Immigrant Community

The experience of immigrants to the United States and the contribution made by these immigrants as they brought their own cultural life to their new country has through the centuries received much acknowledgment, and recently, much study. The contribution of Arab-Americans is no exception. But the specific development of Arab-American theater and the role that theater has played in the establishment of the self-identity of Arab-Americans, and the explanation and realities peculiar to the Arab-American experience, have been little noted. In fact in the last decade Arab-Americans have increasingly produced theater dealing with the Arab-American experience, theater of different types: plays in Arabic by and for Arab-Americans, bilingual productions for wider audiences of both Arab-Americans and non-Arab-Americans, and professional productions in English for the general U.S. public.

Theater is a complex form of expression. Cultures and groups of people develop their own form of theatrical expression to reflect their concern about moral, social, political, and religious issues. The choice of the theatrical form to reflect these concerns fulfills the need to share common experience and to provide entertainment.

Arab immigrants in the United States are undergoing the experience of other immigrant groups who have over the past two centuries struggled to preserve their cultural heritage. Their effort produced new cultural characteristics as what they brought to this country intersected with what they found here, and that new creation contributed in turn to the greater U.S. culture. For example, the African-American community in the United States has its own identity and its own cultural expression. Out of that identity and through that expression it has contributed largely to the wider cultural development in the country. In the experience of many immigrant groups, theater is a natural and important form of expression and has its own contribution to this broader culture.

The phenomenon of the ethnic theater in the United States is well recognized and has been thoroughly studied by theater scholars and anthropologists.[1] But there has been no specific attempt to record, study, or analyze the development of the Arab-American theater movement now emerging in cities and communities across the United States. Arab-American theater is rapidly moving from an exclusive form of entertainment with appreciation only by Arab-American audiences into an art form with broad general interest for all Americans. These Arab-American productions convey through their form and content the experience of Arab-Americans in this country, so making that experience part of the American culture.

Early Arab-American immigrants produced plays about Arab history and its glory in their cultural clubs and organizations. Some ten years ago as I was just developing my interest in this topic I came across, in a book about Kahlil Gibran, a picture of a play produced by Arab-American immigrants in the United States early in this century. The picture showed the actors in authentic costumes and scenery. Unfortunately, I made no note of the book at the time and I have been unable to relocate it since. This picture, though restricted to my own memory, indicates early attempts to produce plays for Arab-American audiences, and so to preserve Arab traditions and culture in the new world.

Arab-American theater audiences are accustomed to watching video-taped Arabic plays produced in the Arab countries, which are now an established part of their entertainment. Also, Arab-Americans have had the chance to see live theater performances produced and

---

1. Graff B. Wilson, *Three Hundred Years of American Drama and Theater,* (Englewood Cliffs: Prentice Hall, 1973) pp. 4–5.

performed by Arab theater groups touring major U.S. cities like New York, Washington, D.C., Boston, Chicago, Houston, San Diego, and Los Angeles. These theater groups visit the United States from different Arab countries such as Iraq, Syria, Lebanon, Palestine, and Egypt. These groups frequently perform musical and comedy productions originally written and successfully performed in the Middle East. These performances have had great artistic and financial success. A major Arabic star usually performs in these productions, a star whom the Arab-American audience would like to see in person. Doreid Lahham from Syria, Adel Imam of Egypt, Saleem al Basri from Iraq, and Fairuz of Lebanon are among the well-known stars that have performed in the United States since the early 1970s. These productions have had an impact on Arab-American cultural life. This study, however, will focus only on the Arab-American theater productions produced for and performed by the Arab-American community.

Theater for and by Arab-Americans

The 1970s and 1980s brought a large wave of Arab immigrants to the United States. Some came to pursue a dream of a better life, others fled political persecution or the destruction and horror of war. Those immigrants concentrated in large numbers in urban areas, with initially unmet social and cultural needs. At once, the communities of Arab-Americans began to produce newspapers, magazines, nightclubs, television, and radio shows for the benefit of the new Arab immigrants. Theatrical productions, naturally enough, also soon appeared to fulfill the cultural and entertainment needs of this community.

In Detroit, amateur groups since 1980 have presented several plays dealing with the complexity of living in the new culture. Most of these plays have been farces and have tried to imitate Egyptian farces as written and produced; a few have tried to deal with political concerns. These plays present social commentary on change in traditional values as they interact with the values of U.S. culture. Titles of some of the plays reflect interesting subjects of the realities of the New World and their concerns, "Party Store" 1983, "*Shūf al-Lotto Esh Sawwa*" (See What the Lotto Did) 1986, and "*Mātlūb Za'īm Lil-Jāliyah*" (Wanted: A Leader for the Immigrant Community) 1988.

These plays are in different Arabic dialects, mostly Iraqi. They concern issues of family, marriage, drugs, working conditions, and so on. They are explicitly critical of people who seek to accumulate wealth at the expense of their cultural and moral values. Arab-American audiences welcomed the plays and attend performances in growing numbers. Some of these productions toured other cities such as Chicago, San Diego, and Los Angeles. Especially significant and interesting is that the performances were usually presented late in the evenings, at nine or ten o'clock, to allow Arab-Americans who work in stores or late factory shifts to attend the performance without missing any part of the play.

That these plays have frequently been videotaped, with copies made available for general market sale, attests to their popularity. They have been commercially successful as well. But the artistic quality and the dramatic treatment of these plays has been generally weak. These plays have fulfilled a need for the immigrant community. They have entertained audiences, while showing them a simplified treatment of the realities and problems of their daily lives. Major writers, actors, and directors of these plays have included Abdul Khaliq Al-Falah, Talal Samona, Hikmat Jajoni, Husam Zoro, Salah Kolatoo, and many others.

One of the plays, whose title comes from a traditional Iraqi proverb, *Shaleelah wa Dhāy'a Rās-ha* (A Tangled Yarn), 1984, written by Husam Zoro and directed by Salah Kalatoo,[2] mocks lawyers, justice, and social problems in Detroit. An Iraqi immigrant works as the secretary of a U.S. lawyer named Mr. Toughman. The lawyer is not interested in justice and truth, but only in making money. He agrees to defend a man on trial for robbery and an associated murder, who claims self-defense. He encourages a woman to divorce her husband, who spends all his time in the coffeeshop rather than at home. He also agrees to represent in court a man who sues U.S. society because it has not fulfilled the promises for which he came to the United States. The secretary, who is an Iraqi immigrant, is in conflict with the lawyer's values and unethical practices. The secretary ends up representing these cases in court because Mr. Toughman has a heart attack.

In the second act the secretary disguises himself as Mr. Toughman,

---

2. Salah Kalatoo, director, "Shaleelah wa Dhaya Ràas-ha," by Husam Zoro, videotape, Baghdad Theater Company, Detroit, 1984.

wearing a black robe and representing the clients and their cases. The judge wears a black robe and a white wig. There is no jury present in the courtroom. The secretary uses his own value system to resolve these cases. He brings the divorced couple back together instead of allowing them to divorce one another. Through side commentary and jokes, he makes a mockery of the judge and the judiciary system in the United States. The real justice and truth that the immigrant community expected and looked for do not exist. The judicial system is filled with bribery and corruption; the real criminal is set free and the victims' rights are taken away.

Although the play presents interesting issues and concerns about people's experience in Detroit, it fails to discuss the issues in enough depth. However, it succeeds through its use of familiar human situations to elicit audience appreciation and laughter.

The play is deceptive however in its setting: a courtroom is used that does not exist in the U.S. judicial system. The factual error reflects the playwright and the director's ignorance of the legal system and cultural reality of this country, which is common to many Arab-Americans. Their attitude toward the culture in which they now live thus comes from assumptions or misunderstanding of the reality of the new culture. The play, then, rather than clarifying the U.S. cultural experience for the audience, encourages them in their misunderstanding of it as it perpetuates ignorance and misinformation.

Bilingual and Musical Productions

Another large community of Arab-Americans lives in Los Angeles. Theater in that area is beginning to present plays in bilingual and musical formats so they may be enjoyed by Arab-Americans born in this country who are not native speakers of Arabic, and also by the general public. These plays appear with the support of the Arab-American Cultural Group, which attempts to promote a better understanding of Arab culture through presentation of music, dance, films, and plays in the L.A. area.

Hammam Shafie, a Palestinian-American actor, dancer, and director, is one of the leading figures in promoting the Arab-American theatrical activity as a way of presenting Arab-American experience and Arab culture. In 1987 he presented his work *Where to Ramallah*. The play centered around a teenager of Palestinian descent who is provoked by the hit song "Walk Like an Egyptian" to imagine a journey to his father's homeland at the turn of the century. Through his walk into the past, the play shows the contradictions between the values and the reality of life in the Arab world. It presents the story of the Palestinian people, revealing the contribution of the Arab regimes to the tragedy of the Palestinian people. The play combined Arab and U.S. music and dance in creating the dramatic effect of the production.[3]

In November 1989, Arab-American theater saw the birth of the Arab-American Children's Theater company which marked an important step in the development of the cultural identity of Arab-Americans. *The Festival: A Musical Play in Two Acts* marked this birth and a new beginning. Hammam Shafie adapted and directed the play from a short story by Amira Assaly, with music composed by Faheem Sadi. This production employed several Arab-American professional talents with about twenty-five Arab-American children who created this production in a teamwork effort.[4]

The Festival treats the issue of growing up in an Arab-American family. A father who is unemployed has four daughters who want to participate in a festival. Each daughter has a different performance talent; playing the piano, folk dancing, singing in Arabic, and the last one is a ballerina. The play encourages the perpetuation of the Arab family's values and heritage in the United States. It stresses the importance of hard work by quoting several Arabic proverbs like "He who seeks shall find." It calls for children to be taught these values in order not to acquiesce to the materialism of U.S. society. This play also incorporates a dream journey, but through a medieval Arabic tale that reflects the values of hard work, honesty, and truth.

The production exposed the audience to Arab culture; at the same time it encouraged the young Arab-American talents to develop several aspects of Arab culture and performing arts. What the Arab-American Children's Theater is doing is very significant and should be supported and encouraged. As Fereal Masre, the producer of the show, said, it is "planting seeds of love for the Arab cultural values and heritage." She also explained that "this is a first full production

3. Telephone interview with Hammam Shafie, February 2, 1990.

4. Hammam Shafie, director, "The Festival," Faheem Sadi, Comp., videotape, Arab American Children's Theater, Los Angeles, 1989. All further references and quotations to this work are from this videotape production.

by Arab-American children," and *"The Festival* gave those children the chance to work creatively with their tradition and heritage." Masre concluded that the project "is a seed which will develop future talents and leadership for this country." (*The Festival,* video copy)

Hammam Shafie explained the importance of *The Festival* as a product of teamwork, a celebration of Arab culture and an accomplishment of Arab-American unity. He declared that the goal of the Arab-American Children's Theater is to provide "a place where kids learn to experiment, explore, and perform their culture, heritage, history, and values which makes it real for them." (*The Festival,* video copy) He promised that this production was just a beginning for the ongoing program, and the second production would come the following spring.[5]

This project involves all the community. Their support and encouragement is the key for its continuity. The bilingual musical theater beginnings are similar to many other ethnic theaters in the United States, like the Mexican-American theater movement in Texas, New Mexico, and other states, which started similar productions in the early 1970s and has been very successful.

Arab-American Theater for General Audiences

My own first attempt to produce a theater piece based on Arab culture to a U.S. audience took place in 1977 in Columbia, Missouri. My wife and I assembled all the Arab students at the University of Missouri with their families to perform a sketch, which I wrote, reflecting our culture, concerns, and dreams.

The first scene of this two part sketch, titled "Wedding," opened with a storyteller introducing an Arab wedding. The women entered in one procession and the men entered in another one through the audience. At the end of the first part, they left in one body again proceeding through the audience, singing and dancing. The sketch included music, dance, and songs from different Arab countries, and the actors wore costumes characteristic of these various countries. Although such an assembly of Arabs would not take place in the

---

5. Personal interview with Hammam Shafie, 15 May 1990. He indicated that there was a delay in producing another project because of financial and personnel support difficulties.

Arab world itself, it represented a yearning for and a romantic attempt to display a united Arab nation.

The second scene, titled "A Slice of Life," began with the story-teller presenting the other reality of life in the occupied Arab land. Although this scene lasted only three minutes in contrast to the twenty minutes of the first scene, with no words spoken in it, it generated intense emotion and dramatic power. It presented the Palestinian struggle for self-preservation and self-determination. Through this sketch the Arab community presented its culture, concerns, and aspirations so as to introduce to a U.S. audience its side on controversial and frequently misunderstood issues.

Arab-American author and theater artist Fareed Al-Oboudi presented the issue of discrimination and prejudice against Arab-Americans, while Arab-Americans were in search of self-identity. Al-Oboudi is U.S. born; he is an actor, writer, director, and teacher of theater. Fareed studied theater at Wayne State University, received an M.A. in acting from the University of Michigan, and an M.F.A. in directing from Michigan State University. He taught theater at Yarmouk University in Jordan and worked professionally in L.A. and Chicago. Fareed made an important contribution to the development of Arab-American theater by writing, producing, acting in, and directing a play in Chicago from June to July, 1988 that dealt directly with prejudice and stereotypes of the Arab-American. He argues that such prejudices contribute to the alienation of the Arab-American.

His play, *Portrait of a Suspect,* was produced at the Chicago Actor's Project Theater, and ran for a month in summer 1988. *Portrait* presented an unnamed Arab-American character, referred to only as "Suspect", who is in search of an identity, struggling to be part of something. But his search leads him to become part of nothing.[6]

Portrait of a Suspect introduces a young U.S. citizen of Arab descent who undergoes three harrowing and painful interrogations. Fareed employs music, slides, and violent dynamic action with flashbacks to create these horrifying experiences. In his production note Fareed describes the essence of the play:

The action of the play for the most part is distilled from larger

---

6. Fareed Al-Oboudi, writer and director, "Portrait of a Suspect," Chicago Actor's Project Theater, Chicago, July 2, 1988.

events. The sense should be concentrated rather than loose. Present and past mix in a series of flashbacks that are presented through audio and visual methods and highly physical stage action.[7]

He advises that the director of this play should do careful research into the subject of "prejudice, human and civil rights, and the political problems generated due to discrimination; moreover the lack of human understanding.... The director should work with his cast on the psychological and physical states of restriction." (p. 1) Fareed asks the director to improvise with his cast to create "the physical and psychological dynamic of restrictive environment." Then he concludes that:

This dynamic and analytical process should ultimately illuminate the frustration encountered by individuals who are victims of prejudice. Prejudice causes utter deprivation and a colossal violation of the human psyche. It leaves many people in states of passive anger, immobile, vindictive or worse violent themselves. (p. 1)

The play conveys to the audience the destructive effect of prejudice on human life. It begins with the sound of body blows made by an audio synthesizer, and these auditory blows become real, individually felt and endured. A sense of personal identification with the main character is created, so forcing each member of the audience into the world of terror that surrounds those who live under prejudice. The play confronts everyone present with the reality of the state of terror created by prejudice and discrimination.

This play employs the flashback technique with the use of slides, both black and white and occasionally color, to reflect happy occasions in Suspect's life. The play's twelve scenes vary in length, and portray a young man undergoing first apprehension, then detention, confinement, and interrogation. The young man's only guilt is his identity. He is an Arab-American.

Fareed Al-Oboudi drew the events of the play from events he

---

7. Fareed Al-Oboudi, "Portrait of a Suspect," (Chicago: unpublished manuscript, 1988), (p. 1). All further references to this work appear in the text.

either personally experienced or read about. During his research for the play, he studied the technique of interrogation used by the United States, Arab regimes, and the Israeli army. The first interrogation in the play, for example, represents an experience of his in Ann Arbor in 1981 while he was a graduate student in theater at the University of Michigan, although the play does not locate the event there.

In the interrogation scenes Suspect finds that his isolation and alienation grow ever larger. First he is arrested by police officers who accuse him of roughing up a woman who is his classmate, and of making obscene phone calls to her.[8] The interrogators call him "faggot," "rag head," and "camel jockey" (p. 12). He is suspected because of who he is and not because of what he did. The police twist his every word to fit their stereotype of an Arab.

In another scene Suspect is interrogated by two Syrians. They accuse him of spying, because while vacationing in Syria, he took photographs in an area that he did not know to be a security zone. His real crime this time is that his U.S. passport has an Arab name. They call him "traitor," (p. 24) and say:

"Your American citizenship is not good in Syria."

"If you were proud, you would have struggled like everyone. You lived in the West for comfort, for money, for sex—."

"Just like a bastard you take your father's name and throw away his honor," and

"You are here because you couldn't be more than a car washer in America." (p. 26)

Their attacks on him are so strong that they expel him now from the people to whom he had believed he belonged. Then the Syrian interrogator goes further. "You are not an Arab and you are not an American. And there isn't something called Arab-American. You are like a cockroach . . ." (p. 30)

Before the third scene of the interrogation, Suspect tells of finding a kitten who has been tortured, explaining that it was too late to save the kitten. As the lights dim gradually to darkness, he weeps:

---

8. The playwright did not refer to the city or state of the police officers for symbolic purposes; these events could have happened in any U.S. city. Personal interview with Fareed Al-Oboudi, July 3, 1988.

"The whole world was cruel . . . My heart ached . . . There are so many things I don't understand, I ask God's guidance . . . I want to live so much because life has so much beauty if people could only see . . . [dark]." (p. 35)

The third scene of interrogation is the ugliest, most violent, and most physical scene of the play. This time Suspect is arrested in Jerusalem while running from a bomb blast. His plea that he is a U.S. citizen is ineffective. They regard him as just another Arab terrorist. The Israeli interrogators treat him like a subhuman, saying: "You are not an American, an Arab is always an Arab." (p. 37) The scene moves in ever greater rhythm as the interrogators beat him, smash him to the ground, and throw filthy water on him until he collapses.

In the last scene, "Limbo," the suspect completes a letter. "I never thought of myself as being a minority. I thought I was a human being . . . because I never belonged to any group and yet I received a label. . . . It's more like an insult not being distinguished in a positve way but rather divided from the rest." He continues "It's easy for people to hate. Those who hate have become not human." The letter concludes: "All my life I've been heading in the wrong direction . . . playing someone who I am not. . . . I just wanted to belong, I wanted to be part of something. Now I'm part of nothing. How hard it is to be a human being without an identity."

Fareed Al-Oboudi takes Suspect through a journey of Arab-American stereotypes from rapist, spy, to terrorist. Through this trip he reveals the pain of alienation. Fareed, like James Baldwin in *Blues for Mr. Charly,* shocks and disturbs. *Portrait of a Suspect* reveals the anger of Arab-Americans victimized by prejudice. Fareed builds the insult of the interrogators to the point that everything looks possible and violence seems logical. The flashback technique and the use of slides support and enhance the content of the play. In a life of alienation, the past is part of the present, it reoccurs from moment to moment, opens the door to alienation and welcomes the audience to enter.

A study of the Arab-American theatrical movement does not reveal a high literary and artistically enduring quality right now, but it mostly does reveal attitudes, values, ideals, and aspirations of immigrants developing a community. It brings to light a new dimension to understanding the growth and development of the self-identity of an immigrant community in the United States. As a theater practitioner and scholar, I find the ongoing movement of evolving cultural character material of great value to be recorded and studied further.

The three types of theater represent a broad spectrum of Arab-American experiences today. They reach out not only to Arab-American audiences, but to the larger world in which they find themselves. And they reveal not only the wishes and dreams of Arab-Americans but their fears, to themselves and to others. Arab-Americans in their developing theater are bringing their past and their values to the U.S. culture of which they are now a part while at the same time they struggle to maintain their own identity and to define for themselves what that identity is. To be an Arab-American, say these plays, is to be both Arab and American and, for the time being at least, to be neither.

Ethnic Archetypes and the Arab Image

Ronald Stockton

Just think Happy—if we guess the identity of the Masked
Woman, we get a herd of camels, an oil concession, a
completely furnished harem, a goat . . .
—Steve Canyon, 1948

Our major cities are turning into war zones, with all the
violence in the streets that we see. We're in Detroit this week,
and this great city is being torn apart by violence. Many
people here are accustomed to the daily sound of gunshots
ringing out, fire bombs being launched, cars being torched.
Why? I'll tell you, pal. Because the largest community of
Arabs outside of the Middle East lives right here in Detroit . . .
—Morton Downey, Jr., November 18, 1988

The word stereotype originated in the early publishing industry and
refers to the wood block from which identical prints were derived
without variation or deviation. The word was popularized by Walter
Lippman in 1922 in his classic work on public opinion. Today it is
routinely used to describe unfriendly, undifferentiated imaging of
cultural or ethnic groups.

Philippe describes stereotyping as "a kind of motionlessness, a
repertory of eternally true types" (1980, 25). Stereotypes of course
can be hostile or nonhostile but we are more concerned with hostile
stereotypes that cause harm or do damage. Examples of nonhostile

stereotypes are that the Irish are cheerful or that Chinese are good at mathematics.

Perhaps the essential quality of stereotypes is that they take people "out of history" and deny them the right to change across time. It is as if somehow their traits were fixed or defined at some ancient moment and since that time their behavior has been pre-determined and ahistorical.

This essay focuses on American images of Arabs, especially in comics and cartoons; but in a sense the topic is much broader. The central thesis is that images of Arabs cannot be seen in isolation but are primarily derivative, rooted in a core of hostile archetypes that our culture applies to those with whom it clashes. The roots of these archetypes lie in ancient conflicts or cultural teachings that go back centuries or even millenia. In one sense their origins are so distant as to be irrelevant to contemporary realities, but their persistence across time attests to their potency and staying power. When conflict or tension emerges they can be conjured up and adapted to new situations.

The concept of generic archetypes is discussed at length by Sam Keen (1986), who focuses on "recurring images that have been used in different times and places to characterize the enemy" (13). Keen believes that in the human psyche—especially in wartime—there is a tendency to generate a hostile Other who somehow represents the negation of our own identity. In portraying such an enemy "the hostile imagination has a certain standard repertoire of images it uses to dehumanize the enemy. In matters of propaganda, we are all Platonists; we apply eternal archetypes to changing events" (13).

This essay will show that two hostile archetypes are particularly significant. The first was traditionally targeted at Africans, who were deemed to be inherently inferior in culture and biology; the second was traditionally targeted at Jews and describes peoples or nations with historically advanced cultures but now somehow believed to be pathologically in error because of some inherent flaw or trait. The two archetypes are typically called racism and anti-Semitism.

In his classic study of prejudice, Allport (1958) hinted at a "reciprocal character" or "complementary" quality in these image clusters, as if they somehow represented distinct poles of undesirability. "Between them they take care of the two major kinds of evil—the more 'physical' and the more 'mental'" (194). Allport also suggested that hostile images may be subject to a process of transference in which themes that originate with one group can be shifted to a completely different target. By way of example he cited California data showing local Armenians being saddled with images that were traditionally anti-Jewish (185).

The data in this study confirm and elaborate upon this Dual Archetype model. The conclusions in this chapter are based upon several hundred cartoons with Arab characters. Typical examples are included for illustration. The cartoons were taken from editorial pages, comic books, and newspaper comic strips. While the sample cannot be considered either comprehensive or scientifically drawn, it is nevertheless both extensive and representative of materials published in the past few decades. In preparing this study, I examined dozens of cartoon anthologies (by artist or by annual selection), scores of comic books with Arab (and non-Arab) characters, standard works on graphic arts and cartoon images, and a personal collection of several hundred political cartoons.

Comic books and cartoons are useful sources of data because they are aimed at a mass audience, use simplified graphic images, and often have action themes with some story or meaning. In attempting to communicate quickly and efficiently they rely upon reductionist images that contain and transmit cultural messages, often without or beyond verbal reinforcement. Analysis suggests that while some Arab-linked themes are unique to that group (such as those dealing with deserts, oil, or camels), an exceptional proportion of all hostile or derogatory images targeted at Arabs are derived from or are parallel to classical images of Blacks and Jews, modified to fit contemporary circumstances.

Classic Studies of Cultural Images

Since the focus of this essay is not limited to existing images but deals more broadly with the adaptation of pre-existing themes to contemporary situations it is important to understand the cultural legacy upon which those images are based. Rather than make an extensive review of the literature, two seminal case studies can be taken as illustrations of core models of classical images of Blacks and Jews. One is Winthrop Jordan's *White Over Black* (1968), an analysis of early American attitudes toward Africans and African-

Americans; the other is Norman Cohn's *Warrant for Genocide* (1966), a British study of European attitudes toward Jews. For comparison, we can also look at John Dower's *War without Mercy* (1986)—a study of the United States' wartime images of the Japanese—to see how certain themes were applied and adapted to a new conflict situation.

Case One: Blacks as a Savage People

Jordan (1968) focuses his analysis on the early formation of Western and American attitudes toward Africans and African-Americans. These attitudes began to take shape even before Westerners first penetrated the African continent in the 1500s. Even then there were "long-standing and apparently common notions about Africa" (34), some of which "derived from traditions which had been accumulating in Western culture since ancient times" (29). Those notions can be compressed into two main themes: the idea of a savage people whose brute instincts dominated their nature and a related concept of biological hierarchies in which certain races stand between civilized beings and animals.

Europeans decided very early that Africans were a savage people and frequently described them as "brutish" or "bestial" (28). They were believed to be "a lewd, lascivious, and wanton people" (32), lower than Europeans in intelligence, sophistication, economic creativity, self-discipline, ability to understand, religious development, and human civilization.

In the eyes of Europeans, it was no accident that Blacks were found on the African continent, a place inhabited by other human-like, black-skinned beings—the simians. There was considerable speculation about possible genetic links between the "man-like beasts and the beast-like men of Africa" (30), especially alleged sexual liaisons between the two. Such views grew from "a centuries-old tradition" about "an ordered hierarchy of sexual aggressiveness" among creatures (490). Beasts occupied one end of this hierarchy—engaging in shameless, promiscuous sexual activity—and humans the other. Blacks existed between the two, sharing characteristics of both beasts and humans.

The quasi-religious concept of a chain of being conveniently reinforced these perceptions. The concept is summarized in a 1799 treatise: "From man down to the smallest reptile . . . Nature exhibits

Peddling with a notions case, Worcester, Massachusetts (1898)

Back peddler, Birmingham, Alabama (ca. 1910)

Peddler showing his wares, Birmingham, Alabama (pre–World War I)

Horse drawn peddler's wagon (pre–World War I)

Ready-to-wear peddling truck (early 1920s)

Mr. Souri in his dry goods store on 36th Street, Georgetown, Washington, D.C. (1909)

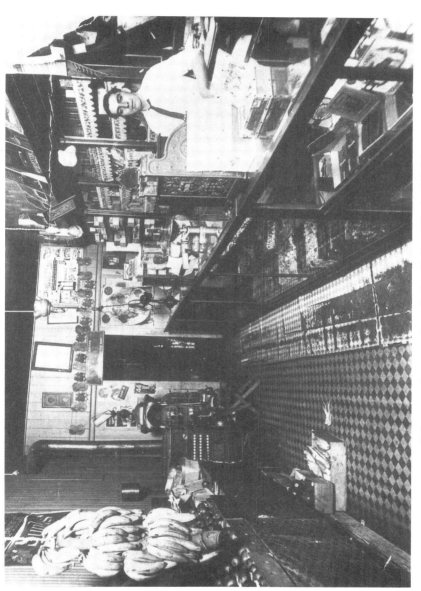

Tobacco and sweets shop, Spring Valley, Illinois (1920s)

Opening day, 1916

Wedding party, Fort Wayne, Indiana (1896)

The Nicola family, Bismark, North Dakota (pre–World War I)

The Boohaker family, Birmingham, Alabama (ca. 1923)

Dedication of St. George Orthodox Church by Bishop Germanos,
Detroit, Michigan (World War I)

Maronite girl, Palm Sunday, Detroit, Michigan (early 1920s)

Making *kibbi*

Immigrants from Zahle, Lebanon, gathering in a popular recreation area, Illinois (1930)

The Lebanese cast of *Hamlet*, Utica, New York (1915)

Posing in the flapper era (1920s)

Edward Najjar, Lebanese Druze doughboy, at Camp Fremont, California (1917)

Arab-American soldier, New Guinea, World War II

Mary, Lester, and Mike Nicola, first-prize winners in the 1917
Fourth of July Parade in Dickinson, North Dakota

to our view an immense chain of beings, endued with various degrees of intelligence and active powers, suited to their stations in the general system" (499). While "rank in creation" was not an inherently racist concept, the charged environment of slavery soon made it so. Also contributing to its transformation was the centuries-old conflict between Europe and the Turks which made nonwestern peoples seem inherently threatening and worthy of subjection. "International warfare seemed above all a ceaseless struggle between Christians and Turks. Slavery, therefore, frequently appeared to rest upon the 'perpetual enmity' which existed between Christians on the one hand and 'infidels' and 'pagans' on the other" (55). Subjection was also ideologically facilitated by the fact that Blacks in the United States were not seen as having the "quality of nationality." In Western thinking, "nations" were more advanced than "peoples." Given that Africans had been denationalized to the extent that "Negro nations tended to become Negro people" (90) they were more easily viewed as inferior and subjectable.

Case Two: Jews as an Inverted People

Classic anti-Semitism tended to see the Jews as an Inverted People whose values were the mirror image of those held by others. This belief originated in pseudo-Christian doctrines (since renounced by the Christian churches) and seen in full bloom in the infamous "Protocols of the Elders of Zion," a nineteenth-century Russian propaganda document. This mind-set held that while other peoples love God, the Jews killed God; while others love children, the Jews sacrifice children in their rituals; while others love their country, Jews betray theirs; while others work hard for a living, Jews cheat and lie for their livelihood; and while other peoples love peace, Jews thrive on war.

In outlining the structure of this logic, Cohn (1966) says that between the French Revolution and World War II "certain ancient and immensely destructive fantasies were reactivated" (19). These fantasies—that Jews were "mysterious beings, endowed with uncanny, sinister powers" (21)—go back to the second century after Christ when the church and the synagogue were competing for converts. During this time Christian leaders often portrayed Jews as "habitual murderers and destroyers" and the synagogue as "the temple of demons . . . the cavern of devils . . . a gulf and abyss of perdition" (21). During the Crusades such images were adapted so that Jews became "agents employed by Satan for the express purpose of combating Christianity and harming Christians" (22). Through their demonical religion they came to possess "limitless powers for evil" regardless of how weak they might seem (22).

According to the Protocols, Jews exercised their power through a mysterious council. Specifically, there was "a secret Jewish government which, through a world-wide network of camouflaged agencies and organizations, controls political parties and governments, the press and public opinion, banks and economic developments" (22–23). The goal of this group was world power. Their strategy was to generate domestic disorder and international war so as to enhance their own influence. Controlling as they allegedly did key international economic structures, they were very successful.

Overall, there were three kinds of classical anti-Jewish sentiments: hostility to the Jewish religion, seeing it as perverted and evil; demonical anti-Semitism, portraying Jews as the source of social disorder and disruption; and economic anti-Semitism, focusing on Jewish wealth and power. In combination, these alleged traits accounted for an exceptional proportion of social ills: bolshevism, capitalism, heavy taxes, debt, stalemated wars, unemployment, ecumenical religion, secularism, sexual license, drunkenness, breakdown of the family, and poor schools.

Cohn argues that these hostile images had exceptional power. "What Jews really were or did or wanted, or what Jews possibly could be or do or want, had nothing whatsoever to do with the matter." Once in place, images "can be deliberately exploited in multitudes of ordinary human beings. This had happened before, during the witch-mania that gripped Europe in the sixteenth and seventeenth centuries. It was to happen again as the myth of the Jewish world-conspiracy began its deadly work" (25).

Case Three: The Monkey Men of Asia

According to Dower's 1986 landmark study of U.S. and Japanese wartime propaganda, U.S. views of the Japanese built upon certain "formulaic expressions" and "archetypical images" whose origins went back several centuries and were long ago used to characterize nonwhites in general (9–10). Dower's argument parallels that of Jordan in suggesting that two beliefs were particularly important: the concept of a hierarchy of races and the idea of savage peoples. He sees a belief in "civilized" versus "savage" peoples as particularly significant for it provides an ideological foundation for racist thinking (149). From it grew the assertion that nonwhites have animal natures that place them in a lower stage of development characterized by primitiveness, immaturity, and serious deficiencies in the mental, moral, and emotional realms (153).

In the 1940s these traditional images were mobilized for war. The Japanese were portrayed as an inherently inferior people, subject to primitivism, childishness, and collective psychic deficiencies (9–10). Politically they were "fired by blind and relentless nationalistic ambitions ... given to 'mad dog' orgies of brutality and atrocity" (20). Constantly abstracted as "the Jap" they were denied "even the merest semblance of pluralism" (79). They were a "numerous and undifferentiated pack, devoid not merely of humanness and individuality but even of gender and age" (93). Their society was an impersonal anthill and their people subject to "sheep-like subservience" (83). They were "primitives or savages" in a tribal, uncivilized sense; they were "infantile or childish as individuals and as a group, collectively abnormal in the psychological and psychiatric sense, and tormented at every level by an overwhelming inferiority complex" (122). Their "suppressed individualism" was reinforced by "a primitive 'group ideology,' sanctified by an archaic communal religion and reinforced by centuries of tyranny" (141). They were "a race suffering from severe collective psychological disorders" (117).

In cartoons the Japanese were depicted as nonhumans or subhumans, "often as animals, reptiles, or insects" or as a "herd" (81). One common image was the octopus, grasping Asia in its tentacles, often reaching out to plunge daggers into the heart of neighboring lands (83–84). The simian personification was particularly popular, "perhaps the most basic of all metaphors traditionally employed by white supremacists to demean nonwhite peoples" (86). And while Hitler and the Nazis also occasionally emerged as simians, "this was a passing metaphor, a sign of aberration and atavism, and did not carry the explicit racial connotations of the Japanese ape" (87).

American Images of Arabs

In 1977, Lipset and Schneider detected in U.S. public opinion a pattern of attitudes toward Arabs that they described as "negative, close to racist" (22). Slade's 1981 analysis added that "The Arabs remain one of the few ethnic groups who can still be slandered with impunity in America" (143). Jarrar (1983) reported that a study of forty-three high school social studies textbooks found Arabs portrayed as "primitive, backward, desert dwelling, nomadic, war loving, terroristic and full of hatred" (387–88). And in 1984 Shaheen analyzed over 200 television programs and found that most Arab characterizations followed what he called "The Instant TV Arab Kit." The "kit" consists of "a belly dancer's outfit, headdresses (which look like tablecloths pinched from a restaurant), veils, sunglasses, flowing gowns and robes, oil wells, limousines and/or camels" (5).

In his classic study of Western attitudes toward the Middle East (including Islam, Turkey, Iran, and Arabs) Edward Said (1979) found a set of collective images applied to Eastern peoples that he summarized under the term "Orientalism." This image cluster contains within itself "the Western approach to the Orient . . . that collection of dreams, images, and vocabularies available to anyone who has tried to talk about what lies east of the dividing line" (73). While some of these views are ancient, many emerged during the thousand-year conflict between Europe and the Middle East, and were associated especially with the Crusades and later wars with the Ottoman Turks. During much of this time Europe was on the defensive, sometimes fearing for its survival. Not until the era of Napoleon did the balance shift so that Europeans became the rulers of the East.

Said's thesis is that Western Orientalist scholarship emerged during this era of Western ascendance, primarily a byproduct of conflict and conquest. Since Europe's primary orientation was in "dominating, restructuring, and having authority over the Orient" (3), Western scholarship had an inherent interest in portraying Arabs as simple, emotional, volatile, backward people, needing protection and elevation. The emergent Western view of the region was "more particularly valuable as a sign of European-Atlantic power over the Orient than it is as a verdical discourse about the Orient" (6). Scholarship became "a system of knowledge" that, "because generated out of strength, in a sense *creates* the Orient, the Oriental, and his world" (40).

Said says the key symbol of this alien world was Islam, a word that even today strikes fear in many Western hearts. Historically Islam represented the aggressiveness of the region, its threat, and its danger.

> Not for nothing did Islam come to symbolize terror, devastation, the demonic, hordes of hated barbarians. For Europe, Islam was a lasting trauma. Until the end of the seventeenth century the "Ottoman peril" lurked alongside Europe to represent for the whole of Christian civilization a constant danger, and in time European civilization incorporated that peril and its lore, its great events, figures, virtues, and vices, as something woven into the fabric of life. (59–60)

In a later analysis of American media and "expert" portrayals of Islam, Said observed that "in no really significant way is there a direct correspondence between the 'Islam' in common Western usage and the enormously varied life that goes on within the world of Islam" (Said 1981, x).

If Said summarizes classic Western images of the generic Orient, the Slade study cited above focuses more specifically on contemporary American attitudes. Slade relied upon a national public opinion poll that asked respondents to say whether certain words applied to different ethnic groups, Arabs being one. Analysis showed that most words associated with Arabs were unfriendly or hostile. *Rich* led the list with 69 percent thinking it applied; in second place with around 40 percent agreement were the words *warlike, mistreat women, treacherous and cunning, powerful, dark and swarthy, barbaric and cruel;* in third place were three positive images (*religious, intelligent, brave*) with 12–20 percent agreement; at the very bottom was *friendly* with only 5 percent thinking it typically Arab. In follow-up questions, 40 percent of respondents felt that most or all Arabs were anti-Christian, 40 percent felt they were anti-Semitic, and 44 percent felt they "Want to Destroy Israel and Drive the Israelis into the Sea." Further analysis suggested that two variables had exceptional power in explaining anti-Arab sentiments, a perception that Arabs were hostile to the West and a feeling that Arab men mistreat Arab women (Slade 1981).

Two Explanations

Explanations of why Arabs behave as they allegedly do tend to fall into two main categories: warped socialization practices and the unhealthy influence of Islam. The socialization argument parallels the pseudoanthropological or pseudopsychological models used against the Japanese (see Dower 1986, chaps. 5 and 6). The Islamic argument is not unlike some forms of religious anti-Semitism.

A classic example of unsympathetic writing is Raphael Patai's lengthy work, *The Arab Mind* (1972). Patai suggests that Arab males are corrupted at an early age by the fact that young boys are breast-fed well into the talking stage. This means that "the verbalization of the one major childhood desire, that for the mother's breast" is followed by "instant gratification." The psychological result is that

> the emphatic verbal formulation of the wish carries in itself, almost automatically, the guarantee of its fulfillment without the need for any additional action on the part of the child . . . It may not be too far-fetched to seek a connection between this situation in childhood and a characteristic trait of the adult Arab personality . . . the proclivity for making an emphatic verbal statement of intention and failing to follow it up with any action that could lead to its realization. (31)

Patai says that later socialization patterns (such as urging younger brothers to compete against the standards of older brothers) also generate sibling rivalries. These rivalries help explain Arab disunity and the "conflict proneness" that is an "outstanding characteristic of the Arab mind" (227). "At the slightest provocation the fighting propensity surfaces . . . and easily degenerates into physical violence" (225).

In Patai's model, Islam contributes to Arab problems by excluding "human will" from society. This exclusion makes long-range planning sinful since "it seems to imply that one does not put one's faith in divine providence" (150). Islam also encourages a willingness to accept "Oriental Despotism" since it teaches that good and evil are defined by an "absolute will" from above (148).

A more contemporary example of this kind of analysis is an article in *Omni* magazine on "The Importance of Hugging" (Bloom 1989). *Omni* is a mainstream popular science magazine not ordinarily given to ethnic bashing. In this case, the author argued that many of the ills of the Middle East are a by-product of child rearing practices. "Why do some societies seem to revel in violence?" he asks. His answer: societies that hugged their kids were relatively peaceful while "cultures that treated their children coldly produced brutal adults" (30). Islamic cultures "treat their children harshly. They despise open displays of affection. The result: violent adults. . . . Could the denial of warmth lie behind Arab brutality? Could these keepers of the Islamic flame be suffering from a lack of hugging? Could that deprivation help explain their thirst for blood?" (30). His conclusion: "In much of Arab society the cold and even brutal approach to children has still not stopped . . . and the Arab adult, stripped of intimacy and thrust into a life of cold isolation, has become a walking time bomb. An entire people may have turned barbaric for the simple lack of a hug" (116).

Explanations focusing upon Islam often emphasize the allegedly violent nature of the religion. Laffin (1975) suggests that in the Koran violence is "the most positive form of prayer" and as such "forms a thread in the normal fabric of life" (106, 108). For a non-Muslim to look for reason in such a conclusion is "to expect something logical from the fundamentally illogical" (131). A study of U.S. K-12 text-books (Al-Qazzaz 1983) found something similar, a "singular emphasis on war as an instrument for the spread of Islam." Such an approach, the author observed, "tends to create a misleading mental image in which Islam is associated primarily with holy war and violence" (376).

In the factional realm, similar images also persist. When Leon Uris (1985) described the Palestinian people in his best-selling novel *The Haj,* he drew together some of the most hostile and derogatory stereotypes imaginable. In one typical passage he described pre-1918 Palestine as "a mucky, diseased swamp" and "a backwater" covered with "a curtain of darkness." It was "devalued to bastardy and orphanhood . . . reduced to sackcloth and ashes." The political system was characterized by "total cruelty, total corruption." The local rulers had "no more compassion than the blistering sun" and showed "little mercy to the weak." People lived in "a system of absolute social order" in which "each man had a specific place in the tribe into which he was locked from birth to death. The only way to rise was to destroy." There was "no room for democratic principles" since "the law of the desert was absolute." The local Arab was a "thief, assassin, and raider" to whom "hard labor was immoral" (16–17). Uris also explained that "hatred is holy in this part of the world" and that for Muslims, "hatred of the Jews is sacred" (52, 55).

Themes Shared and Derivative

Each ethnic group has culturally assigned image themes unique to itself. Such themes are reserved for the group and cannot be easily transferred to others. To depict aggression or hostility, for example, one can portray a Black as a violent savage (in the jungle or in the street), a Jew with a knife ready to assault an unsuspecting innocent, and an Arab holding a sword dripping with blood. But Arabs cannot be accused of killing God, Jews cannot be shown in a jungle, and Blacks cannot be shown manipulating power from behind the scenes.

On the other hand, certain images or themes are more generic and *can* be transferred or adapted to different groups. Where depiction of Arabs is concerned, at least six image themes seem exogenous or derivative. These images are so similar to stereotypes of other groups that they almost certainly are adaptations.

Sexual depravity. One almost universal theme of hostile stereotyping is that our "enemies" are driven by crazed animal passions unchecked by social limits (Keen 1986, 58–60, 129–34). "Their" women are either shamefully promiscuous or have a thin veneer of pseudo-modesty which they take off as easily as a dress; their men view women as nothing but objects of pleasure, as chattel to be passed from one to another, or as booty to be taken by the strongest. Living as they do with the often unattractive or unsophisticated women of their own kind, the men are driven to the verge of madness by the beautiful women of our own people. Sometimes this lust is rooted in a pathological desire to possess and despoil, sometimes in a primitive drive to have that which is higher on the evolutionary scale, sometimes simply by the beauty of blond hair. Almost always their relations with "our" women have political overtones, the assertion of power, or a challenge to authority.

These themes were used against Jews and Blacks and are used against Arabs as well. Nazi propaganda often portrayed the lustful Jew enticing young girls, leering at a beautiful but modest Aryan woman, flirtatiously seducing an innocent, or forcing himself upon an unwilling victim (Bytwerk 1983). In action stories set in Africa it frequently happens that a blond female (Tarzan's mate, Jane, for example) is kidnapped or captured by vile natives whose evil intentions one can see only too clearly. Her pathetic cries as she is dragged off into the darkness are strikingly similar to action stories set in the

Arab world. The reader of these stories inevitably cringes with contempt at the brutality of her treatment, and at the inability of these savages to contain their lust. Occasionally a variant story will occur in which a white woman is captured or enchanted by a dashing Arab sheikh of the desert, is well treated, and falls in love with him. No such variant ever occurs with white women in Africa.

In an earlier era, Thomas Jefferson (1787) offered an explanation for this behavior. He hypothesized that Black males preferred white females over Blacks for reasons including "flowing hair, a more elegant symmetry of form, their own judgement in favour of the whites, declared by their preference of them, as uniformly as is the preference of the Oran-ootan for the black women over those of his own species" (138). In *The Haj* Leon Uris writes of Gideon, the Jewish hero in 1920s Palestine, and his relationship with promiscuous Palestinian women. As Uris describes it, Gideon "knew many women . . . frequently a dozen times a day" although "no Arab man ever knew or suspected" (23). Arab men, for their part, would raid Jewish settlements and would always "save one of the Jewish women for men's sport." (31).

Attitudes toward Arab women are illustrated in figures 1–5. They frequently appear as a faceless, indistinguishable mass, as in a Steve Canyon classic, available in contemporary reprint (fig. 1); in an adventure story about Sinbad they sit nude in their harem bath discussing past and future infidelities (fig. 2);[1] in a contemporary adventure story set in North Africa during World War II, an American unit meets an Arab father and his seemingly modest daughter Azir. That evening Azir undresses and performs for the soldiers as the embarrassed American hero tries to deal with the shameless father (fig. 3); later, Azir embraces and fondles an American sentry to distract him so he can be strangled.

---

1. The term harem is misunderstood in the West. In a bedouin tent there is a cloth that separates one side from the other. One side is the public area where guests are received. Men and women alike can be on that public side although it is mostly for men. The other section is for women and children only. It is where food is prepared and where women sit to chat. The two sections are a few feet from each other so that people on different sides can exchange comments or share conversations. The harem of Western imagination is in contrast a luxurious place where the multiple wives of a powerful man lounge carelessly on pillows awaiting their turn to be called for wifely duty. The women are always young, always attractive, and frequently seminude. Much of their time is spent bathing and perfuming in anticipation of their call. For an honest perspective on the institution of the "harem" see Croutier 1991.

Fig. 1

Fig. 2

The attitudes of Arab men toward women range from the shameless pandering of Azir's father to pathological possessiveness. When a blond woman ventures into the Middle East, an Arab ruler decides to add her to his harem—without bothering to ask her views on the

Fig. 3

matter (fig. 4); when Tarzan ventures into a nightclub to find another Westerner he is confronted by an Arab horde who accuse him of "insulting" a seminude belly dancer they had enslaved for their pleasure. The invective against Tarzan is typical of that used by cartoon Arabs (fig. 5). When the Arabs push Tarzan too far, the text tells us that his anger explodes like "a desert storm."

Creature Analogies. While Arabs are sometimes subjected to the racial simian analogy they are more frequently subjected to vermin images closely paralleling the painful Jewish experience. This has been especially true in situations involving violence or war. Palestinians in particular have been portrayed as rats malevolently entering a house or caught in a trap, or as fleas infesting a region and being exterminated.

In the wake of the 1982 Israeli invasion of Lebanon, several cartoons portrayed Palestinians in this manner. A classic by Scrawls asks the difference between a rat and Arafat and finds the rat more

Fig. 4

Fig. 5

lovable (fig. 6). Szep used the simian analogy to show Palestinian apes cheering bombastic Ape Chieftan Arafat (fig. 7).

Among less flattering camel images was an Oliphant cartoon showing an Arab household complete with tent, faceless wives in black, and a scruffy male with a profile strikingly similar to his beast (fig. 8). Oliphant originally set the scene in Libya but apparently liked it so much that he later placed it virtually unchanged in Saudi Arabia. During the Gulf War the camel theme was especially popular, relaying an image of a people wedded to desert-style warfare (fig. 9). A widely distributed T-shirt also showed an Iraqi soldier on a camel, both in a gun sight, with the slogan "I'd Travel Ten Thousand Miles to Smoke a Camel."

But this reference to a classical cigarette slogan was not entirely good for the company. In earlier times, cigarettes were associated with the Arab world and the Arab image was a boost to sales. But today is different and in the 1980s, Camel Cigarettes found themselves burdened with a negative "camel" logo. Their solution was to contain the damage by an aggressive "Joe Camel" advertising campaign. Their "Smooth Character" attracted beautiful women, drove fast cars, wore tuxedos, and was a war hero. He quickly became a popular figure and surveys showed his recognition at an exceptionally high level. Perhaps there is some truth in the old piece of advice: When the world gives you lemons, make lemonade.

Physiological and psychological traits. Here the parallel between the depiction of Jews and Arabs is striking. The physiological traits of the generic evil Jew are well-known: thick lips, weak chin, crooked nose, shifty eyes, unkempt hair, scruffy beard, vile leering mouth, crooked teeth. The generic Black also has unpleasant physical qualities: thick lips, heavy brow, ugly teeth, stupid expression, stooped shoulders, bent knees, long arms (Hardy and Stern 1986).

The generic Arab shares with Jews thick lips, evil eyes, unkempt hair, scruffy beard, weak chin, crooked nose, vile look. He also shares with Blacks thick lips, heavy brow, stupid expression, stooped shoulders. This double overlap suggests that image transfer may be working at multiple levels. It may be that in earlier eras Jews were saddled with the images of despised Africans and that those images are now being transferred to Arabs. Certainly, Jewish images during the era of Rembrandt are completely different from Jewish images today. Likewise, Arab images earlier in this century were much more benign.

Fig. 6

Then exotic, nonhostile themes were dominant, including the romantic sheik and the friendly native. The noticeable shift came after the 1967 war when political tension apparently revived certain hostile images and grafted them onto a new target.

It is ironic but not illogical that Jewish images would be superimposed on Arabs. It was not until the late 1800s that the word *Semite* changed from a linguistic term incorporating both Arabs and Jews into a more specialized term applying only to Jews (Kraemer 1967). Earlier, Shakespeare's Arab Othello and his Jew Shylock were—in spite of vastly different personalities—both transplants from the Middle East whose alien values left disorder and tension in their wake. That cartoonists should follow the connection by using parallel depictions is not surprising.

In 1989 a national monthly on Middle East affairs published a cartoon on "The Arab Mind." The similarity with a cartoon ninety years earlier on "The Jewish Mind" is striking (figs. 10 and 11). "Reading the Arab Mind" shows a generic cartoon Arab—prominent nose, thick lips, heavy eyebrows, shifty eyes. Inside the mind are predictably simplistic ways of thinking: fanaticism, vengeance, double

Fig. 7

PERHAPS VE COULD INTEREST YOU IN GLOBAL SUPREMACY THROUGH PHARMACEUTICAL INVESTMENT, JA?'

Fig. 8

Fig. 9

talk, fratricidal hatreds. The parallel with the generic "Jewish mind" a hundred years earlier is striking. In the Jewish mind are worship of money, propensity to theft, and unwillingness to serve one's country. The common physical features of Arab and Jew include a curved nose and facial hair. Both minds center upon socially hostile orientations to the world and rigid mental compartmentalization with thought processes alien to normal humans. The pervasive theme in stereotyping—that the group shares a common mind set that allows for little individual variation—is clearly present. The fact that "the Arab Mind" was published by a Jewish group merely shows that stereotypes are culture wide and do not exempt any subgroup from being affected by such thinking.

Savage leaders. A common scene in racist comics or cartoons has the witchdoctor or chief—driven by wild xenophobic passion and bravado—renouncing whites and calling upon the natives to destroy them or drive them out. The witchdoctor or chief is usually depicted with his arm flailing wildly in the air, his face contorted with hatred. The natives—dangerous in their simplistic acceptance of whatever they are told—respond with hysterical passion, often jumping into the air or chanting slogans such as "kill, kill" (Hardy and Stern 1986).

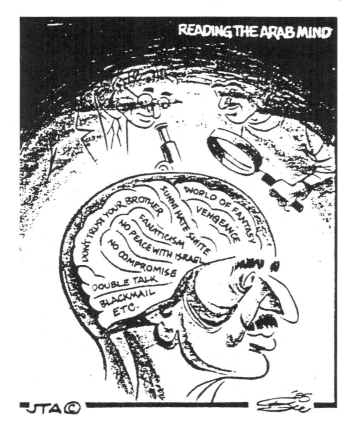

Fig. 10

Depictions of Arab leaders often rely upon similar images. In action stories a common theme has a tribal chieftan or megalomaniacal dictator calling upon his people to attack or drive out foreigners (often religious or Crusade-linked words are used, such as "jihad" or "infidel"). The motive of the ruler is often personal, perhaps an imagined slight or a desire to maintain his power unchecked by the civilized ideas that might be brought in by outsiders. The unstated but obvious weapons of the leader include the simplemindedness of the people, their innate xenophobia, their prejudice against foreigners, their antipathy to structured norms. Their response is enthusiastic, passionate, irrational, dangerous. In a comic-book style biography distributed by the Catholic church, even the gentle St. Francis is

Les qualités du Juif d'apres la méthode de Gall

Fig. 11

threatened as he tries to mediate the Crusades, and is nearly killed for his effort (fig. 12).

In a 1988 story, America's counter-terrorist group (code named GI JOE) must go into an Arab Emirate where a ruler named Sharif "has been known to behead jaywalkers." Sharif's band of followers (the word army would be too dignified) are called Guardians of Paradise (fig. 13). The term Paradise is itself an ironic word to describe the mound of useless sand Sharif controls. The Guardians cheer wildly when he urges them into battle, with assurance that the infidels are "weak and cowardly" and that "a special place is promised in paradise for all who fall in the cause." In the final confrontation, dozens of Guardians die as two courageous Americans—one male, one female—stand against them.

Fig. 12

Fig. 13

The related theme of the blustering Arab is used to describe that most dangerous of all Middle East cartoon creatures, the desert Bedouin. This prototypical Arab is known for ruthlessness, cruelty, deceit, and a tendency to view life as a cheap commodity. The way to deal with such people (according to cartoonists) is to recognize that while they appear tough and aggressive they are in truth weak and cowardly. The bluff and bluster is neutralized if one stands up to them. In a Lawrence of Arabia retelling, Lawrence is "tested" by a stream of invectives. He maintains his poise and punches out his assailant. This action astonishes a second tormentor and wins the admiration (and political support) of the Prince, who has been watching secretly from the sidelines (fig. 14).

A more contemporary story occurs when Batman visits Beirut to find Robin's long lost mother. When he encounters a terrorist army his comment—"this is going to be easier than I thought"—is painfully reminiscent of a parallel mindset during the 1983 marine mission to that troubled land (fig. 15). President Reagan's masterful understatement when 241 marines died in their barracks was that "the situation in Beirut was much more difficult and complex than we initially believed" (Reagan 1990, 461). Reagan went on to explain that Arab "depravity," "ancient tribal rivalries," and "pathological hatred" had produced an "irrationality" that challenged the "moral" commitments upon which American policy was based. "How do you deal with a people driven by such a religious zeal that they are willing to sacrifice their lives in order to kill an enemy simply because he doesn't worship the same God as they do?" (462–63).

Later in the Batman story, when Bruce Wayne (Batman) arrives in Beirut and hails a taxi, he is able to converse freely with the driver (readers are told) because he is fluent in Farsi. Readers are *not* told that Farsi is a non-Arabic language spoken in Iran but not Lebanon. When Ayatollah Khomeini then hires Batman's nemesis, the Joker, a murderous sociopath, to be Iran's UN ambassador, the new ambassador appears at the General Assembly wearing a Saudi-style headdress rather than an Iranian-style turban.

The blurring of identities and sharing of themes is also seen in the similarity between the anti-Arab concept of the "Law of the Desert" and the anti-African "Law of the Jungle."

In parallel but bizarre ways Blacks and Arabs are shown with norms of life that civilized Westerners cannot understand. Their rules of social order dehumanize people, elevate the most evil elements of society, and promote regimented, mindless obedience. Ultimately, their way of doing things is counterproductive and contrary to their own interests, but they can never recognize this.

Fig. 14

A war of darkness against light. The war theme has been attached to the Arab image since the time of the Crusades, but there is a twist of demonization in contemporary depictions which is more intense than justified by a conflict that ended 800 years ago. The Arab desire to conquer is attributed to a pathological desire to destroy civilization or to cause ill for humanity. Somehow Arabs allegedly believe that generating social disruption and disorder will promote their own selfish or parochial interests. They are not just enemies in a temporal sense but are enemies in a metaphysical sense as well.

One cannot help but note the striking parallel between this theme and how Jews were depicted in the *Protocols* and in Nazi propaganda. Like Jews, Arabs allegedly engage in war and terrorism to undermine social order itself. They kill because they enjoy it, just as medieval Jews allegedly sacrificed Christian children as a part of their faith. Like the Jews before them, Arabs are portrayed as an Inverted People.

Deceit. One of the vilest anti-Semitic (and later Nazi) accusations against Jews was that they were perfidiously deceitful where war and peace were concerned. In particular, they would allegedly wrap themselves in the mantle of peace while secretly working for war (Cohn 1966; Gitelman 1988). They were a people whose very God was war, and who would thrive on the destruction of the nations.

Fig. 15

Similarly, deceit is one of the main traits of cartoon Arabs. They pretend to want peace, but work for war. Arab leaders are shown firing at the dove of peace and shrinking in horror at a small desert flower labeled "peace." In a Herblock classic not reproduced ("Operation Peace") Doctors Arafat, Assad, King Hussein and others carve up a female victim with a palm branch in her fallen hand, proclaiming with crocodile tears that "unfortunately" the victim died.

Conversely those who break rank and really do seek peace are quickly martyred. In "The Sting of Death" an Arab delegate attending UN Peace Talks is assassinated (fig. 16). And in a story set in Israel, the army discovers that a violent terrorist is really El Rachmi, the gentle West Bank businessman who was pretending to help keep the peace (fig. 17).

Fig. 16

Fig. 17

Secret power. Is it possible for those who are in power to be controlled by elements unseen? Is it possible for small, powerful groups to have puppets who do their bidding? If so, what would be the nature of those secret power brokers?

In the *Protocols* Jews are seen as the secret rulers of the world, a people who have a centuries-long plan and a centuries-old organization for controlling and manipulating those who appear to rule. Their power is based partially on their wealth but even more on their cunning and their ability to support policies that appear to benefit general society but in reality weaken those societies and allow Jews to occupy the vacuum. *The International Jew* (undated, ca. 1920), a famous series of articles published in Henry Ford's newspaper, the *Dearborn Independent,* contains a U.S. variant. Volume 1 has articles on "The Jewish World Program," "Jewish Imperialism," "The Jewish Plan to Split Society," "Jews and the Russian Revolution," "Jews and American Farms," "Jewish Power and the World Press," "Jewish Political Power," and "The Jewish Mark on Red Russia."

The image of Arabs as a secret power bloc is somewhat different. Their power is seen as based on their oil and on the moral weakness and naivete of Western leaders. They buy support and friends with their vast wealth. Their property and investments in the United States enable them to manipulate existing political structures. The image of Arabs as power brokers is often represented by bags of currency, vast checks, offers to purchase whole industries, direct payoffs, and secret board meetings where decisions are made. Much of this is definitely reminiscent of the Jewish Elders.

One parody of this stereotype in the mid-1970s by *Mad* magazine suggested a commemorative stamp ("Sucking Up To The Arabs") to show things "the way they are" (fig. 18). Several cartoons in the mid-1980s showed Jesse Jackson as the paid agent of Arab money. One Szep masterpiece entitled "Jesse of Arabia" showed Jackson in an Arab headdress. Another showed Jackson leaving an Arab embassy with bags of money with the chant of Jackson supporters in 1984, "Run, Jesse, Run," as the theme.

Hatred of Israel. While on the surface this theme seems unique to the post-1948 world, in fact its essential components and the images used to illustrate it are very similar to the images of Jews as the enemies of God. Just as Jews were accused of deicide, Arabs are sometimes accused of intended genocide. We must also remember that to many Christians, hating Israel—a nation believed to have been selected by God—is no less than hating God.[2] One does not want to conjure up pseudoparallels where they are weak or ques-

---

2. Simon 1984 and Stockton 1987 present distinct approaches to the belief that the creation of a Jewish state in Palestine in 1948 was the fulfillment of God's will.

Fig. 18

tionable or to engage in the rhetoric wars so harmful where discussions about the Israeli-Palestinian dispute are concerned, but the image of Arabs as the destroyers of God's people has been so strongly stated that the possibility of an image transfer must be considered.

The parallel theme of terrorism is also used. Terrorism is a frightening word, often ill-defined, that conjures up images of demonical souls determined to inflict pain on the innocent for no reason other than to see people suffer. Terrorists allegedly enjoy violence, exacting a particular pleasure at seeing the innocent suffer. They are often portrayed as leering gleefully at their evil deeds. It is one of the most pervasive themes used against Arabs (fig. 19). The fact that Arabs are more often the victims of brutality than its perpetrators is largely overlooked.

After the Algiers Conference of 1988 when the PLO renounced terrorism, recognized Israel, accepted the right of Israel to exist as a Jewish state, and called for a negotiated settlement between Jews and Palestinians, Israeli intelligence concluded that "the PLO has undergone a genuine change and is truly interested in a peaceful settlement with Israel" (*New York Times,* April 2, 1989, p. 6). Cartoonists saw it differently. Most portrayed the Palestinian effort as a

Fig. 19

charade or as a tactical shift, a "fashion statement" if you will.
Yassir Arafat was often shown in designer sunglasses or wearing a
stylish "peace" keffiya, recently purchased (fig. 20). And of course,
the fact that Arafat was not assassinated reinforced the belief that
he was only putting on a performance for Western consumption. To
many observers, the assumption that Arabs lie was so ingrained that
they were unable to see historical events in terms other than that of
a pre-existing mind set. The devious smile on Arafat's face—similar
to that in other cartoons at the time—leads one to ask, "Would you
buy a used car from this man, much less a peace treaty?" It was
not until 1993 when Israeli leader Rabin shook hands with Arafat
that Palestinian statements were granted credibility by cartoonists.

The Cost of Hostile Images

A skeptic might ask what difference it makes if we harbor stereotypes.
Is it not natural that we generalize about others and hold unfriendly

ARAFAT'S NEW FASHION STATEMENT

Fig. 20

views of foreign or alien peoples, especially those from regions with whom our nation may have tense relations?

We would have to answer "yes" to these questions, but we would also have to point out that what is natural is not necessarily desirable. There are four reasons why one might want to minimize or resist harsh stereotyping.

First, especially where domestic populations are concerned, the costs to the victims are considerable. An estimated two million Arab-Americans (Naff 1983, 9) and over three million Muslims from a variety of ethnic backgrounds (Haddad 1986, 1) are subjected to hostile and derogatory imaging. The harm to children alone is enough to justify a reconsideration of techniques by cartoonists.

Second, entrenched stereotypes (even demonologies) play definite roles in historical outcomes, rationalizing and justifying policies otherwise unacceptable. In the case of Africans, it facilitated the acceptance of slavery, an intolerable institution if applied to whites; in the case of Jews, the outcome was centuries of persecution and ultimately the murder of millions of innocent individuals; with Japan, it led to conflict conducted with such fury that Dower (1986) called it "a war without mercy."

It is important to remember that while government policies are not simple outgrowths of public opinion, governments operate within parameters defined by what the public will tolerate. If the public is willing to dehumanize a population—be it domestic or foreign—then exceptional latitude is allowed where human rights are concerned. Slavery, brutal war, mass murder, assassination, and indifference to suffering become more acceptable.

A third outcome is inept policy making. As Dower argues about World War II, the Japanese and the Americans misunderstood and underestimated each other. Japan was convinced that the United States was a weak, fading, decadent culture, incapable of sustained resistance. Americans for their part believed Japan was a backward land, doomed to technological ineptness and organizational malfunction. As Dower says of U.S. decision making, "racist anti-Japanese myths overrode rational intelligence gathering" and "prejudice masqueraded as fact" (101, 102). The Japanese went to Pearl Harbor assuming the United States would surrender; the United States was convinced Germany was behind the attack since Japan was incapable of such a sophisticated maneuver. Both sides were wrong, and both suffered dire consequences as a result.

Finally, stereotyping leads to what theologian Allan Boesak (1979) calls a false "innocence." By portraying others in a hostile way or by portraying ourselves as blameless victims of some Manichaean opposite, we engage in a process of self-denial and mutual dehumanization. Faced with issues "too horrendous to contemplate" we deny responsibility for our own actions. "This pseudoinnocence cannot come to terms with the destructiveness in oneself or in others and hence it actually becomes self-destructive" (4).

Put another way, if stereotyping requires misrepresentation of the enemy, it also requires misrepresentation of ourselves (Keen 1986, 23). If our enemies are irrational, aggressive, expansionist, and brutal then it follows that we are rational, accommodationist, peaceful, and gentle. If our enemy abuses women, then it must be that we respect women. If our enemy is racist or intolerant, then it follows that we are egalitarian and open minded. If our enemy has cruel rulers who devalue human life, then our rulers must be pious souls who put human life above all else. As Dower (1986) says, those who live in the realm of stereotypes "reveal more about themselves than about the enemy they are portraying" (27).

BIBLIOGRAPHY

Allport, Gordon. *The Nature of Prejudice.* Garden City, N.Y.: Doubleday Anchor, 1958.
Al-Qazzaz, Ayad. "Image Formation and Textbooks." In Ghareeb, *Split Vision,* 369–380, 1983.
American-Arab Anti-Discrimination Committee (ADC). *The Uprising in Cartoons.* Washington, D.C.: American-Arab Anti-Discrimination Committee, Issue Paper 21, 1988.
Appel, John, and Selma Appel. "The Arab Image in American Film and Television." Washington, D.C.: American-Arab Anti-Discrimination Committee, n.d.
————. *Jews in American Graphic Satire and Humor.* Cincinnati: American Jewish Archives, 1984.
Balch Institute. *Ethnic Images in Advertising.* Philadelphia: Balch Institute, 1984.
Bloom, Howard. "The Importance of Hugging." *Omni* (February, 1989): 30–31.
Boesak, Allan Aubrey. *Farewell to Innocence: A Socio-Ethical Study on Black Theology and Power.* Maryknoll, N.Y.: Orbis Books, 1979.
Bytwerk, Randall. *Julius Streicher: The Man Who Persuaded a Nation to Hate Jews.* New York: Stein and Day, 1983.
Caniff, Milt. *Steve Canyon Magazine.* Princeton, Wis.: Kitchen Sink Press, 1948. Reprint.
Christian Nationalist Crusade. *Protocols of the Learned Elders of Zion.* 1903. Reprint. Eureka Springs, Ark.: Christian Nationalist Crusade, n.d.
Cohn, Norman. *Warrant for Genocide: The Myth of the Jewish World-Conspiracy and the Protocols of the Elders of Zion.* New York: Harper and Row, 1966.
Croutier, Alev. *Harem: The World Behind the Veil.* New York: Abbeville Press, 1991.
Damon, George H., Jr., with Laurence D. Michalak. "A Survey of Political Cartoons Dealing with the Middle East." In *Split Vision,* ed. Edmund Ghareeb, 143–56, 1983.
Dower, John. *War Without Mercy: Race and Power in the Pacific War.* New York: Pantheon Books, 1986.
Feiffer, Jules. *The Great Comic Book Heroes.* New York: Bonanza Books, 1965.
Ghareeb, Edmund. *Split Vision: The Portrayal of Arabs in the American Media.* Washington, D.C.: Arab-American Affairs Council, 1983.
Gitelman, Zvi. *A Century of Ambivalence: The Jews in Russia and the Soviet Union, 1881 to the Present.* New York: Schocken, 1988.
Haddad, Yvonne Y. "A Century of Islam in America." Washington, D.C.: The Middle East Institute, 1986.

Hardy, Charles, and Gail Stern. *Ethnic Images in the Comics*. Philadelphia: Balch Institute, 1986.

Hess, Stephen, and Milton Kaplan. *The Ungentlemanly Art: A History of American Political Cartoons*. New York: Macmillan, 1975.

The International Jew: The World's Foremost Problem. Dearborn, Michigan: The Dearborn Independent, 1922. Reprint.

Jarrar, Samir Ahmad. "The Treatment of Arabs in U.S. Social Studies Textbooks. In *Split Vision,* ed. Edmund Ghareeb, 381–90, 1983.

Jefferson, Thomas. *Notes on the State of Virginia*. 1787. Reprint ed. William Peden. New York: W. W. Norton & Company, 1954.

Jordan, Winthrop. *White Over Black: American Attitudes Toward the Negro, 1515–1812*. Chapel Hill: University of North Carolina Press, 1968.

Keen, Sam. *Faces of the Enemy: Reflections on the Hostile Imagination*. San Francisco: Harper and Row, 1986.

Kraemer, Joel L. *Historic Confrontations Between Jew and Arab*. Hadassah Education Department, 1967.

Laffin, John. *The Arab Mind Considered: A Need For Understanding*. New York: Taplinger Publishing Company, 1975.

Lendenmann, G. Neal. "Arab Stereotyping in Contemporary American Political Cartoons. In *Split Vision,* ed. Edmund Ghareeb, 345–54, 1983.

Lippmann, Walter. *Public Opinion*. 1922. Reprint. New York: Free Press, 1965.

Lipset, Seymour Martin, and William Schneider. "Carter vs. Israel: What the Polls Reveal." *Commentary* (1977): 21–29.

Michalak, Laurence. *Cruel and Unusual: Negative Images of Arabs in American Popular Culture*. Washington, D.C.: American-Arab Anti-Discrimination Committee, Issue Paper 15, n.d.

Naff, Alixa. "Arabs in America: A Historical Overview." In *Arabs in the New World: Studies on Arab-American Communities,* ed. Nabeel Abraham and Samir Abraham. Detroit: Wayne State University Center for Urban Studies, 9–29, 1983.

Patai, Raphael. *The Arab Mind*. New York: Charles Scribner's Sons, 1972.

Philippe, Robert. *Political Graphics: Art As a Weapon*. Oxford: Phaedon Press, 1980.

Press, Charles. *The Political Cartoon*. Madison: Farleigh-Dickenson University Press, 1981.

Reagan, Ronald. *Ronald Reagan: An American Life*. New York: Simon and Schuster, 1990.

Said, Edward W. *Orientalism*. New York: Vintage Books, 1979.

———. *Covering Islam*. New York: Pantheon, 1981.

Shaheen, Jack. *The TV Arab*. Bowling Green, Ohio: Bowling Green State University Popular Press, 1984.

———. "Palestinians on the Silver Screen in the 1980's." *American-Arab Affairs* 28 (1989): 68–80.

———. "The Comic Book Arab." *Link* (Nov.–Dec., 1991): 1–11.

————. *The Influence of the Arab Stereotype of American Children.* Washington, D.C.: American-Arab Anti-Discrimination Committee, n.d.

Simon, Merrill. *Jerry Falwell and the Jews.* Middle Village, N.Y.: Jonathan David Publishers, 1984.

Slade, Shelly. "The Image of the Arab in America: Analysis of a Poll." *Middle East Journal* 35 (1981): 143–62.

Stockton, Ronald R. "Christian Zionism: Prophecy and Public Opinion." *The Middle East Journal* 41 (1987): 234–53.

Uris, Leon. *The Haj.* New York: Bantam Books, 1985.

Zogby, James. *The Other Anti-Semitism: The Arab as Scapegoat.* Washington, D.C.: American-Arab Anti-Discrimination Committee, n.d.

Anti-Arab Racism and Violence in the United States

Nabeel Abraham

Few people would dispute that racism, prejudice, and hate violence continue to be features of our society. If anything, one is likely to hear that such phenomena are on the upswing. No one would doubt, for example, that African-Americans continue to encounter prejudice and hostility in the contemporary United States. Or that Jews face anti-Semitism, even though the evidence suggests anti-Jewish bigotry has been on the decline until recently. Or that Hispanics, Asians, and Native Americans, as well as women and gays, confront prejudice and bigotry. These matters are largely taken for granted, much like environmental pollution and government waste.

At issue is the extent of the racism in contemporary society, particularly its nature and scope. This study addresses this question in relation to anti-Arab racism. The discussion of racism and hate violence in general tends to focus mainly on the activities of fringe white supremacist and racist groups.[1] A study undertaken by the Center for

---

This essay was written before the Gulf crisis occurred. A postscript has been added to cover some of the war's impact on Arab-Americans. For a detailed account of this period see the author's "The Gulf Crisis and Anti-Arab Racism in America" (1991).

An earlier version of the present paper was excerpted in the Italian publication *Invarianti,* under the title: "Razzismo e violenza antiaraba negli Stati Uniti" (Rome, Autumn-Winter 1990–91).

1. The term *racism* is used here broadly to mean an irrational attitude of hostility (i.e., prejudice) directed against racial, ethnic, and national groups or their supposed characteristics, suggesting a denial of human worth as well as human and civil rights.

Democratic Renewal (CDR) and published by the National Council of Churches recorded nearly 3,000 acts of "bigoted violence" occurring in the United States during the period 1980 to 1986. According to its author, the CDR report is "the first national overview of bigoted violence to cover a several-year period since the re-emergence of hate groups in the 1970s" (Lutz 1987, Foreword). The picture that emerges is that "members of far-right, racist and anti-semitic organizations" constitute the main source of racism and hate violence in contemporary society. Their crude racial and anti-Semitic doctrines along with acts of violence against African-Americans, Jews, Hispanics, Asians, and gays make white racist and neo-Nazi groups logical candidates on which to pin much of society's racism and hate violence.

But how accurate is this picture? A careful reading of the CDR and other reports raises some doubts. For one, the CDR report notes that while "[t]here are no areas of the country where white supremacist organizations have been extremely active without correspondingly high levels of bigoted violence," the converse is *not* true, since "there are areas of the country which have experienced high levels of bigoted violence without correspondingly high levels of organized white supremacists" (Lutz 1987, 17). In another report on hate violence the reader learns that "anti-Semitic vandalism, overwhelmingly, is not the work of organized hate groups. Rather these incidents are most often the work of teenagers unaffiliated with hate groups; year after year, some 80 percent to 90 percent of those arrested for such crimes have been aged 20 or younger" (Anti-Defamation League n.d., henceforth ADL). Although this observation applies narrowly to anti-Semitic incidents, it seems likely that it is equally true of racist vandalism and violence generally. This conclusion is indirectly supported by the fact that the Ku Klux Klan (KKK) and various neo-Nazi organizations have been in decline since the early 1980s. In 1987, the KKK numbered only between 4,500 and 5,500 members, "its lowest total in 14 years," while neo-Nazis could "claim no more than 400–450 members . . ." In brief, "[t]he overall pattern of decline has been steady and has brought the hate movement back down to where it was when it began its mid-70s effort at resurgence" (ADL 1987, 1–2).

If claims about right-wing and racist groups appear exaggerated, the tendency remains nonetheless to view such groups as the main source of racism in contemporary society. Conventional wisdom narrowly ascribes racism and hate violence to white supremacist and neo-

Nazi groups.[2] Yet there are glaring discrepancies in this view as well. The CDR report and ADL studies make no mention of the activities of Jewish extremist groups such as the Jewish Defense League (JDL).[3] The latter group is said to be "one of the most active terrorist groups in the United States," responsible for killing seven persons and wounding at least twenty-two between 1968 and 1985 (Hoffman 1986, 11, 15; Friedman 1986, 1988a). According to an authoritative 1987 study by John W. Harris, Jewish extremist organizations committed "approximately 20 terrorist incidents and numerous other acts of violence, including extortion and threats . . ." or about a quarter of the total terrorist acts committed on the U.S. mainland during the 1980s. In 1985, when terrorism in the United States had decreased sharply, Jewish extremists carried out four of the seven reported terrorist acts, resulting in at least two deaths and several serious injuries (Harris 1987, 6).[4] As will become evident below, Jewish extremist groups constitute an undeniable source of anti-Arab hate violence not discussed in conventional accounts of racist violence in the United States.

Curiously, the CDR report makes a single passing reference to the JDL, ironically placing it in a favorable light. The report refers to a 1986 incident in Los Angeles in which: "A security guard was assaulted by an American Nazi Party member during a clash between white supremacists and the Jewish Defense League members . . ." (Lutz 1987, 24). Even more bizarre is the description of the 1985 murder of Arab-American activist Alex Odeh (see below) on the same page of the report. The murder is cited without mentioning that the JDL was implicated in the bombing (among other bombings that year) that killed Odeh. It seems odd that a major report on racist violence would omit a deadly source of hate violence in the United States.

---

2. A recent study, for example, lists sixty-seven "racist and anti-Semitic hate organizations" that openly advocate or engage in acts of violence. All are extreme rightwing, Christian-hate, and neo-Nazi groups; no Jewish extremist groups are mentioned. (See ADL 1988a, 1988b.)

3. Equally curious was the CDR report's tendency to label abortion clinics bombed by antiabortion fanatics "women's health clinics", another indication that ideological considerations were taken into account in the study. The ADL issued a "listing" of JDL leader Meir Kahane's "racist, violent, and anti-democratic statements," without delving into the violent activities of Jewish extremist organizations (see ADL 1985).

4. See also the testimony of FBI executive assistant director Oliver B. Revell, before the House Subcommittee on Criminal Justice (U.S. Congress 1988, 9–12).

The omission of Jewish extremist groups from the discussion of hate violence is odd for another reason. Whereas white racist groups have experienced a marked decline in membership in recent years and remain indisputably on the fringe of society, Jewish extremist groups like the JDL and the Jewish Defense Organization (JDO) have expanded their base of support among mainstream Jews.[5] Rabbi Meir Kahane, founder and spiritual advisor of the JDL, and long considered a dangerous demagogue by leaders of mainstream Jewish organizations, continued nevertheless to receive wide acceptance and financial support from U.S. Jews right up to his assassination in early November 1990. Journalist Robert Friedman observes:

> While the Brooklyn-born rabbi's supporters in Israel are mainly poor Sephardic slum youth, in the United States, where he raises money, Kahane has over the years attracted an odd collection of admirers, including former Haagen-Dazs ice cream president Rueben Mattus, 1987 Tony Award-winner Jackie Mason and attorney Barry Slotnick, who last year [1987] successfully defended subway gunman Bernard Goetz and reputed mobster John Gotti. (1988a, 45)

Friedman cites a poll appearing in the Israeli magazine *Monitin* at the time which revealed "21 percent of the Israeli public approves of [Kahane's] fiercely anti-Arab views" (1988a, 45).

According to an Israeli reporter, in February 1990 Kahane appeared at a synagogue in Silver Spring, Maryland, where he spoke to an audience of 600 persons "who clap[ped] their hands enthusiastically" to his declaration that "Israel will be a democracy for Jews only. The Arabs will enjoy the status of resident aliens, that is without rights . . ." Kahane added. The reporter added, "I have no doubt

---

5. A feature story on the JDO in a mainstream Jewish community newspaper noted that the organization numbered "more than 3,000 members nationwide and [has] chapters in the United States, France, Mexico and South America . . ." The story, which was favorable, added that the JDO "trains Jews to fight anti-Semitism with more than words" (Applebaum 1990). For a more balanced picture of the JDO's previous record, see the testimonies of Bonnie Rimawi and her attorney, Michael Smith, before the House Subcommittee on Criminal Justice (U.S. Congress 1988, 141–47, 159–70; cf. Ridgeway 1985; Friedman 1986).

there exists in the U.S. a substantially large group of Jews which accepts all his opinions" (Tal 1990).[6]

Suppose that the conventional view of racism and hate violence were modified to include Jewish extremist groups, would it then adequately reflect the reality of anti-Arab racism in the United States? Only if anti-Arab racism were a priori limited to the fringe of society. But this is an untenable position. As the discussion below reveals, anti-Arab racism, like other types of racism, permeates mainstream cultural and political institutions. But unlike other forms of racism, anti-Arab racism is often tolerated by mainstream society, a fact that has been recognized by a number of commentators.[7] After surveying the attitudes of 600 people in the United States in a telephone poll in the fall of 1980, researcher Shelly Slade concluded, "The Arabs remain one of the few ethnic groups who can still be slandered with impunity in America" (1981, 143). The survey revealed, inter alia,

A large percentage of the respondents [felt] that the Arabs can be described as "barbaric, cruel," (44%), "treacherous, cunning" (49%), "mistreat women" (51%) and "warlike, bloodthirsty" (50%). Furthermore, when asked how many Arabs are described by a long list of traits, a large percentage view[ed] "most" or "all" Arabs as "anti-Christian" (40%), "anti-Semitic" (40%) and "Want to Destroy Israel and Drive the Israelis into the Sea" (44%). (1981, 147; cf. Suleiman 1988)

Similarly, recalling her attitude toward Arabs as a reporter for the *Chicago Daily News* in 1969, nationally syndicated columnist Georgie Ann Geyer writes:

---

6. In his capacity as member of the Israeli Knesset, Kahane submitted a "Proposed Law for the Prevention of Assimilation between Jews and Non-Jews and for the Sanctity of the Jewish People," which called for, inter alia, "separate beaches . . . for Jews and non-Jews"; "Jews and Jewesses . . . are forbidden to marry non-Jews"; "Jews and Jewesses . . . are forbidden to have full or partial sexual relations of any sort with non-Jews"; "A non-Jew who has sexual relations with a Jewish prostitute or with a Jewish male shall be punished with fifty years' imprisonment . . ." These and other racist ravings can be found in Kotler 1986, 199–201ff., and in Kahane 1981; see also the recent work by Friedman, 1990.

7. This is, of course, not to suggest that other forms of racism (e.g., anti-African-American racism) are not found in mainstream society, only that anti-Arab racism is *openly* tolerated.

The Arab world was set up—largely subconsciously, to be sure—in the minds of the American people and even of the American press as a kind of "outcast" world. The unspoken expectation of editors, friends and even of oneself was that the Arabs were a decadent and backward people, left behind by history and even slightly abhorrent in their ancient and odd habits of past times. (Ghareeb 1983, vii)[8]

Important work has already been done in the area of anti-Arab (anti-Muslim, anti–Middle Eastern) bias and stereotypes in the news media, literature, and Hollywood. There is little need to rehearse it here.[9] Stereotypes, however, constitute only one aspect of the more fundamental problem of anti-Arab racism, which for our purposes also includes anti-Muslim and anti–Middle Eastern attitudes. This essay seeks to extend the discussion beyond stereotypes to anti-Arab racism and violence, subjects which have received little attention in the past. The very fact that anti-Arab racism has often been tolerated in mainstream society makes this form of racism a good gauge of the true situation in the United States.

The chapter begins with a review of anti-Arab racism and violence for the years 1980–1986, the same period covered by the CDR study. The review makes no claim to be exhaustive, limiting itself mostly to salient incidents. The review demonstrates that the conventional view of racism and hate violence as propounded in the CDR and similar reports is too narrow to adequately account for anti-Arab racism and violence. An analysis of the various sources of anti-Arab racism follows. The analysis reveals further inadequacies in the conventional view of racism: namely that anti-Arab racism in contemporary society is not only a fringe phenomenon, but extends to mainstream society as well.

---

8. Two decades later, Flora Lewis could still write in her syndicated column:
   Many Mideasterners bemoan the fact their region seems to be losing significance now that they can't play Cold War tag. No doubt many more, muzzled by dictatorships, bemoan the fact their region hasn't joined the march to democracy. They suffer most from their own *sick* societies. (*New York Times,* Apr. 28, 1990; emphasis added)
9. On how the U.S. news media portray the Arabs, see Said 1981; Suleiman 1988; Ghareeb 1983; and my essays in *Lies of Our Times* (a monthly of the Institute for Media Analysis, NY, 1991–94). For a detailed examination of Hollywood's Arab stereotype, see Michalak 1984; Shaheen 1984. On the Arab stereotype in popular literature, see Terry 1985 and Christison 1987. An illuminating study of the cultural antecedents of anti-Arab, anti-Muslim attitudes in Western culture is found in Said 1978.

In "The Zone of Danger"

For the better part of the 1980s, Arab-Americans lived in an increasing state of apprehension as the Reagan administration waged its "war on international terrorism." The fear reached its zenith in 1985 and 1986. The hijacking on June 14, 1985, of TWA Flight 847 to Beirut by Lebanese Shiite gunmen highlighted the predicament. The hijacking began with the beating death of a young American aboard the plane, and ended seventeen days later with the release of thirty-nine remaining U.S. hostages. The incident received extensive coverage in the news media, much of it unashamedly sensationalist and hysterical. An editorial in the Richmond, Virginia, *News Leader,* for example, suggested one Lebanese Shiite prisoner be executed every fifteen minutes until the hostages were released (June 21, 1985). The *New York Post,* famous for its shrill tone, ran a front page photo of a Dearborn, Michigan, man of Lebanese Shiite ancestry posing with the likeness of an AK-47 machine gun, wearing a camouflage vest, bandoliers, and bullets under a banner headline, "'U.S.-Nation under Attack'/Beirut U.S.A." (June 19). The photo was obtained by an unscrupulous reporter who persuaded the Lebanese-American to pose for his camera. According to the accompanying article, the Dearborn man allegedly boasted that 5,000 armed Lebanese Shiites were poised to defend themselves in the Detroit suburb. Even the normally staid *Wall Street Journal* was not immune to the hysteria of the hour. In an editorial titled, "The Next Hijacking," the *Journal* unabashedly called for U.S. military retaliation, starting with "strikes against Syrian military targets inside Lebanon" (June 18).

The media hype may have contributed to the outbreak of violent attacks against Arab-Americans and Middle Easterners that coincided with the hijacking, making 1985 a milestone in the history of violence against Arabs and other Middle Easterners. According to the Los Angeles Human Relations Commission, twelve (16.9 percent) out of a total of seventy-one religiously motivated incidents that took place in Los Angeles County in 1985 "were directed against Islamic mosques, centers or individuals of the Islamic faith." Commission officials noted this was the first time that any anti-Islamic incidents had been recorded in the six years for which records had been kept. According to the commission's annual report the anti-Muslim incidents appear "to have been provoked by a number of events in the

Middle East," specifically, the TWA and Achille Lauro hijackings, and the Rome and Vienna airport attacks (see below). "In each case, Americans were killed" (Baker 1986).

Between June 16 and 22 Islamic Centers in San Francisco, Denver, Dearborn, and Quincy, Massachusetts, were vandalized or received telephone threats. Arab-American organizations in New York and Detroit were also threatened. On June 22 the Dar as-Salaam Mosque in Houston was firebombed, resulting in $50,000 worth of damage.[10] A week later on June 30, a woman known to be dating a Palestinian was raped in Tucson by two men who lightly carved a Star of David on her chest. On August 16 a bomb placed outside the door of the Boston office of the American-Arab Anti-Discrimination Committee (ADC) detonated, severely injuring the two policemen called to remove it (U.S. Congress 1988, 57, 58, 64).[11]

Although not every incident mentioned can be demonstrably attributed to the 1985 TWA hijacking, a pattern is nevertheless discernable—terrorist incidents and other events occurring in the Middle East, especially those involving U.S. citizens and played up by the administration and the press, could trigger threats and violence against Middle Easterners anywhere in the country.[12] Because of the ongoing turmoil in the Middle East, it was only a matter of time before someone was seriously hurt, or worse.

In autumn 1985 another Middle Eastern hijacking occurred, and again violence against Arab-Americans and other Middle Easterners ensued. But this time the outcome was far more tragic. On the morning of Friday, October 11, a bomb went off at the Los Angeles

10. According to the president of the Islamic Society of Greater Houston, Sayed M. Gomah, "The force of the blast moved the room's 15×30 foot wall nearly four inches from the foundation. The bomb went off less than one hour after the congregation of Dar us-Salem—which means the House of Peace—had left from the evening prayer. . . . Three young men, one an Air Force veteran, were convicted in the bombing" (U.S. Congress 1988, 200–201).

11. See also "Men Carve Star Symbol on Woman During Rape Outside of Restaurant," *Arizona Daily Star* (Tucson), July 2, 1985, and Lerner 1986.

12. George Ball, former undersecretary of state in the Johnson Administration, speaking before the annual convention of the ADC on September 5, 1985, made this apt observation: "[Americans] were totally unprepared for the fortnight-long ordeal of the hostages on TWA Flight 847; in part because no one in authority even tried to explain the causal connection between the incident and our automatic support of Israeli projects and ambitions . . ." (Ball's address is reprinted in *The Washington Report on Middle East Affairs,* Nov. 4, 1985).

office of the ADC, killing the organization's forty-one-year-old regional director Alex Odeh. Odeh was blown in half by the force of the booby-trapped bomb wired to his office door (Palermo and Jarlson 1985; Reyes and Jones 1985; Pinsky 1986; Friedman 1987a). The day before, Odeh had appeared on a local television news program where he opined that the Palestine Liberation Organization (PLO) and its leader Yasser Arafat were not behind the hijacking of the Achille Lauro cruise liner in the Mediterranean. The murder of one of the ship's passengers, Leon Klinghoffer, had been confirmed on Wednesday, October 9. Odeh's statements condemning the hijacking and terrorism in general were cut from the interview, possibly contributing to his murder, though it is difficult to be certain about this.

Especially distressing to Arab-Americans was the lack of attention devoted to Alex Odeh's murder by the U.S. news media in comparison to that given to victims of Middle Eastern violence generally. In a memorial address for Alex Odeh on January 31, 1986, syndicated columnist and media critic for the *Nation,* Alexander Cockburn, compared the media's coverage of Alex Odeh's murder to that given to the murder of Leon Klinghoffer a few days before. "In the first three days after the killings, the *New York Times* devoted 1,043 column inches to the Klinghoffer killing and twelve and one half inches to the murder of Alex Odeh. Comparative figures for the *Washington Post* were 620 inches for Klinghoffer and 30 inches for Alex Odeh."[13]

Although most of the news reporting was straightforward, the *New York Post,* known for its sleazy sensationalism, ran the Odeh story under the headline, "Arafat Fan Killed, 7 Arabs Injured in Cal. Bomb Blast" (Oct. 12, 1985). The callously insensitive headline was set in boldface type. The *Post* shamelessly twisted Odeh's comments on the hijacking of the Achille Lauro, telling readers Odeh "had publicly praised Yasser Arafat's role in the seajacking," *without* once mentioning that Odeh was praising the PLO leader's mediation efforts, not his involvement in the actual hijacking. In contrast, the *Los Angeles Times* reported that Odeh had in fact said, "... we commend Arafat for his positive role in *solving* this issue" (Oct. 13, 1985; emphasis added).

The FBI considered Odeh's murder to be the top terrorist act of

---

13. Cited in *ADC Times,* ADC, Feb. 1986, 15.

1985 in the United States. The agency strongly hinted that the JDL or a similar Jewish extremist group was behind the bombing (Cummings 1985).[14] The Odeh murder was clearly and indisputably a political killing, an assassination, because of who the victim was, what he was doing, and where he was at the time of his tragic death. For this reason, the murder of Alex Odeh was (and continues to be) highly significant for Arab-Americans. Other killings of Arabs have not been as clearly political in motivation, such as the slaying of two Yemenis in Dearborn in 1976 (described below). The 1985 murder of Alex Odeh is surely the best known, but probably was not the first politically-motivated murder of an Arab-American. That dubious distinction belongs to another, less well known murder.

On April 6, 1982, a mysterious fire engulfed the Tripoli Restaurant in Brooklyn, New York, killing one woman and injuring eight others. The Lebanese restaurant was located on Atlantic Avenue, on the edge of a Brooklyn Heights Arab-American neighborhood. Callers claiming to speak for the JDL said the organization was behind the blaze. One caller alleged the restaurant was "the underground headquarters of the Palestine Liberation Army."[15] Lending credence to the suspicion that the JDL was probably behind the fire is that it occurred only two days *after* unidentified gunmen murdered Israeli diplomat Yaacov Bar-Simantov in Paris. Several days earlier on March 31, the Israeli embassy in the French capital was hit by machine gun fire. Responsibility for the attacks was claimed by a shadowy group in Beirut calling itself the Lebanese Armed Revolutionary Faction.[16]

In the eighteen months following the Odeh murder hostile attacks

---

14. In Los Angeles, JDL head Irv Rubin told reporters shortly after the blast: "No Jew or American should shed one tear for the destruction of a PLO front in Santa Ana or anywhere else in the world. The person or persons responsible for the bombing deserves our praise for striking out against the murderers of Americans and of Jews." (cited in *New York Post,* Oct. 12, 1985)
Not one to mince words, Rubin also told the *Washington Post,* "I have no tears for Mr. Odeh. He got exactly what he deserved" (Oct. 13, 1985).
15. *ADC Issues* no. 9 (Washington, D.C.: ADC). A former JDL member recalls that during 1982 "fifty good, dedicated JDL people . . .
would prowl the streets of New York at night in search of Arab or Russian victims. That summer there were twelve to fifteen bombings. We had an underground bomb lab in a house in Borough Park crammed with explosives, Tommy guns, Uzis . . .
(Friedman 1988a, 46)
16. *New York Times,* Apr. 4; *Christian Science Monitor,* Apr. 2, 1982.

against Arab-Americans and Arab organizations tended to follow a fairly predictable pattern. Less than two months after the Odeh killing, the Washington headquarters of the ADC was severely damaged by a mysterious fire that gutted major parts of the building.[17] The still unsolved fire occurred on Friday evening, November 30, five days after Egyptian army commandos stormed a hijacked Egyptian airliner on the Mediterranean island of Malta. The rescue operation resulted in fifty-nine dead from among the mostly Egyptian passengers and crew.[18]

The Washington fire, coming so soon after the death of Alex Odeh, sent shock waves throughout the Arab-American community.[19] It also appears to have prompted FBI director William Webster to warn that Arab-Americans and others advocating "Arab points of view have come within the zone of danger" by supporters of Israel.[20] Webster's warning came in a question-and-answer session with reporters at the National Press Club on December 10, 1985. The FBI director also revealed that following the murder of Alex Odeh in October he had brought together forty experts from around the coun-

---

17. "There's too much there for it to have been accidental but not enough to declare it arson, so we are classifying it at the present time as suspicious," was how Ray Alfred, a Washington, D.C. Fire Department battalion chief, assessed the fire. (cited in Stuart 1985)

18. Earlier that month, "Los Angeles police dismantled a bomb found on the steps of a school adjoining the Masjid al-Mumin Mosque in the city's downtown area..." (Pinsky 1986, 12)

19. Typical of the level of concern at the time was the assessment of Ismael Ahmed, director of the Arab community center in Dearborn, who observed: "The atmosphere that Arab Americans live in is really a very frightening one.... People have ideas of who and what Arab Americans are that don't come close to reality" (cited in McGraw 1986).

Concern ran so high that forty Detroit Arab community leaders decided to sponsor an antiracism rally, as well as issue a holiday message to Michigan residents from the Arab-American community. The message ran in the local papers during the Christmas holiday. In Washington, a group of Arab-Americans led by ADC chairman James Abourezk organized a nationwide group called the "Ad Hoc Coalition Against Terrorism in America." The group sponsored a full page advertisement in the Sunday *New York Times* for Jan. 5, 1986. Under a banner headline that read, "Don't Let Terrorism Spread Into America," the advertisement carried the names of some one hundred prominent Americans, including many American Jews and several rabbis.

20. Cited in *New York Times,* Dec. 11, 1985. On the same day the U.S. Commission on Civil Rights issued a statement condemning acts of violence as well as "vicious" stereotypes aimed at Arab-Americans. The Commission also promised to hold hearings in February 1986 on the subject (see 169). Webster subsequently informed a congressional subcommittee that there appeared to be "no relationship" between the fire and terrorist groups. ("FBI Chief Doubts Terrorists Caused Blaze," *New York Times,* Mar. 15, 1986).

try "to marshall our resources in this area."[21] Violence against Arab-Americans and their property continued, nonetheless.

In the early weeks of January 1986, the Reagan administration openly raised the possibility of a retaliatory strike against Libya following Arab terrorist attacks at the Rome and Vienna airports on December 27 in which 12 persons died and 114 were wounded.[22] On January 7, President Reagan announced publicly that there was "irrefutable" evidence linking Libyan leader Muammar Qaddafi to the airport attacks.[23] The tension of the period was reflected in the following headlines: "Libya Jets Buzz U.S. Plane on Patrol in Mediterranean" (*New York Times,* Jan. 15); "Shultz Supports Armed Reprisals" (*New York Times,* Jan. 16); "U.S. Navy Starting Maneuvers Off Libya" (*New York Times,* Jan. 24).

In reality the Reagan adminstration had targeted Libya as part of its "war on international terrorism" early in its first term in 1981. The record is replete with government disinformation and deception. In August 1981, the U.S. Navy shot down two Libyan planes over the Gulf of Sidra during provocative war games off the Libyan coast. By November President Reagan accused Colonel Qaddafi of sending "hit teams" to assassinate him and other top administration officials. "We have the evidence and he [Qaddafi] knows it," the President stated. The allegation, which proved to be an utter fabrication, stimulated anti-Arab, anti-Middle Eastern hysteria among the news media and the public at large.[24] When aid for the Nicaraguan Contras was

---

21. *New York Times,* Dec. 11, 1985.

22. The attacks, which were completely incomprehensible to many observers, appeared to be the work of a renegade Palestinian faction led by Abu Nidal. Their purpose was to discredit the mainstream wing of the PLO and block its attempts to gain admittance to the U.S. sponsored Arab-Israeli peace process. (See my discussion of this incident, Abraham 1986.)

23. In private, however, the president resisted calls for a direct military strike "pending a 'smoking gun'—some evidence linking Qaddafi to the airport bombings" (Hersh 1987, 71). Another investigator found: "The Italian and Austrian governments stated that the terrorists were trained in Syrian-controlled areas of Lebanon and had come via Damascus, a conclusion reiterated by Israeli defense minister Yitzhak Rabin." Officials of both governments reiterated months later the same position, in the words of the Austrian Minister of Interior, that "there is not the slightest evidence to implicate Libya" (Chomsky 1986, 135–36).

24. In a January 1986 interview, FBI assistant director Oliver B. Revell dismissed as "a complete fabrication" allegations that Libya's Col. Qaddafi had sent suicide terrorists into U.S. streets ("Terrorists Trained Abroad are Known to Live Here," *Washington Times,* Mar. 27, 1986). Revell has repeated the statement on other occasions.

in jeopardy in 1984, Qaddafi again became part of the White House agenda. Following the 1985 TWA hijacking, Libya once again became an issue, even though, according to Seymour Hersh, "[t]here was no evidence linking the hijacking to Libya, but within the Reagan Administration feelings ran high that action must be taken, and striking against Iran and Syria wouldn't do." Hersh notes that following the December 1985 airport atrocities "secret White House planning escalated dramatically . . ." At a top-level government meeting "a decision was made to provoke Qaddafi by again sending the Navy and its warplanes on patrol in the Gulf of Sidra. Any Libyan response would be seized upon to justify bombing" (Hersh 1987, 26, 48).[25]

On the night of January 17, 1986, Moustafa Dabbas, the fifty-one-year-old publisher and editor of *Arrayh* (The Aim)—Philadelphia's only Arabic-English newspaper—was beaten and mugged by several men. Dabbas says one of the men first inquired as to whether he was the editor of *Arrayh*. When he replied that he was, "the men beat him unconscious, leaving him with a fractured skull, a gash under one eye, and bleeding from the ears" (Lerner 1986, 21). According to another report, Dabbas "was nearly beaten to death and spent several days in intensive care with a blood clot on the brain, a fractured skull, 17 stitches and other complications."[26]

Dabbas, an immigrant from Syria, had experienced harassment before, but nothing like the assault against his person.[27] In the nation's capital ten days earlier (January 7, 1986) "two ADC staff members were forced off the road on the way home from work by a car which sped away afterwards." In Milwaukee two days later, a Palestinian grocer was shot in the head by gunmen who took no money.[28]

By late January concern was still running high among Arab-Americans. The prevailing mood caught the attention of *News-*

---

25. See also Noam Chomsky's excellent discussion of Libya in the Reagan administration's demonology (1986, chap. 3).

26. Rimawi (1986). Rimawi herself encountered repeated death threats, which forced her to resign from her job as ADC regional coordinator for New York City.

27. Philadelphia police treated the incident as a robbery, "but Dabbas claims that nothing was stolen from him. 'I was attacked because I am the tongue of the Arab community here,'" he insisted. In 1975, the year after Dabbas started his printing business, his printing machines were vandalized or stolen on two occasions, apparently by the local JDL, which boasted about the theft in the Philadelphia newspapers (Lerner 1986, 21).

28. The Washington incident is found in Friedman 1986; the Milwaukee incident was reported by Schidlovsky 1986.

week magazine, which observed that "the animosity grows with each new terrorist outrage overseas."[29] In Flint, Michigan, three Arab-Americans, two men and a woman, were arrested in the Hyatt Regency hotel on January 21 after an employee reported to local police that the three were part of a "Qaddafi hit team." According to a news story, "The three, all of whom are U.S. citizens, said the police abused them verbally and refused to explain the charges." The men told the Washington-based ADC that they were beaten by jail guards; one man reportedly suffered a fractured foot which went unattended until the next morning.[30] Mosques in southern California were also vandalized in late January. In Milwaukee, a Libyan student was allegedly harassed by the FBI and the Immigration and Naturalization Service (INS) because of his nationality. Threats and abusive telephone calls were received by Arab-American community activists across the country (U.S. Congress 1988, 64–66).

During this tension-filled period, NBC television aired with great fanfare on February 9 the film "Under Siege," a made-for-television movie about a foreign (read "Arab") terrorist group that launches a wanton killing spree in the nation's capital. To the dismay of Michigan's large Arab-American community, the shadowy group's ringleader is discovered to be hiding out in a predominately Lebanese Shiite neighborhood in Dearborn, Michigan. Arab-Americans across the country were not amused, and flooded local television stations with angry protests.[31] Their anger stemmed from the fact that they had been the *victims* of terrorism on U.S. soil, not its perpetrators, as the entertainment industry and certain government officials would have the public believe.[32]

---

29. "Arab-Bashing in America," *Newsweek,* Jan. 20, 1986.

30. Hundley 1987a. The news report is based on information gleaned from the 1986 annual log of anti-Arab harassment issued by the Washington-based ADC (cf. Rimawi 1986).

31. News stories in papers across the country in 1986 indicate the extent of Arab-American outrage. "TV Film on Terrorism is Criticized," *USA Today,* Feb. 10, 1986; "Arab-Americans Irate About Terrorism Film," *Washington Times,* Feb. 10; "TV Station 'Under Siege,'" *Houston Post,* Feb. 11; "Terror Film Ignites Protest," *New York Daily News,* Feb. 11; "Villainous Images," *Detroit Free Press,* Feb. 9; "Arab Leader Urges TV Movie Sequel," *Detroit News,* Feb. 10.

32. In his testimony before a House Subcommittee, California congressman Mervyn Dymally summarized the extent of "Arab terrorism" said to have plagued the country:

We have the image that Arab groups are hard at work doing bad things in the U.S. . . . According to FBI statistics there have been no acts of terrorism by Arab groups

Two days after "Under Siege" aired, several Arab-American leaders, joined by Alex Odeh's widow and brother, appeared by previous arrangement before the U.S. Commission on Civil Rights, where they demanded an investigation into pernicious media stereotypes, as well as harassment, discrimination, and violence against Arab-Americans. The Arab-American witnesses faulted the news and entertainment media, Jewish groups, politicians, and government agencies. ADC chairman James Abourezk, a former senator from South Dakota, accused President Reagan of exacerbating anti-Arab stereotypes, observing that the President had "'created a cowboy anti-Arab atmosphere' with his statements on terrorism" (Thornton 1986).[33]

In March and April (1986) U.S.-Arab tensions in the Middle East reached an all time high. On March 25 and 26, the U.S. Navy attacked four Libyan ships in the Gulf of Sidra, destroying two; survivors were left to die. U.S. planes also conducted raids against the Libyan mainland, flying some eight miles into Libyan airspace. The attacks left more than fifty Libyans dead, with no U.S. casualties. The attack failed to provoke a Libyan counterattack or ignite terrorism against U.S. civilians, its apparent goal, according to some knowledgeable observers. "The Gulf of Sidra operation . . . was plainly timed to stir up jingoist hysteria just prior to the crucial Senate vote on Contra aid, coinciding with a fabricated Nicaraguan 'invasion' of Honduras," Noam Chomsky observed (1986, 142–45). Hersh added, "Qaddafi's failure to rise to the bait frustrated the N.S.C. [National Security Council] staff." "The basic question for N.S.C. aides remained: how to convince the reluctant President that bombing was essential" (1987, 74).

In early April, bombs placed by unidentified terrorists aboard a TWA flight enroute from Rome to Athens (April 2), and in a West Berlin nightclub (April 5), left one U.S. citizen dead in each incident

---

against other non-Arab groups or individuals in the U.S. in the period of the FBI records which extends from 1977–1985.

He added that there had been several "acts of violence within the Arab-American community." These consisted of "a sit-in at the Saudi Arabian embassy," and assaults by pro- and anti-Qaddafi Libyan nationalists on each other; not quite the image of Arab terrorism so familiar to the public mind (cited in U.S. Congress 1988, 90).

33. See also, "Arab-Americans Call for Full Inquiry into Rights Violations," *ADC Insider's Report,* March 1986; and James Zogby, "Statement to the U.S. Commission on Civil Rights," *Issues 86,* Washington, D.C.: Arab American Institute, March 1986.

out of a total of five dead and scores wounded. The nightclub was frequented mostly by African-American GIs and Third World immigrants, making it an unlikely target of Libyan attack. Calling Libya's Colonel Qaddafi the "mad dog of the Middle East" in a nationally televised address, President Reagan vowed to retaliate if evidence revealed Libya was behind the bombings.[34] A week later (April 14) U.S. fighter planes bombed Libya in retaliation for Qaddafi's alleged complicity in the bombing of the West Berlin disco. Commenting on the attack, Chomsky observed:

> The April 14 attack was the first bombing in history staged for prime time television. As the subsequently published record shows, the bombing raids were carefully timed so that they would begin precisely at 7 P.M. Eastern Standard Time—as they did (*New York Times,* April 18, 1986); that is, precisely at the moment when all three national television channels broadcast their major news programs, which were of course preempted as agitated anchormen switched to Tripoli for direct eyewitness reports of the exciting events. (1986, 147)

Two days after the attack in the Gulf of Sidra, Joel Lisker, chief counsel of the Senate Judiciary Subcommitee on Security and Terrorism, raised the specter of Middle Eastern terrorists residing in the United States, saying, "You have a cadre of individuals with Middle East connections, some of whom are American citizens, some of whom are 'green carders' [permanent residents], who have been trained in the Middle East since they've been here." Lisker's warning bears an eerie resemblance to government claims in the arrest of seven Arabs and a Kenyan in Los Angeles some nine months later (discussed below). Lisker also added that radical states like Libya, Syria, and Iran "could call upon any of their nationals in the United States

---

34. Reagan later claimed to have "direct," "precise," and "irrefutable" evidence linking Libya to the La Belle disco bombing. In fact, as Chomsky reports, there was never any proof of Libyan involvement:

> In an interview on April 28 with a reporter for the U.S. Army journal *Stars and Stripes,* Manfred Ganschow, chief of the Berlin Staatschutz and head of the 100-man team investigating the disco bombing, stated that "I have no more evidence that Libya was connected to the bombing than I had when you first called me two days after the act. Which is none." (1986, 149–50)

'presumably to act in solidarity . . . with Arab nationalism, or anti-U.S. sentiment, because of what is happening in the Gulf of Sidra'" (McCaslin 1986). Ten days later on April 28, Attorney General Edwin Meese said he would study the issue (see below).

Given the climate of jingoism prevailing in March and April 1986 and the previous pattern of anti-Arab violence in the country, it was highly likely that anti-Arab threats and attacks would result again. Indeed, that is what happened. On the night of the U.S. raid, the Washington headquarters of the ADC received threatening calls with references to Libyans. In Dearborn, Michigan, several persons were arrested for vandalizing Arab-American businesses, homes, and the Arab community center. Bomb threats were received by the Detroit ADC office, the Dearborn Arab community center (ACCESS), and the local Arab-American newspaper, a routine occurrence during heightened Middle East tensions.[35]

Two days before the U.S. bombing, five Arab students from the University of Syracuse, New York, "were beaten by a gang of Americans" in a bar, one student almost losing an eye, in an outburst of anti-Arab hostility. Similar attacks were reported in Detroit and New Haven, Connecticut, in ADC's "Harassment and Violence Log Sheet" (U.S. Congress 1988, 67–69). A closing note in the Detroit entry in the log for this period states:

> Many incidents occur that are not reported to ADC, but only to the police. Dearborn Police said on TV that there are more incidents than usual of anti-Arab attacks. Detroit FBI Director Walton petitioned the public not to direct hostility against Arabs in Detroit, since they had nothing to do with the current crisis. (U.S. Congress 1988, 69; see also Campbell 1986; Hamm 1986)[36]

Perhaps the most graphic anti-Arab attack during this time oc-

---

35. During the 1985 Achille Lauro hijacking, for example, a caller telephoned the Houston Islamic Center threatening, "For every American killed, 10 of you . . . pigs will die." In early 1986, when promotions for the NBC movie special "Under Siege" were airing, another caller warned the same center to "go back to your home country or die" (U.S. Congress 1988, 202). The pattern was repeated elsewhere.

36. In another report, ADC found that:
nearly 40% of all 1986 incidents of anti-Arab violence and harassment reported to the National Office were directly attributable to heightened tensions surrounding the U.S. bombing of Libya in April 1986. The incidents included acts of vandalism and threats of violence. (ADC 1987, 29)

curred in the Detroit suburb of Westland. The home of a Palestinian immigrant family was broken into shortly after the April 14 bombing of Libya. A smoke bomb was thrown into the house and the words "Go Back to Libya" were daubed on one of the walls. Frightened, the family fled after contacting the police. Although the working-class family had not been politically active or visible, it had experienced acts of vandalism in the past. The mother told a reporter that their house had been broken into and a bedroom set afire the previous year (1985).

> Her front window has been shot full of BB holes on numerous occasions, her mailbox was stolen, and the family car was smeared with eggs and painted with slogans revolving around the "Arab Go Home" theme. Her six-year-old son has asked her to change his name to something that "sounds more American" and requested that she not speak to him in Arabic outside the home or send him to school with pita bread. Classmates call him "camel jockey" and "Qaddafi's brother." (Lerner 1986, 24)

Another barometer of the level of anti-Arab hysteria following the U.S. raid on Libya is the sad, but somewhat farcical incident that occurred aboard Delta flight 136 from Ft. Lauderdale to Boston on May 1, 1986. Rema J. Simon, a twenty-three-year-old Arab-American, had been reading a book, *Palestine Is, But Not in Jordan,* at the gate area. After boarding the plane, she resumed reading the book. About ten minutes later Simon was approached by an airline employee who asked her to leave the plane with him. In the jetway she was informed that "a passenger had expressed concern about the book" she was reading. After leafing through the book, the airline employee asked Simon to "put it away", adding, "[t]his is a sensitive subject at airports." An apprehensive passenger apparently had insisted on assurances that Simon was not a terrorist. "He also told Delta that he was afraid that the book was about Col. Mu'ammar Qadhafi" (U.S. Congress 1988, 145–46; cf. Hentoff 1986). The fact that Simon was not searched indicated that the threat she posed must have appeared extremely minimal to airline security.

Simon's experience was not an isolated one. A public relations manager for the airline, Richard Jones, indicated that "a group of Delta passengers [was] recently singled out because they were 'Middle

Eastern looking.'" The airline also admitted to having evacuated an airplane because a "Hispanic-type" person was among its passengers. In similar fashion, "a security officer at Philadelphia International Airport admitted that 'Arabic-looking' passengers were being routinely stopped and searched." More generally, a check by ADC revealed that the Federal Aviation Administration (FAA) acknowledged "having received numerous complaints from Arab-Americans who have alleged discriminatory practices, and has pinpointed examples of local officials who have instituted their own profiles, some of which are based on ethnicity" (ADC 1986, 32).

Tensions remained high weeks after the April 14 attack on Libya, as illustrated by the following developments.

April 17. Gunmen in Beirut murdered three hostages (two Britons and a U.S. citizen) in retaliation for the U.S. raid on Libya.

April 18. Nearly 300 dependents of U.S. embassy officials and other nonessential personnel were evacuated from Sudan out of concern for their safety following the wounding of an embassy employee in the capital, Khartoum.

April 23. President Reagan stated he was prepared to use military force against Syria or Iran if presented with solid evidence that either had supported terrorism against U.S. citizens.

April 24. ABC News quoted a U.S. State Department intelligence assessment that claimed Qaddafi was "more dangerous" now than before the U.S. bombing, and that the Libyan leader was seeking "personal revenge" against President Reagan for the death of his daughter and the wounding of his two sons.

April 25. Former Democratic presidential nominee Walter Mondale said the United States should indict Qaddafi and post a reward for his apprehension if evidence links him to the murder of U.S. citizens.

April 25. Secretary of State George Shultz recommended the use of covert action, in conjunction with expanded economic sanctions and the threat of further military action, in order to weaken the Libyan government.

April 25. Arthur L. Pollick, a U.S. communications officer at the U.S. embassy in North Yemen, was shot and wounded by unidentified gunmen. At the same time the secretary general of the Council of U.S. Muslim Associations in Pacifica, Cal-

ifornia, reported receiving several "threatening phone calls ask-
ing, 'Is this the Shiite terrorist's heaven? Why are you killing
American boys in Beirut? Why don't you go back there with
a car bomb?'" On April 27, a rock was hurled at the Muslim
leader while he was working on his parked van, smashing a
window (U.S. Congress 1988, 68).

April 28. Attorney General Meese said he would discuss with the
INS and the FBI whether the number of Libyan nationals in
the United States should be reduced in order to lessen the
possibility of domestic terrorist activity.[37]

How much of this anti-Arab hysteria spilled over into the tragic
murders in Philadelphia the following month is difficult to gauge. On
May 27, 1986, Dr. Ismail al-Faruqi, age sixty-five, and his wife Lois
Lamya, age sixty, were brutally slain in their suburban Philadelphia
home. The couple's pregnant daughter was severely injured but survived the assault by the lone knife-wielding attacker. The al-Faruqis
were both internationally recognized Islamic scholars. In addition,
Ismail al-Faruqi, a Palestinian who had served as the last Arab
governor of Galilee in 1948, was also an outspoken critic of Israel.
Although an arrest was subsequently made in connection with the
slayings, the alleged murderer's motives remained shrouded in mystery
beyond his assertion that "voices" told him to kill Ismail al-Faruqi.
It is far from certain that there was any connection between this
incident and the political climate prevailing at the time. However,
"sources close to the investigation" indicated at the time "that Dr.
al-Faruqi's views on politics and religion [were] . . . considered possible keys to the slaying."[38] The sudden and brutal nature of the

37. Chronology, *The Washington Report on Middle East Affairs.* May 19, 1986, 7.

38. "Congressional Hearings on Anti-Arab Violence," *ADC Special Report,* August
1986, 9. There is some dispute over the extent of al-Faruqi's political visibility. He had
expressed strong views on Israel in an article published in 1983 ("Islam and Zionism," in
Voices of Resurgent Islam, ed. John L. Esposito. New York: Oxford University Press).
This article was later excerpted in the *Near East Report* (Jan. 27, 1984), the newsletter of
the American Israel Public Affairs Committee (AIPAC), the principal pro-Israel lobby in
the United States. One longtime friend reported al-Faruqi's views on the Arab-Israeli
conflict had provoked death threats from persons claiming to represent the JDL ("The al-
Faruqi Murders," *ADC Special Report,* Washington, 1986, 7). In contrast, scholar Ralph
Braibanti asserted al-Faruqi had not been "actively engaged in the politics or diplomacy
associated with" the Palestine issue. "The emphasis of his career . . . was teaching Islam,
organizing structures to institutionalize that teaching, and encouraging students every-
where" (*The Washington Report on Middle East Affairs,* Aug. 11, 1986).

murders, occurring when they did, gave many Arab-Americans across the country pause.[39]

Several weeks later on June 17 a mysterious fire damaged the offices of the United Palestine Appeal (UPA), the second Arab-American organization in the nation's capital to be struck in six months. The blaze caused over $60,000 in damage. The police ruled arson was the cause, but added the curious statement that there was "no evidence the blaze was set by terrorists."[40] A former building custodian was later charged in the case, but his actual motives have never been established. UPA director Bishara Bahbah told the *Washington Post,* "We can't help but think it [the fire] might be motivated by the fact that we're Palestinians, but we do not know."[41]

The mounting violence and harassment of the previous twelve months, beginning with the June 1985 TWA hijacking, prompted Congressman John Conyers (D-Mich.), chairman of the House Subcommittee on Criminal Justice, to hold hearings on anti-Arab violence, the first of their kind ever. Part of the impetus behind the hearings was a Secret Service internal memo revealing that because the Odeh murder investigation "has failed to identify the perpetrators . . ." the "FBI have suspended active investigation of this case due to lack of investigative leads" (deletion in the original).[42] The document heightened concern in the Arab-American community, prompting calls for a congressional hearing, in the words of Congressman Conyers, to "bring the FBI into the real world of catching criminals and murderers" (Shea 1986).

The hearings were held on July 16, 1986. The Subcommittee on Criminal Justice heard testimony from over a dozen witnesses, including the widow of Alex Odeh, several victims, three current members of Congress, a former U.S. senator, an FBI official, and two representatives from the American Jewish Committee (AJC).[43] Norma

---

39. A little known fact is that al-Faruqi's son, who was stationed with the U.S. Army in New Mexico, had "died mysteriously in a car accident which [curiously] has since been linked to food poisoning" weeks prior to the murder of his parents (U.S. Congress 1988, 202).

40. "Arson Damages Palestinian Office in D.C.," *Washington Post,* June 18, 1986.

41. "Arson Damages Palestinian Office . . .," *Washington Post;* cf. *ADC Insider's Report,* July 1986, 32.

42. The document, dated January 7, 1986, was obtained by a third party through a Freedom of Information Act request.

43. The congressmen were: Rep. Nick Rahall II (D-W.Va.), Mary Rose Oakar (D-Oh.), and Mervyn Dymally (D-Calif.).

Odeh encapsulated the frustrations of Arab-Americans when she told the Subcommittee: "While our government apprehends terrorists half way across the world, it seems helpless in the face of domestic terrorism directed against Arab Americans" (U.S. Congress 1988, 106–7).[44]

The toughest questioning in the daylong hearings was directed at Oliver Revell, FBI executive assistant director, who insisted his agency had not terminated the Odeh murder investigation, claiming it is the "highest priority investigation in our domestic terrorist program, and it will continue to be so until it is solved." Revell added the surprising revelation that the bureau's investigation "extends beyond the boundaries of the United States" (U.S. Congress 1988, 11).[45] Taking issue with the bureau's performance was California congressman Mervyn Dymally. In his testimony before the subcommittee, Dymally observed:

> The FBI records show that the majority of recorded terrorist incidents against Arab Americans have been traced to just one extremist group. I have been able to find no record of arrests in any of the incidents of terrorism against Arab Americans and Arab diplomatic missions. (U.S. Congress 1988, 91)

ADC chairman James Abourezk echoed Dymally's observations: "Despite assurances from the FBI that these cases are top priority, not one of the perpetrators responsible for the bombings, harassment and violence so far has been apprehended or convicted" (U.S. Congress 1988, 57). By January 1987, frustration with the lack of progress in the then two-year-old Odeh case was so acute that ADC offered a $100,000 reward for information leading to the arrest and conviction

---

44. The reference was to the U.S. Navy's interception on October 10, 1985, of an Egyptian plane carrying four Palestinans suspected of hijacking the Achille Lauro cruise liner. James Zogby, director of the Arab American Institute, struck a similar chord, saying "Every time a Palestinian greengrocer in Dearborn writes a check to the PLO, the FBI is swarming all over the place . . . Why haven't the FBI caught the Jewish terrorists?" (Cited in Friedman 1986.)

45. Relying on information supplied by former JDL members, the *Los Angeles Times* reported on July 17 that "as many as a dozen people in Israel have been questioned about the bombings—at the request of the F.B.I.—by the Israeli police and officers of Shin Bet," the Israeli secret police. (Cited in "Congressional Hearings on Anti-Arab Violence," *ADC Special Report,* Washington, Aug. 1986.)

of those responsible for Alex Odeh's murder.[46] The investigation remains open.[47]

Sources of Anti-Arab Racism and Hate Violence

The review of anti-Arab racism and hate violence reveals a number of salient features. First, Arab-Americans, Muslims, and other Middle Easterners were victims of hate violence that was for the most part not mentioned in the studies on the subject cited earlier (Lutz 1987; ADL n.d., 1987, 1988a, 1988b). From March 1985 to June 1986 alone, the period documented in the ADC Harassment Log that was presented to the congressional hearing, Arab-Americans and Muslims experienced: Four bombings (one against a mosque and another against an Orthodox church); four cases of arson; three deaths; ten cases of serious bodily assault and seven other injuries; fifteen acts of vandalism (six committed against Muslim leaders and places of worship); twenty threats (five directed at Muslim leaders and places of worship); five complaints of harassment (two against law enforcement authorities); and at least one break-in (U.S. Congress 1988, 61–70). It is important to emphasize again that these incidents represent only those that came to the attention of ADC, and that presumably many other, less dramatic incidents went unreported. Although these incidents probably represent a peak period of anti-Arab racism from 1985 to 1986, anti-Arab racism and hate violence is virtually absent from Lutz's study which claims to be "the first national overview of

---

46. The reward was announced by the ADC in an op-ed (Jabara 1987).

47. In early 1989 federal authorities were preparing to try a man said to be a "prime suspect" in the Odeh slaying on other charges. The defendant, Robert Manning, along with other JDL terrorist suspects, had taken refuge in the Jewish settlement of Kiryat Arba on the Israeli-occupied West Bank (*Detroit Jewish News,* Jan. 6, 1989). Manning was extradited to the United States on July 19, 1993 to stand trial for the murder of Patricia Wilkerson, a secretary from Manhattan Beach, California. Manning's wife, Rochelle, was still fighting extradition in October 1993 for the same charge. (*ADC Times,* Sept. 1993, p. 9; *Jerusalem Post* International edition, Oct. 9, 1993, p. 3).

An internal 1987 FBI memorandum revealed that Israeli authorities had impeded a high level federal investigation into the Odeh and other JDL bombings. The document, which was obtained by the *Village Voice,* stated: "Numerous leads have been forwarded through [FBI headquarters] to the Israeli Secret Intelligence Service in Washington, D.C. Response to these leads is crucial for the solution of the 25 terrorist incidents and other criminal activity perpetrated by the JDL" (Friedman 1987a); (cf. "FBI Memo: Israelis Hampering Probe," *Washington Post,* Nov. 19, 1987).

bigoted violence to cover a several-year period [1980 to 1986] since the re-emergence of hate groups in the 1970s" (1987, Foreword). The pattern extends to the scholarly literature as well. A major volume on violence in the United States, for example, carries an oblique, one-sentence reference to the murder of Alex Odeh, devoid of any context of violence directed at Arab-Americans (Gurr 1989, 222–23).

A second feature of anti-Arab violence is that it does not fit the conventional model of racist violence presented in the CDR and other reports on hate violence. Virtually none of the anti-Arab violence, vandalism, arson, and the like was perpetrated by organized, right-wing Christian supremacist and neo-Nazi groups. This is, of course, not to suggest that Arab-Americans and Middle Easterners generally are outside the ambit of right-wing hate violence, but rather that as far as can be determined most of the violence directed at Arab-Americans has not come from this quarter. As we have seen, much but by no means all of the serious violence has emanated from Jewish extremist groups. Although such groups clearly fall on the fringe of society, and properly should be classified as some of the most active and dangerous right-wing hate groups, conventional accounts of hate violence neglect to mention them in this context. For example, there is only cursory mention of the JDL in Gurr (1989), and even then the organization is discussed only in the context of "American terrorism in foreign causes," not under "rightwing extremism," where it properly belongs.

A third aspect of anti-Arab racism and violence is that it is definitely not limited to fringe groups, but stems from mainstream institutions as well, often stimulated by the jingoism of the White House. This point was stressed by several of the witnesses who testified before the congressional hearing on anti-Arab violence. They blamed the news and entertainment media, the Reagan administration, and even politicians in general for creating, in the words of ADC's James Abourezk, "an atmosphere which leads the public to believe that all the violence abroad and the potential violence at home is perpetrated solely by Arabs" (U.S. Congress 1988, 56). In all fairness, the news media, while generally following the administration's cues on the Middle East and international terrorism, have tended for the most part to present a sympathetic portrait of Arab-Americans and their concerns in the eighties.[48]

---

48. Two notable exceptions that stand out for their mean-spirited and dishonest por-

There is a tendency to depict anti-Arab hate violence as an outgrowth of the Arab-Israeli conflict. This was the tenor of the testimony at the congressional hearing on anti-Arab hate violence. In Congressman Dymally's words, "the failure to distinguish between . . . Arab Americans . . . and the policies of Arab states and individuals in the Middle East" has led to the "scapegoating" of Arab-Americans. Thus, "[g]iven the fact that a peaceful resolution to the Middle East problem is not likely to come along any time soon," Dymally predicted, "it is likely that there will be further acts of terrorism against Arab-Americans" (U.S. Congress 1988, 93–94).

In his congressional testimony ADC president Abdeen Jabara distinguished between two types of anti-Arab attacks: 1) "spontaneous racially or religiously motivated vandalism, graffiti-writing or slurs," which are largely stimulated by an "anti-Arab or anti-Muslim tone" in the media and in the administration; and 2) premeditated "politically motivated violence" aimed at curtailing the political activity of Arab-Americans. The latter is the "more serious" of the two (U.S. Congress 1988, 126).[49] As will become apparent below, Jabara's distinction, while useful, does not account for yet another type of anti-Arab hostility and violence not stemming directly from the Arab-Israeli conflict, but from domestic xenophobia. Ultimately, however, all types of anti-Arab hostility rest at a deeper level on a bedrock of anti-Arab and anti-Muslim racism found in U.S. society.

Perhaps the clearest expression of the thesis that anti-Arab hostility is an offshoot of the Middle East conflict was put forth by Helen Hatab Samhan, deputy director of the Arab American Institute. In a 1987 article, Samhan asserted that "[w]hat is called racism against Arabs in America today is in fact not racism in its classical

---

trayal of Arab-Americans as potential terrorists, drug dealers, and gun runners are: Ehud Yonay, "The PLO Underground in California," *New West* (Feb. 26, 1979) and Allan Lengel and Frank Kuznik, "The Middle East Connection: How the Arab Wars Came to Detroit," *Monthly Detroit* (Feb. 1984). It may be more than coincidental that these magazines are slick regional publications serving markets where large and visible Arab-American populations reside. The major media, as we have seen, have tended to echo Washington's jingoistic anti-Arab, anti-Middle Eastern line *during* international crises.

49. In subsequent statements, Jabara drew a further distinction beetween "racially or ethnically motivated" and "religiously motivated" attacks, with the latter being "attacks on Islamic mosques," but this distinction merely subdivided the category without adding anything new ("'Arab-Bashing' Described to Conyers' Group," *Detroit News,* July 17, 1986).

sense." The roots of "anti-Arab attitudes" are in politics, not ethnic prejudice, she argued.

> The origins of what can be called political racism lie in the Arab-Israeli confilct and, as such, constitute an ideological struggle more than an ethnic one. Arab Americans who choose not to be active in Palestinian or Arab issues or organizations are not, in most cases, victims of this political racism. Conversely, non-Arab Americans sometimes are. (1987, 11)

How valid is Samhan's contention? A careful examination of the sources of anti-Arab bigotry would reveal that her contention is overly narrow. Anti-Arab racism does not emanate from a single source, and certainly is not limited to passions stemming from the Arab-Israeli conflict. Several types of anti-Arab racism and violence can be discerned. The first, and most obvious, is the political violence of Jewish extremist groups, which is correctly viewed as emanating directly from the Arab-Israeli conflict; this is where Samhan's thesis applies. The second is a more nativistic violence which is xenophobic and local in nature; this is where her thesis falls flat. The third is a form of jingoist hostility and violence usually associated with international crises involving U.S. citizens, another area which Samhan's thesis overlooks. I shall discuss each type, before turning to the role of political leaders and the news media in creating a cultural climate conducive to anti-Arab racism and violence.

Ideologically Motivated Violence

Anti-Arab attacks instigated, sponsored, and organized by the JDL and other Jewish extremist groups clearly fall under the category of political racism and violence. The extremists perceive their actions to be a part of the wider Arab-Israeli conflict and the ongoing struggle against the "enemies of Israel" and the Jewish people as a whole. In this sense, their actions are ideologically motivated and premeditated, not merely spontaneous outbursts stemming from anger, fear, or ignorance.

Examples of their extremism abound. Throughout the 1970s and early 1980s, the JDL concentrated its attacks against Soviet cultural, transportation, and diplomatic interests in New York and Washington.[50] It subsequently expanded to Arab and other targets. Aside from the anti-Arab attacks mentioned previously, the JDL is suspected in the bombings of several Arab diplomatic missions, the homes of alleged Nazis, and an apartment on the Arizona State University campus. In the Arizona bombing, automobiles belonging to Arab students living in the building were daubed with the slogan "Death to the PLO" and Stars of David.

The JDL, or splinter groups like the JDO and Jewish Direct Action (JDA), are believed to have been behind two bombings preceding the October 1985 bombing that killed Alex Odeh. In the early hours of August 15, 1985, Tscherim Soobzokov, a former Nazi, was killed in an explosion when he stepped outside of his Paterson, New Jersey, home. His wife, daughter, a four-year-old grandson, and neighbor were injured in the blast. On September 6, a bomb went off in front of the home of Elmars Sprogis of Brentwood, New York, a former Latvian police officer cleared of aiding the Nazis. Sprogis was injured along with a passerby whose legs were blown off in the explosion. According to the FBI, each of the bombs had a similar signature; they were either made by the same person, or the makers had the same teacher (Friedman 1986). These incidents coincide with the resignation in August 1985 of Rabbi Meir Kahane as head of the JDL, which he founded in 1968.

In addition, the JDL is thought to have been behind attacks against Gulf Oil gas stations in the Northeast in August 1975. In the same month a mysterious fire hit Gulf's huge Philadelphia refinery. An anonymous caller later announced, "This was done in protest of Gulf Oil's submission to and financing of Arab propaganda against the Jewish people and the nation of Israel in the U.S. and the world" (ADC n.d.). In March 1987 a grand jury convened to hear "evidence relating to a wide range of JDL activities," including the murder of Alex Odeh (ADC 1987).[51]

---

50. Evidence has recently surfaced indicating Kahane's JDL was secretly funded by Israeli rightwing leaders beginning in the late 1960s. Leaders like Yitzhak Shamir and Geula Cohen secretly "masterminded the league's often violent campaign against Soviet targets . . ." (Friedman 1988b). The *New York Times* (June 6, 1970) editorialized that the JDL attacks were "directly in the totalitarian tradition"; the *Chicago Tribune* added, "The JDL's insistence on condemning all Russians simply because they are Russians is fanaticism in the extreme" (Feb. 21, 1972). (Cited in ADC n.d.)

51. Subsequently, New York JDL leader Victor Vancier and two associates pleaded

Since the objective of terrorism is to silence opposing viewpoints through intimidation, it need not always take the form of outright physical violence. More often the mere threat of bodily harm will suffice. Not surprisingly, Jewish extremist groups regularly intimidated Arab-Americans and other perceived enemies through abusive phone calls and letters, home and office break-ins, publication of hit lists, and, in at least one instance, infiltration. In his public pronouncements, JDL leader Victor Vancier talked openly

> about silencing a prominent Palestinian-American professor who is an outspoken supporter of the PLO. "I think the man is a monster. And that means anything goes. I believe the Arabs are the new Nazis, the heirs of the Third Reich. I don't wish him well to say the least." (Friedman 1986)[52]

The threat was an unmistakable reference to Columbia University professor Edward Said, undoubtedly the most prominent Palestinian in the United States. Said's office had been ransacked and his apartment building broken into months before Vancier's death threat. The head of the JDL's all-Russian Brighton Beach Chapter, a recent immigrant himself, echoed Vancier's threats, telling a reporter, "I don't lose sleep over murdered Nazis or American Arabs who support the PLO. They have been responsible for the deaths of so many people." These aims and sentiments were in keeping with the JDL founder's 1979 call for the creation of a terrorist underground in the United States that would "quietly and professionally eliminate those modern day Hitlers . . . that threaten our very existence" (Friedman 1986). In 1986, the FBI

> uncovered a JDL plot to assassinate ADC founder James Abourezk . . . who says the FBI called him after foiling it. In ad-

---

guilty to Federal charges that they took part in a series of "terrorist bombings" in the New York area since 1984. They pleaded guilty to "racketeering charges involving acts of bombing, arson, extortion and fraud. Each faced a possible maximum prison sentence of 20 years." Vancier received a ten-year sentence. Another defendant, Jay Cohen, age twenty-four, committed suicide before sentencing (*New York Times,* Aug. 14 and Oct. 27, 1987).

52. According to Friedman 1986, as far back as 1974 Kahane was calling for "the creation of a 'world-wide, Jewish anti-terror group' that would 'spread fear and shatter the souls' of Israel's Arabs, forcing them to flee for their lives."

dition, the FBI thwarted a plot by a Kach member from Israel who was in Los Angeles allegedly recruiting militant Jews to kidnap two Israeli Arab businessmen working in California. (Friedman 1987a)

Kach is the name of Meir Kahane's political party in Israel. More recently, following the assassination of Meir Kahane in November 1990, Kach issued a hit list containing the names of eight prominent Arab and Jewish critics of Israel. Among those targeted were Edward Said and *New York Times* columnist Anthony Lewis.[53]

Another target of JDL-style terror tactics was Bonnie Rimawi, former coordinator of the New York ADC office. Shortly after Rimawi opened the office in March 1985, she was subjected to a series of threats, intimidations, and prank newspaper advertisements. Her office experienced several attempted break-ins (including one successful entry), and was infiltrated by a man who was later identified as Mordechai Levy, head of the JDO. Among the hundreds of harassing calls Rimawi received were two collect calls purporting to be from the Committee against Rape and the Rape Center. Two weeks after the Odeh murder in October 1985, Rimawi was terrified to learn that her name appeared on an enemies list published on the front page of *American Jewish Life*, a New Jersey monthly newspaper. Rimawi was described as a "PLO organizer" under the heading "enemies of the Jewish people," a veritable death sentence under the circumstances. Another enemies list bearing Alex Odeh's name had circulated in southern California before his murder. Rimawi quit her job shortly thereafter (U.S. Congress 1988, 141–45, 159–70).[54]

Mainstream Jewish organizations have consistently disavowed the actions of Jewish extremist groups. They were, for example, quick to disassociate themselves from the Odeh murder. AJC leader Hyman Bookbinder telephoned the leadership of the ADC "to express [his] horror." AJC also denounced the bombing. Other Jewish leaders did the same.[55] Nevertheless, establishmentarian Jewish organizations

---

53. *Detroit Free Press,* Dec. 5, 1990, 17a.

54. Rimawi retained an attorney who helped her obtain a front-page retraction from an initially reluctant publisher. The retraction appeared in the December 20 issue of *American Jewish Life.*

55. See the testimonies of AJC leaders David Gordis and Hyman Bookbinder in U.S. Congress 1988, 39–54 and 80–83; see also Pinsky 1986.

have participated in the vilification of Arab-Americans and others, thereby helping to create the very climate of hostility and violence that they purport to deplore. These organizations have engaged in a form of ideological warfare that is in some ways more insidious than that practiced by the extremist groups.

The ADL of B'nai B'rith, a tax-exempt Jewish religious and educational organization, offers a case in point. The ADL has used its highly respected position as one of the nation's leading civil rights organizations to denounce prominent Arab-Americans, as well as U.S. critics of Israel, as PLO propagandists. For example, the director of the ADL's Michigan office, Richard Lobenthal, publicly accused the ADC on at least two occasions of being "a mouthpiece for the PLO." In an interview with the *Christian Science Monitor* he openly criticized the ADC, noting that unlike his own organization "that group" is not actively battling discrimination, the implication being that it is merely fronting as an antidiscrimination group for a hidden political agenda (White 1982). In a letter to the editor rebutting Lobenthal's accusation, then ADC executive director James Zogby charged the ADL with being "a significant source of anti-Arab defamation in the United States . . ." The League, Zogby asserted,

> freely attaches "pro-PLO" or "pro-terrorist front" labels to American activists and organizations which support the Palestinian cause. In addition, the ADL frequently "suggests" that various Arab-American organizations "might have" petrodollars or illegal Arab connections. (Zogby 1982)

The ADL also has vigorously criticized U.S. academics and universities in a manner that is considered intimidating. In 1981, the ADL attacked the highly acclaimed documentary film "Women Under Siege." The film, by noted author Elizabeth Fernea, focused on the lives of Palestinian women living in refugee camps in southern Lebanon. The ADL charged that Fernea's work amounted to "unabashed propaganda for the PLO." The allegation prompted the film's major funder, the National Endowment for the Humanities, to denounce the film, even though impartial viewers considered it a fair treatment of a rarely explored topic.

In November 1984, the Middle East Studies Association (MESA) passed a resolution criticizing the ADL for defaming various students, teachers, and researchers as "pro-Arab propagandists." The ADL had asserted that these individuals "use their anti-Zionism as merely a guise for their deeply felt anti-Semitism" (cited in Winkler 1985; see also Campbell 1985). MESA members had become alarmed after a confidential list of allegedly anti-Israel, pro-Arab individuals and groups was circulated among student leaders at various college campuses by the ADL's New England Regional Office. MESA also cited American Israel Public Affairs Committee (AIPAC) in the same resolution for soliciting "unbalanced information on students, faculty, and other parties on American university campuses" (cited in Winkler 1985).

The activities of the two organizations, both among the most prominent Jewish organizations in the country, struck many Middle East academics as having the hallmarks of McCarthyite-style blacklists. Indeed, the ADL ultimately issued a handbook titled, *Pro-Arab Propaganda in America,* which amounted to such an enemies list. It included thirty-one organizations and thirty-four individuals, mostly Arab-Americans, who purportedly constitute the "pro-PLO support network" in the United States (ADL 1983). AIPAC also issued two similar lists (AIPAC 1983; Kessler and Schwaber 1984). (For other examples of intimidation by AIPAC and ADL, see Findley 1984; Aruri 1985; Tivnan 1987; Friedman 1987b; Marshall 1989.)

In late 1988, B'nai B'rith International, the world's largest Jewish organization and the organizational parent of ADL, issued a fundraising letter to 14,000 of its members that claimed: "The Arab presence on the college campus is poisoning the minds of our young people." The letter pointed out (erroneously) that "Arab money is pouring into college campuses all over the United States . . ." Raising the specter that the "dream of Judaism is in danger," the letter asked readers to "join forces and attack the evil," which presumably included the "Arab presence" as well as "cults and cultists." When the ADC criticized the letter, B'nai B'rith offered a partial apology, claiming the letter was prepared by an outside contractor, and that "the choice of words and sentiments they convey do not reflect our views" (Goldman 1989). The ADC later pointed out that the 1988 letter was similar to one issued in 1987. The 1987 letter employed many of the "same phrases, sentences, terms, and blocks of information" but did not include the "poisoning the minds" phrase (Cook 1989).[56]

---

56. In a similar vein Martin Peretz, the editor-in-chief of the *New Republic,* pandered to anti-Arab racism and hatreds in a solicitation letter he sent to Jewish Americans in

Smears, enemies lists, and other forms of vilification can create a climate conducive to violence. In April 1980 the Washington, D.C. office of the Palestine Human Rights Campaign (PHRC) was fire-bombed. The JDL took credit for the bombing. James Zogby, who was at the time director of PHRC, described the circumstances surrounding the bombing in his testimony before the House Subcommittee on Criminal Justice:

> ... for three years prior to the bombing ... the PHRC had been subjected to a campaign of vilification ... The PHRC, for example, was termed a terrorist group and a PLO front by AIPAC. I was accused of being an agent of the PLO, an agent of Libya, an agent of Cuba, all of these by the ADL, the Anti-Defamation League. (U.S. Congress 1988, 113)

There are also indications that the ADL, for one, has spied on Arab-Americans and other critics of Israel, passing on information to the FBI and other government agencies. As far back as 1975 a Chicago newspaper story reported that an ADL spokesman "said that he also keeps files on the more active Arabs living here and routinely passes them on to the FBI" (Young 1975). The article made the following important observations: "FBI officials said they have uncovered no concrete evidence of terrorist activity by Arab-Americans." Unidentified "Israeli intelligence sources ... believe the main thrust of Arab activity in the U.S. is not terrorism." If taken at face value, such observations imply that the ADL's surveillance amounts to spying on people for merely exercising their constitutionally guaranteed rights of free speech and assembly, a conclusion that seems to have eluded the writer of the story. There is also reason to believe that similar information is passed on to the Israeli government.

Suspicions of ADL spying were confirmed in 1993 when San Francisco police raided two California offices of the organization.

---

summer 1991. Referring to "the vainglorious but failed Arab civilization," to "the defeat of Arab nationalist fanatics in the Gulf," to "the logic of Arab politics" that "inevitably" led to Iraq's invasion of Kuwait, Peretz pitched his magazine as being "on the watch for the safety of the Jewish state." When ADC questioned his resorting to such stereotypes, Peretz did not deign to respond. On this score, one need only replace the word "Arab" here with "Jewish" to imagine the howls of protest and charges of "anti-Semitism" that would emanate from respectable journals like the *New Republic*.

"They left with boxes of files a prosecutor later described in court as 'contraband,' including leaked copies of confidential law enforcement reports, fingerprint cards, driver's license photographs and individual criminal histories drawn from police records" (McGee 1993).

The San Francisco police had acted on an earlier tip from the FBI that a detective on the force, Thomas Gerard, had sold confidential police files on local antiapartheid groups to a South African intelligence agent. Gerard's accomplice was Roy H. Bullock, who worked as an undercover spy for ADL. "Over a thirty-year period," Bullock "compiled computer files for the ADL on 9,876 individuals and more than 950 groups of all political stripes, including the NAACP, the Rainbow Coalition, ACLU, the American Indian Movement, the Center for Investigative Reporting, Pacifica, ACT UP, Palestinian and Arab groups, Americans for Peace Now, and anti-apartheid organizations" (Friedman 1993). Bullock was also suspected of "tapping phones, accessing answering machines, and assuming false identities to infiltrate organizations," Friedman adds.

The investigation revealed that the ADL ran a nationwide spy network that included obtaining confidential law enforcement files, among them FBI files. Investigations by the FBI and San Francisco police further revealed that the ADL passed information to the Israeli and South African governments. "What's more, Israel apparently used tips from the ADL to detain Palestinian Americans who traveled there" (Friedman 1993; McGee 1993). "This collaboration continues and has resulted in harassment of Arab-Americans," reports Abdeen Jabara, an attorney for plaintiffs in a civil suit—one of two against the ADL. "After the ADL provided information to the federal authorities on seven Palestinian men and one Kenyan woman living in California, the targets were rounded up in dragnet arrests and charged with violating the McCarran-Walter provision" (Jabara 1993). Oddly, the San Francisco District Attorney dropped its criminal investigation by late 1993, because, as the District Attorney explained, "the group does many good things" (*New York Times* 1993b).

The overall effect of the ADL's practices is to reinforce the image of Arabs as terrorists and security threats, thereby creating a climate of fear, suspicion, and hostility toward Arab-Americans and others who espouse critical views of Israel, possibly leading to death threats and bodily harm.

The ideologically motivated hostility and violence of Jewish extremist groups and its less lethal corollary among mainstream Jewish organizations constitute an important source of anti-Arab racism and animosity. It would be wrong, however, to consider this source the *only* or even principal source of anti-Arab racism in the United States.

Anti-Arab Xenophobia

A second type of anti-Arab racism consists of locally inspired hostility and violence toward Arab-Americans, Muslims, and Middle Easterners and their institutions. It usually occurs when they are ethnically visible. This type of hostility may have little, if anything, to do with the Arab-Israeli conflict, U.S. involvement in the Middle East, or other overt political or foreign policy considerations. It is based on perceived differences of race, culture, ethnicity, and religion. Its source is rooted in racist nativistic attitudes found in society. An extreme case in point was the murder of two Yemeni immigrant workers in Dearborn in spring 1976.

In the early hours of May 17, Saleh Nagi Shahbain, age thirty-four, was brutally gunned down by a shotgun blast to the chest. His assailants were never apprehended. Three weeks later in the predawn hours of June 5, another Yemeni, Ali Shebrin Eleshemmam, age twenty-two, was also brutally slain by a shotgun blast, this time to the head. The assailants, reported to be two white men, were never apprehended (Magnusson 1976).[57] Nor were their motives ever established, though some suspicions centered on local rednecks seeking to avenge some perceived wrong.[58] Nothing in the victims' backgrounds indicates they knew their assailants. The circumstances of the attacks—both took place in a long-established Arab immigrant neighborhood during the early morning hours while the victims were on their way to work—suggests they were chosen at random.

Such attacks, if shown not to be ordinary crimes (i.e., not linked to the victims' ethnicity), properly belong to the category of nativistic

---

57. See also, "Yemeni Immigrant Killed in Dearborn," *Detroit News,* June 6, 1976.

58. Some "people in the neighborhood" attributed the slaying to "growing hostility between the Arab group and surrounding Southern white factory workers..." (*Detroit Free Press,* June 6, 1976). Others speculated that "the two Arabs were gunned down by pimps who resent Arab dealings with their prostitutes" (*Detroit Free Press,* June 8). The stabbing of a white youth, allegedly by Arabs, after the second murder lent some credence to suspicions that the murders were related to Arab-white hostilities.

xenophobia and racism, rather than Samhan's (1987) "political racism." Admittedly, sometimes the line distinguishing the two types of anti-Arab hostility and violence can be extremely blurred, as when bigoted people act on jingoistic impulses prompted by news of events taking place in the Middle East, and by the tone of political leaders and opinion shapers in the media (matters to which we return). But it does not follow, as James Zogby, director of the Arab American Institute, has contended, that there is no "strong nativist anti-Arab sentiment in this country, and despite our intense problem in the media, it has not translated into a hate-the-local-Arab problem" (cited in Hundley 1987b). Zogby allows for one exception—the Detroit Arab-American community, whose visibility makes it a target of attacks. But the reasoning here is circular (Arabs are attacked only when they become visible) and begs the question why the hostility exists in the first place.[59]

U.S. history is replete with xenophobia and racism. That it tends to surface with the arrival of new immigrants should not obscure the fact that cultural racism, bigotry, and prejudice are deeply embedded in U.S. culture. Even slight cultural differences are sufficient to form the basis for prejudice and discrimination; all the more so when the newcomers are perceived as coming from radically different cultural, religious, and/or linguistic backgrounds.[60] This appears to be the situation in Dearborn, Michigan, the site of the largest concentration of Arab Muslim immigrants in North America.

In April 1986 *Michigan Magazine,* the Sunday magazine supplement of the *Detroit News,* ran a cover story on the Detroit Arab community. Although uneven, the story was generally sympathetic. Two months later (June 15), the magazine published a letter in reaction to the story. The letter is worth quoting in full:

   Too bad the Arab issue (April 6) was so one-sided, playing

---

59. One could conceivably put forth the argument (untenable in my opinion) that there is something unique about the character or behavior of Detroit's Arab-Americans that renders them the object of scorn and violence, but I doubt this is what Zogby had in mind.

60. The classic example is that of the nineteenth-century Irish immigrants who encountered considerable hostility from the predominately Anglo-Saxon Protestant majority, eventually becoming in turn the victimizers of later immigrants, e.g., the Italians. For an overview discussion, see Fredrickson and Knobel 1980.

for sympathy from all who read it. However, it's hard to give sympathy when you see the Arabs take over. It's difficult to sit on your porch and watch women and children urinate in the street, on sidewalks and against trees. It is equally difficult to understand them when they take flowers off your porch, vegetables from gardens and fruit from your own trees and be told by them that it is their right to take if they wish to.

You should devote an issue to the Arab who takes everything— free lunch, clothes, food, ADC welfare and, of course, opens a business and pays no taxes.

The letter was signed, "A Lifelong Dearbornite, E.L.M.," and closed with this postscript: "To sign and give my phone and address would constitute suicide! What I have written is true—we older citizens cannot speak out because of reprisals."

As the postscript indicates, the author is probably suffering from a severe case of xenophobia. The greater issue, however, is why the editors of *Michigan Magazine* chose to publish the letter (without comment) in the first place. It is very doubtful they would have run a similar letter about African-American or Jewish women urinating "on sidewalks and against trees." (Note the allusion to animal-like behavior.) The fact that the letter with its wild allegations ran in a major daily in a city with a large and vocal Arab-American community is indicative of the level of racism (and cynicism) found at the highest echelons of mainstream society. Along similar lines, the University of Toledo, Ohio, school paper, the *Collegian,* ran a classified advertisement on January 17, 1985, for a roommate that stated in bold letters "No Arabs." One need only imagine the public outcry had a similar notice read "No Blacks," or "No Jews," to appreciate the level of complicity on the part of the school paper in this bit of racism.

E. L. M.'s racist and xenophobic attitudes, though extreme, are unmistakably common in the Dearborn area. For example, in a news story about rising housing assessments in nearby Dearborn Heights, an irate homeowner threatened to "bring down the neighborhood and sell [her house] to the first Arab or black that wants to buy it" (cited in Hitsky 1982). The comment was reported rather matter-of-factly, and provoked no reaction from the paper's readership.

In 1985, first-time mayoral candidate Michael Guido scored a decisive lead in the local elections when he distributed to every Dearborn household an eight-page campaign brochure titled, "Let's Talk About City Parks and the Arab Problem." Guido targeted the city's estimated 15,000 Arab-Americans, insinuating that their increasing numbers "threatens our neighborhoods, the value of our property and a darned good way of life." In the same brochure, Guido promised to get tough with noisy Arab neighbors who, he claimed, neglect to maintain their property and violate overcrowding ordinances. He also took issue with local Arab-American community leaders, who, he said, "continually badger and browbeat our government for tax funds." Guido's election victory in the tight November 1985 race, where he carried 56 percent of the vote, is universally attributed to the anti-Arab posture he adopted late in his campaign (cf. Turque 1986a and 1986b).

The Guido brochure tapped a reservoir of xenophobic, racist attitudes lying just beneath the surface. These attitudes surfaced in early 1988 when Mike Hammoud, a young Lebanese-American, and his American fiancée took over a long-established Polish bakery in Dearborn. Hammoud's plan was to retain the bakery's distinctive ethnic flavor that had made it a tradition in the neighborhood. The gesture was met with hostility by patrons of the bakery. "We've gotten up to 50 calls a day from people who say things like 'Stupid Arabs go home,'" Hammoud told a local newspaper. The paper noted that "[o]ther Arab-owned businesses in Dearborn faced similar problems when they were opened" (Eberwein 1988). Richard O'Neill, vice president of the Dearborn Chamber of Commerce, rejected the notion that the harassment stemmed from xenophobia, claiming that "Arabs are disadvantaged because they can't assimilate as quickly as, say, the Irish or the Polish" (Eberwein 1988), his assertion being itself an indication of the racist mentality of the town.

In another example of latent anti-Arab racism, Dearborn officials and residents opposed a proposal by a Muslim group to build a school on a vacant lot in east Dearborn, the predominately Arab part of town. The local newspaper observed that city planning commissioners "seemed to apply unusual scrutiny to the proposal and adopted an attitude that forced the proponents to take on an almost defensive posture."[61] On the west side of town, where fewer Arabs

---

61. Editorial, *Dearborn Press & Guide,* May 11, 1989. See also a related news story,

reside, a local neighborhood association raised objections to the presence of an Afghan family in the neighborhood, claiming the extended family's large size "would set a precedent" leading to "lower property values," a recurrent theme in Dearborn politics. The neighborhood association was not deterred when the city's legal department ruled that the family had not violated the housing code.[62]

According to Zogby (Hundley 1987b), such racist attitudes are to be expected because they occurred in a city where Arabs are highly visible (Arabs make up about 15 percent of the city's 100,000 residents). Overall, Zogby contends, Dearborn is an aberration because there is no "strong nativist anti-Arab sentiment" in the country. But anti-Arab attitudes do exist in areas of the country where Arabs do not constitute a large and visible community. In Chapel Hill, North Carolina, a Muslim group's request to build a mosque initially was met with opposition from residents, much like the Muslim school proposal in Dearborn. A planning board member objected on the grounds that a mosque's "architecture is not appropriate for the neighborhood."[63]

The rejection is typical. In Brownstown Township, a distant Detroit suburb, a group of mostly Pakistani and Indian Muslims were denied a permit to hold a religious gathering by local authorities. Residents had expressed "fears that the gathering of local Moslems might attract terrorist, Beirut-style violence, might create traffic congestion." A more immediate fear, one opponent confided, was that the Muslims were trying to "take over" the neighboring housing subdivision (Thurtell 1985). In Chicago, the owner of a west side grocery placed a sign in the window of his closed store that read: "This store is being remodeled. No Arabs will be involved." In other words, the store has not been bought out by Arabs (Kass 1990).

Such crude racist and xenophobic attitudes have little to do with

---

"Islamic School Spurs Controversy," (*Dearborn Press & Guide,* June 12, 1989), where residents at a public meeting called to examine the Muslim rezoning proposal complained that "the immigrants . . . refuse to adapt to our way of living," and have turned the area into a "pigpen."

62. "Yacoobis Hot Topic at Meeting," *Dearborn Press & Guide,* Oct. 6, 1988. Residents at a neighborhood association meeting "shouted accusations that the Yacoobis were living as a 'tribe' or were 'running a boarding house.'" The Yacoobis were once a prosperous family who had fled the Soviet invasion and ensuing war in their native Afghanistan.

63. "Residents Opposed Proposal to Build a Student Mosque," *New York Times,* Feb. 12, 1990.

the Arab-Israeli conflict and U.S. involvement in the Middle East and more to do with homegrown nativistic racism. Because of its sporadic and infrequent nature, xenophobic or nativistic anti-Arab racism does not easily lend itself to good documentation. Nevertheless, it can be virtually found at random almost anywhere in the country at any given moment. When this type of racism combines with foreign policy it can make for a volatile mixture of jingoistic racism.

Jingoistic Racism

The third type of anti-Arab racism and violence is jingoistic racism. In many ways similar to xenophobic nativism, jingoistic racism is a curious blend of knee-jerk patriotism and homegrown white racism toward non-European, non-Christian dark skinned peoples. It is a racism spawned by political ignorance, false patriotism, and hyper ethnocentrism. Unlike the ideologically motivated violence of Jewish extremist groups, which is largely premeditated, jingoistic violence tends to be spontaneous, reactive, and episodic. It almost always occurs during heightened international tensions (hijackings, hostage takings, and military conflict), especially if U.S. citizens are involved, and political leaders and the news media react sharply to the crisis. During such moments, the "redneck" may lash out at the "enemy" never knowing the difference between an Arab and an Iranian, a Sunni and a Shiite, a Palestinian and a Pakistani.

Anti-Arab jingoistic racism seems to have been behind the outburst of vandalism and violence against Arab and Middle Eastern community buildings, mosques, and businesses that accompanied such events as the hijacking of the TWA flight to Beirut and the U.S. military strikes against Libya. A more recent example occurred in late summer 1989, during an especially tense moment following the kidnapping in Lebanon of a Shiite Muslim cleric, Sheikh Abdul Karim Obeid, by Israeli soldiers. In retaliation, Lebanese militants executed William Higgins, a marine officer held hostage since February 1988, and threatened the life of another U.S. hostage. Tense days followed the July 31 execution as the nation's leaders considered various responses. Meanwhile, in Brooklyn, New York, handwritten flyers urging violence against Arabs circulated in parts of the borough, the *New York Times* reported. In addition

A banner pro-claiming "Shiite Hunting Season" was draped on a chain-link fence on Bradley Avenue, across from the Staten Island Expressway. Another banner that said "F-14 Beirut" and was signed "Loyal Americans of Bayside" was hung over the Long Island Expressway in Queens. (Lee 1989)

Several days earlier, the *Times* added, Mayor Ed Koch told a rally that the United States should carpet bomb Lebanon's Bekaa region and other areas unless the U.S. hostages were freed.

The pattern of jingoistic violence, as already noted, had become fairly predictable. Events occurring in the Middle East, particularly violence against U.S. citizens, often trigger jingoistic violence against Arabs and others who could conceivably be confused with them, such as Muslims, Iranians, or Pakistanis. Admittedly, it is not always easy to determine whether an anti-Arab incident is due to jingoistic racism or to xenophobic nativism, or whether the attack arose from a personal dispute. Jingoistic hostility, like xenophobic reactions, almost always is accompanied by references to the victim's ethnicity. International tensions, however, need not be high for outbreaks of anti-Arab violence to occur. In mid-June 1988, when little seemed to be happening in the Middle East, vandals broke into the home of a Lebanese family living in Dearborn Heights, Michigan, a white, middle-class neighborhood. Using black and brown shoe polish, the vandals daubed the slogans: "Go Back to Iran," "Go Home," and "Go Back to Khomeini," in addition to stealing money and jewelry from the house (Prater 1988). This incident, with its mixture of jingoistic and xenophobic overtones, was clearly rooted in the deep-seated anti-Arab, anti-Middle Eastern racism that appears to be wide-spread in contemporary U.S. culture.

A more typical example of jingoistic anti-Arab racism occurred after the 1983 bombing of the U.S. Marine base in Beirut. Arab-Americans throughout the country experienced jingoistic sentiments, even in remote places like Vicksburg, Mississippi, where a highly assimilated Arab-American received a telephone call, warning: "From now on, for every American boy that's killed in Lebanon, a Lebanese home is going to burn in Vicksburg" (Orfalea 1988, 251).

Arab-Americans: Cultural Villains, Political Lepers

To varying degrees, all forms of anti-Arab racism feed off the many negative Arab stereotypes, especially prevalent after the October 1973

Arab oil embargo, permeating U.S. culture. Successive administrations, along with numerous congressional figures and political aspirants, have manipulated those images to gain elective office and/or to garner public support for domestic or foreign policy objectives. The history of this demagoguery is now largely forgotten. Yet its impact has no doubt left a deep, if subtle, mark on the political consciousness of Americans, contributing to the public's tolerance of anti-Arab racism. Three minor but egregious examples are:

A Nixon cabinet officer attempted to denigrate consumer advocate Ralph Nader by calling him a "dirty Arab."

Jimmy Carter's chief domestic advisor, Stuart E. Eizenstat, once suggested in a leaked internal memo that the Arabs be blamed for the country's energy problems.

Reagan's first Secretary of Labor, Raymond Donovan, himself embattled by scandal for most of his tenure, staged a "Friends of Donovan" bash for 900 supporters in October 1982 that included three men dressed as Arab sheiks, handing out fake money.[64]

Similar examples of blatantly anti-Arab stereotyping and scapegoating have emanated from virtually every level of government. Terrel Bell, a former Reagan cabinet officer, wrote in his memoirs that midlevel rightwing staffers in the White House and Office of Management and Budget "delighted" in making racist and derogatory slurs about African-Americans and other minorities. "Arabs," Bell disclosed, "were called 'sand niggers' in discussions about State Department issues in the Middle East."[65]

An equally telling, if somewhat humorous, incident involved the highest echelon of the United States Information Agency (USIA). An internal USIA memorandum obtained through the Freedom of In-

64. In what must be considered another unflattering moment for U.S. journalism, the *Washington Post* ran a lengthy, lighthearted story on the event in its Style section under the heading, "Ray Donovan Gets a Fair Sheik" (Oct. 14, 1982). Among those in the "hooting and hollering sellout crowd" of 900 were the U.S. attorney general, the head of Health and Human Services department, the director of the CIA, and the White House chief of staff. Then-presidential counselor Edwin Meese delivered a tribute to Donovan. The latter was described by the *Post* as a "continuing embarrassment to the administration through persistent allegations that he had past ties to organized crime."

65. Cited in "Racist Jokes in White House Reported in Book," *New York Times,* Oct. 21, 1987. Bell served as secretary of education in the first Reagan administration, 1981 to 1984.

formation Act and dated January 8, 1986, carried disturbing news: A food vendor, whose name "could be of Palestinian or Middle-Eastern origin," had positioned himself in front of the USIA building in Washington, where he "can observe movements of the Director [Charles Wick], official visitors, Agency personnel." The vendor was described as "a possible threat to personnel or physical security." Thus began a two-year campaign to remove all vendors from the area around the USIA building. In an effort to persuade District of Columbia agencies to take action (they had ultimate jurisdiction over the matter), one USIA official wrote: "We remain convinced that vendor operations in front of USIA are inappropriate and harmful to the national interest." The official added that "vendor tables and other equipment could be used to hide explosive devices." District of Columbia officials were unswayed by the paranoia, and allowed the vendors to remain (Corn and Morley 1988).

Even in Michigan, home to the largest community of Arab-Americans in North America, the governor was not averse to resorting to anti-Arab demagoguery. William Milliken, one of the longest serving governors in the history of the state, brazenly told a news reporter that if one were looking for a scapegoat for Michigan's economic ills, he would "point to the damn Arabs." Aside from the slur itself, the governor's remark was noteworthy in that it was not made in reaction to the 1973 oil embargo, but in late 1981 in reference to the economic hard times then rocking Michigan's economy. Much had happened in the interim, including the flight of U.S. manufacturing industry to the Sun Belt and abroad, as well as the influx of better quality import goods, among other developments in the state's economy. The governor's attempt to scapegoat the Arabs for Michigan's economic troubles caused an uproar in the state's Arab-American community, which ultimately forced Milliken to issue a public apology to the community (Crutchfield 1981).

In the 1984 presidential campaign, Walter Mondale returned $5,000 in contributions because they were from five citizens of Arab ancestry. He later apologized after Arab-American groups publicly criticized him. His rival, Gary Hart, quickly paid off a $700,000 loan to a Washington, D.C. bank because of reports it was owned by Arab interests.[66] The tone had been set by an earlier controversy

---

66. "Only later did it dawn on campaign aides that someone might make an issue of

over Arab financial contributions to Operation Push, the Chicago organization headed by Jesse Jackson, another Democratic presidential contender. To his credit, however, Jackson refused to succumb to Arab baiting his rivals.

In the 1983 Philadelphia mayoral race, candidate Wilson Goode returned over $2,000 in campaign contributions collected at an Arab-American fund-raiser after his Republican opponent openly charged him with accepting "Arab money." Goode, who won the race, never apologized, resisting for several years offers to meet with representatives of the local Arab-American community.[67] In the 1986 election year, young Joe Kennedy's first-time congressional campaign returned a $100 personal contribution from James Abourezk, a prominent Arab-American and a former senator from Kennedy's political party. In fact, Kennedy had originally accepted the donation, thanking Abourezk for his "thoughtfulness." Some two months later, however, Steve Rothstein, a Kennedy campaign aide, notified Abourezk that his contribution was being returned, adding that the Kennedy campaign did not want to become involved in the Middle East in "this way," citing Abourezk's association with the ADC (Robinson 1986).

Writing in the *Boston Sunday Globe* for April 27, Abourezk speculated that the Kennedy camp feared that his name would hurt fund-raising efforts among U.S. Jews. It is worth noting that Rothstein's phone call came on April 16, the day after the U.S. bombing of Libya, indicating that perhaps the Kennedy campaign was worried about fund-raising among all segments of his potential supporters due to anti-Arab racism in general. Unlike Goode, however, Kennedy later apologized, offering to accept the donation after embarrassing reports appeared in the press.[68]

the fact that in 1982 the bank was sold to a group of Middle Eastern investors," the *Wall Street Journal* reported (Mar. 23, 1984). The rival Mondale campaign reportedly leaked word of the potentially embarrassing connection to the press. "'We didn't know it was an Arab bank,' said Kenneth Guido, special counsel to the Hart campaign. 'We got Hart out of it as soon as we knew'" the *Journal* reported.

67. Goode never really offered an explanation for his action, other than to say, "I am very pro-Israel. I believe that the existence of the Jewish state in the Middle East is a must for this country," (quoted in "Goode Plans to Return $2,000 Raised," the *Philadelphia Inquirer*, Oct. 16, 1983).

68. In May 1986 a candidate for Maryland's 4th congressional district, Robert Neall, returned a $500 contribution to the National Association of Arab Americans (NAAA), "because it's better to be safe than sorry." The day before, Neall was the subject of

Curiously, the 1988 presidential campaign was largely devoid of the overt Arab baiting and the campaign contribution rejections that marked previous elections. The reason for this is a matter of speculation. The protests of Arab-American groups and civil liberties organizations doubtlessly played a role in curbing such practices. The declining serviceability of anti-Arab and anti–Third World jingoism in the twilight years of the Reagan administration may have also played a role, though a limited one (cf. Chomsky 1991, chap. 8). The one brazen attempt at Arab baiting seems to have failed to elicit much support. Early in the campaign, Republican presidential contender Pat Robertson demanded Secret Service protection, because, as an aide put it, his pro-Israel views might make him a target of "more fanatic Arab groups" (Associated Press 1987).

There was, curiously, a brief return to the Arab baiting of the 1970s and 1980s during the 1990 Republican primary in California's 44th Congressional District, demonstrating once again that anti-Arab racism was still a potent force in U.S. politics. In that race, candidate Randy "Duke" Cunningham distributed campaign literature that brazenly Arab baited his rival, Joe Ghougassian. One flyer posed the following question in bold type: "Which candidate for Congress is bankrolled by Arab oil interests?" The flyer was adorned with an oil barrel spewing dollar bills from an attached faucet, with the likenesses of Saudi Arabia's King Fahd and Libya's Muammar Qaddafi. The flyer pointed out that Ghougassian was born and raised in the Middle East (he was an Egyptian-born Armenian), adding disingenuously that he "has been out of the United States for the last 8 years in Arab countries." While factually true, the statement failed to note that Ghougassian had spent that time as a Reagan appointee, first as head of the Peace Corps in Yemen, and later as U.S. ambassador to Qatar. Unlike anti-Arab smear campaigns of the past, this one received considerable media coverage that tended to balance Cunningham's insinuations with countervailing facts (Fikes 1990, Huard 1990). Moreover, the smear campaign was also denounced by an appropriate high-level official, namely, Ed Rollins, national cochairman of the Republican Congressional Campaign Committee. As the politically conservative

---

criticism by the *Baltimore Sun* for accepting money from an organization with "ties to the Palestine Liberation Organization." *ADC Insider's Report* (Washington, D.C.: ADC) June 1986, 14.

Washington Times observed, Rollins's sudden denunciation of campaign smears based on a candidate's "racial, ethnic or religious background" was "an abrupt turnabout by the former political director in the Reagan White House" (Hallow 1990).

Paradoxically, as anti-Arab baiting and campaign fund rejections diminished in the late 1980s, government surveillance and harassment of Arab-Americans increased. As far back as the late 1960s, Arab-Americans had been the subject of FBI and INS scrutiny. During the Nixon years, special measures were undertaken against Arab foreign students, Arab immigrants, and Arab-Americans. The measures included entry restrictions on foreign nationals, FBI surveillance, information gathering on political activities and organizations, and even restrictions on Arab access to permanent resident status (Bassiouni 1974; cf. Hagopian 1975–76).[69] Ostensibly the measures were designed to prevent Arab terrorists from operating in the country. In reality, the argument was specious, as there have never been any recorded instances of Arab terrorism occurring in the United States until the 1993 World Trade Center bombing. Most FBI surveillance and questioning has focused on constitutionally guaranteed activities of free speech and association, not unusual by the standards of FBI practice, but hardly the kinds of activities associated with apprehending terrorists.

The case of Noha Ismail, a Minnesota librarian, is an example. Ismail, a Palestinian-American and a mother, had long been active in Arab-American causes. Although her activities fell entirely within the scope of the U.S. Constitution, and she had never violated any law, Ismail nevertheless was placed under surveillance by the FBI. The *Minnesota Star and Tribune* learned that the FBI had been questioning Ismail's neighbors as to whether they had any reason to believe she was a terrorist. The newspaper ultimately condemned the surveillance, forcing the FBI to issue a rare apology to Ismail.[70]

L.A. Eight

The most alarming example of government harassment of Arab-Americans to date occurred in 1987. On the morning of January 26,

---

69. The FBI's role as the country's "political police" is meticulously documented by Churchill and Vander Wall 1988; 1990. See also Gelbspan 1991; O'Reilly 1989; Criley 1990.
70. See the *Washington Report on Middle East Affairs,* Sept. 8, 1986, for details.

scores of INS, FBI, and police agents raided several houses in the Los Angeles Arab-American community, arresting six Palestinians along with the Kenyan wife of one of the arrested men. Several days later, another Palestinian was arrested while sitting for an exam at Cahffey Community College in San Bernardino County (Pell 1990). The wife of one of the arrested Palestinians recalled how they arrested her husband: "The INS men barged into our apartment and began to look for guns. . . . They were very disappointed that we didn't have weapons. . . . We asked them what right they had to enter our home, but they just laughed" (*Nation* 1987).

The eight were held in detention for nearly three weeks. They were allowed to see their lawyers and relatives only "shackled hand and foot," with "chains around our waists." Khader Musa Hamide, thirty-two at the time, the alleged ringleader, described his detention:

> They put two of us in a six-by-ten cell for 23 hours a day. For the first two days, the lights were on 24 hours a day and a camera was pointed at my head. We were allowed no phone calls, not even to our attorneys. I did not know day from night. I did not know where my wife was. I did not know where my friends were. . . . some of the guards called us many racist names and made sure we could hear the racist jokes they were telling. (Cited in Hentoff 1987)

The arrests reportedly were the culmination of a three-year-long FBI probe into the activities of Arab-American activists (Pell 1990). The L.A. Eight, as they came to be known, were originally charged under a little-used section of the 1952 McCarran-Walter Immigration Act, "which allows the government to deport aliens who 'knowingly circulate, distribute, print or display' material that advocates 'the overthrow . . . of the Government of the United States' or who advocate or teach the 'doctrines of world communism'" (*Nation* 1987). In court, government attorneys could produce nothing more than magazines and other printed literature to link the defendants to the Popular Front for the Liberation of Palestine (PFLP), a Marxist organization.

Unable to make the subversion allegations stick, the INS dropped them against six members of the group, charging them only with technical violations of their visas. The other two, Khader Musa and

Michel Shehadeh, permanent residents of the United States, were subsequently charged with being affiliated with the PFLP. Under the Immigration Act of 1990, the INS filed new accusations against the two. In theory the new act largely invalidated the ideological grounds for deportation and exclusion set forth in the McCarran-Walter Act. Nonetheless, the act contains a "terrorist activities" provision, under which the INS accused Musa and Shehadeh with raising money for a "terrorist organization"—the PFLP (ACLU 1992).

Nearly seven years after it began, none of the eight has ever been charged with any criminal wrongdoing (ACLU 1992; Mydans 1991). By 1993 the case continued to attract national attention (Cole 1993; *New York Times* 1993a). In that year sixty professors of immigration law wrote to the U.S. Attorney General protesting the INS's pursuit of the case against Musa and Shehadeh and its distortion of the 1990 Immigration Act (Lewis 1993).

In a chilling footnote to the L.A. Eight arrests, government agents also detained a twenty-two-year-old college student, holding her overnight. Charges were never brought against her. Born in the Palestinian town of Ramallah, she grew up in San Diego, California. She recounted her experiences in an affidavit and in an interview with *New York Times* columnist Anthony Lewis (1987):

I was studying, alone in the school library, on the night of Jan. 28. At about 8:30 a large man, 6 feet tall, came up and shoved a paper in front of me. It said "subpoena" and had my name on it. He flashed what looked like a badge and said, "Evelyn [not her real name], we want you to come with us."

He had a gun in a holster at his waist. He took my left arm and handcuffed me to his right arm. Another man—he also showed a gun—came over and grabbed me roughly by the right arm. They took me out to a dark burgundy car, cuffed my hands in front of me and shoved me into the back seat.

Evelyn spent the next twelve hours in a mysterious house somewhere in the suburbs. "I was taken into...a big bare room with a cement floor. There was a big metal desk. The room also had a metal pole set in the cement floor. It had a hook at the top, sort of like a tether ball pole." The description evokes images of an Orwellian police state. In a "dimly lit room," Evelyn was "thrown into a gray metal chair, still handcuffed"; "a bright fluorescent light" focused on her face.

> They threw a picture down on the desk. It was a picture of me, my husband and X (the friend who had been arrested). They slapped it and said, "Who is this man, identify him." I refused and said what they were doing to me was illegal. One said, "Honey, we are the law."

By midnight, Evelyn was left handcuffed to the hook on top of the metal pole, her "left arm was stretched up to reach it." She was left in that uncomfortable position for the next three hours. When the men returned, she asked to use the bathroom, but was not allowed to. Evelyn was told her husband was in custody, which was a lie, and was offered a deal if she would be a witness against one of the L.A. Eight. She refused. Around half past eight the following morning she was dropped off about two miles from her home. The experience so terrified Evelyn that she initially refused to talk publicly about it.

Many civil libertarians and others who rallied in support of the L.A. Eight feared that the arrests were a test case by federal authorities, a first step in a broader plan to silence and curtail the political activities of Arab-Americans who opposed U.S. foreign policy. Concern was heightened when a copy of a secret INS plan was obtained by the *Los Angeles Times* shortly after the arrests of the Palestinians. The internal government document, written the previous year, revealed the existence of an interagency contingency plan to apprehend, detain, and deport large numbers of Arab and Iranian students, permanent residents, and even U.S. citizens during a presidentially declared national state of emergency. Oakdale, Louisiana, was designated as one of the major detention sites. According to the plan, a "target group . . . considerably less than 10,000 persons" was scheduled for detention and deportation (INS 1986).

Further evidence that the arrests were "part of a secret plan aimed at chilling dissent by foreigners living in the United States" surfaced in May 1989 when sections of National Security Decision Directive (NSDD) 207 along with other documents were obtained by the American Civil Liberties Union through a Freedom of Information Act request. According to researcher Eve Pell (1990):

NSDD 207, titled "The National Program for Combatting Terrorism," assigned the Justice Department the task of keeping terrorists from entering the country and of expelling those already here. However, one of 207's mandates doesn't mention terrorists at all; it simply orders "expulsion from the United States of alien activists not in conformity with their immigration status." That means targeting politically active aliens—people who exercise free speech rights guaranteed to citizens—and checking to see if they are in technical violation of their visas and, if so, expeditiously deporting them.... To carry out these tasks, the Justice Department created a secret interagency group, chaired by an official from the INS and called the Alien Border Control Committee.

The similarities between the measures outlined in the secret government documents (targeting Middle Easterners, imprisoning the accused, opposing bail, using secret evidence, invoking the McCarran-Walter Immigration Act) and the government's actions in the L.A. Eight case are striking.

Using tactics outlined in the INS contingency plan, the government has also sought to deport another Palestinian, Fouad Rafeedie. Rafeedie, a Cleveland grocer, immigrated to the United States in 1975 from the West Bank town of El Bireh. In 1986, the thirty-one-year-old Rafeedie took a two-week trip abroad, where he attended a PFLP youth conference in Syria. The INS alleges he concealed this fact from border officials when he reentered the United States. Nearly a year after he returned to Cleveland, "the INS charged him with being 'excludable' as a subversive person or one whose admission would be prejudicial to the public interest" (Lewis 1988; Pell 1990). The summary exclusion procedure is authorized by the McCarran-Walter Immigration Act, a vestige of the McCarthy era. Rafeedie is the first resident alien to be charged with this section of the Act, which only applies to persons charged under its ideological provisions (Committee for Justice 1990, 2).

Clearly, attitudes of elected officials toward Arabs and government surveillance and harassment of Arab-Americans are indicative of general cultural attitudes. There is every reason to believe that such attitudes tend to trickle down the social pyramid, fueling and sanctioning popular attitudes.

Gulf War Postscript

Anti-Arab racism and hate violence reached an all time high during the Gulf war. From the outset of the crisis in early August 1990, Arab-Americans were subjected to threats, vandalism, violence, and other forms of harassment. Anti-Arab hostility intensified after the commencement of the air war on January 17, 1991. Prior to the invasion of Kuwait on August 2, 1990, the ADC had recorded only five anti-Arab hate crimes for 1990. After the invasion, the ADC recorded eighty-six incidents between August 2 and February 2, 1991, while many others went unreported (ADC 1991a, 1991b; Abraham 1991). Forty-eight of the incidents (56 percent) were directed at Arab-American organizations, political activists, and others who publicly dissented from official U.S. policy. After the outbreak of war in January 1991, Arab and Muslim community organizations in Texas, Oklahoma, Michigan, and California were vandalized, bombed, or harassed in some way. Being highly visible, such targets were inviting, and thus the incidents surrounding them were not entirely unexpected.

Less prominent targets, however, were also attacked. Arab-owned businesses in Michigan, Florida, Ohio, Texas, and California were vandalized, several were destroyed by arson, though local police were reluctant to link some of the arson cases to ethnic hostility. Jingoism seems to have been behind many of these incidents.

Most revealing were attacks directed against ordinary persons who fit the Arab stereotype. These incidents reveal the depth of anti-Arab racism and bigotry in U.S. society. The ADC logged thirty-six incidents (42 percent) against ordinary Arab-Americans and others who were mistaken for Arabs during the period between August 8, 1990 and February 2, 1991.

During the Gulf war itself many Arab-Americans feared for their safety. This was especially true among Arab immigrants, who were terrified by the manifestations of jingoism they witnessed. Immigrants were particularly vulnerable to taunts, jeers, verbal harassment, and even physical abuse because they tend to wear Middle Eastern clothing and concentrate in readily identifiable neighborhoods like east and south Dearborn, Michigan. But even in their homes, Arabs were not always safe from the swelling tide of jingoism that swept the country during the war. From coast to coast, neighbors, driven by a combination of personal enmity, xenophobia, and hyperpatriotism, harassed their Middle Eastern neighbors. Many Arabs received harassing phone calls, others saw their houses egged, or their car tires slashed.

As in previous years, the White House, Congress, the news media, and political commentators often set the tone. President George Bush repeatedly taunted and demonized Iraqi leader Saddam Hussein, calling him "the new Hitler of the Middle East." The loyal press amplified White House accusations of Iraqi atrocities against the Kuwaitis and exaggerated Iraqi military threats to Saudi Arabia and other states in the region. Latent fears of a recurrence of the oil shortages and attendant price hikes were also stirred up by the Bush administration. Such scare tactics played on deep-seated anti-Arab, anti-Muslim, anti–Third World sentiments rampant in U.S. society (Abraham 1991; Chomsky 1991).

The White House compounded matters when it ordered the FBI on the eve of the war to place Arab-Americans under surveillance. In this, the Bush administration was following in the footsteps of its predecessors. By one estimation, the FBI contacted at least forty Arab-American community leaders, activists, and others during the Gulf war. It also harassed antiwar demonstrators as well (MSN 1991). After the war, President Bush sent a crime bill to Congress that loosely defined a terrorist as anyone who had raised money or recruited members for any organization that had engaged in violence. The bill also effectively called for the establishment of a secret government tribunal to hear terrorist deportation cases. The legislation would empower the government to detain suspected terrorists indefinitely, employing secret hearings and secret evidence (Cook 1991; Johnston 1991). Fortunately, the legislation did not see the light of day. The offensive legislation, called Terrorist Alien Removal, was roundly condemned by the civil liberties organizations as well as the major media. The *New York Times* editorialized that "This bill would make the United States look as foolish and unjust as Kuwait does with its postwar kangaroo courts" (NYT 1991).

The war brought to the surface latent anti-Arab sentiment. Anti-Arab slurs and other derogatory references were openly expressed on radio talk shows, bumper stickers, T-shirts, pins, and posters. A popular poster depicted a bedouin on a camel in the crosshairs of a rifle atop the slogan "I'd Fly 10,000 Miles to Smoke a Camel." Stand-up comedians pandered to the racism of their audiences, resorting to crude anti-Arab jokes. Radio stations played popular tunes altered with an anti-Arab message; in some cases the songs had already been retrofitted with anti-Iranian lyrics from the previous decade, like "Bomb Iran," a takeoff on the Beach Boys classic "Barbara Ann."

Overall, the Gulf period marked a continuation of the previous trends in anti-Arab racism and violence. In comparison to the previous highwater mark of anti-Arab racism, 1985 to 1986, the Gulf crisis was relatively less lethal. Although there were many reports of assaults against Arab-Americans, few resulted in serious injuries and no one was killed. There were only five reported firebombings and cases of arson against Arab-owned businesses, and only one pipebombing. No Arab or Islamic community organizations were bombed, though many received threats and an incendiary device that apparently failed to explode was discovered at the American Muslim Council in San Diego. Five incidents during this period can be traced to the assassination of Rabbi Meir Kahane, the former leader of the JDL. His murder in November 1990 triggered a rash of death threats and harassment against prominent Arab-Americans and others, including a drive-by shooting in which no one was hurt. These incidents were clearly ideologically motivated hate crimes, having little connection to the Gulf crisis.

Conclusion

Do anti-Arab racism and hate violence exist in contemporary U.S. society? The answer, unfortunately, is in the affirmative. Moreover, far from being a fringe phenomenon, anti-Arab racism is found at the highest levels of mainstream society. In magnitude, anti-Arab racism and hate violence is miniscule compared with racist violence directed at African-Americans and other minorities. Yet anti-Arab racism is unique in that it has been largely tolerated by mainstream society.[71]

Arab-American leaders, among others, have tended to attribute the phenomenon of anti-Arab racism to fallout from the Arab-Israeli conflict. There is some validity to this claim, but it is not the full picture. To be sure, ideologically inspired Jewish extremist groups appear to have been responsible for some of the lethal violence di-

71. I have discussed how Arab-Americans cope with their alienation and marginality in U.S. society elsewhere (1989).

rected at Arab-Americans and others sympathetic to the plight of the Palestinians. But this is only a small fraction of the overall violence and racism affecting Arab-Americans, Muslims, and Middle Easterners over the past two decades.

Upon close inspection much of the anti-Arab racism and violence appears to be the result of a volatile mixture of jingoism combined with domestic racism. Arab-American spokesmen have correctly associated this kind of violence and hostility with events occurring in the Middle East. It is important to note, however, that anti-Arab cultural racism is an essential component of the mixture. Anti-Arab racism alone has been behind much of the vandalism, slurs, threats, and attacks against Middle Easterners and their institutions even during times of relative calm in the Middle East. Racism makes possible not only the demagoguery of politicians and political commentators, but the extremist and jingoistic hate violence directed at Arabs as well.

The existence of anti-Arab racism can be inferred from the following incident and the reactions to it in the press. On October 18, 1983, Israel Rubinowits, a twenty-two-year-old Israeli, entered the public gallery of the House of Representatives carrying a bomb. Rubinowits was discovered and arrested, receiving a six-month sentence after pleading guilty to the lesser charge of disturbing Congress. His sentence was ultimately suspended when he agreed to be deported from the country, promising never to return. Even though the incident occurred at the height of the Reagan administration's war on terrorism, it was deliberately played down by the administration and the press, as noted by David Sadd of the National Association of Arab Americans (NAAA) in his testimony before the House Subcommittee on Criminal Justice:

> The *Washington Post,* which reported the story the next day, ironically buried it on the obituary pages in the third section of the newspaper. A follow-up story 10 days later in the Metro section added little new material. The *New York Times* finally managed to cover the incident by November 2. (U.S. Congress 1988, 79)

What if Rubinowits had been an Arab or a Muslim? Would the Reagan administration have treated the matter so lightly, even if the individual in question were determined to be mentally unstable?

Would members of congress have remained as tight-lipped as they had? Would the press have covered the story in as cavalier a manner? It is doubtful. One shudders to imagine the outburst of national hysteria that would have occurred had the would-be bomber been a Palestinian, Libyan, or Lebanese Shiite. But one need not resort to conjecture when history offers many real examples, like Reagan's fabled Libyan hit teams, which generated national alarm and paranoia unprecedented in recent memory.

There is an interesting footnote to the story of Israel Rubinowits. Two years after the incident, then-House Speaker Jim Wright made a passing reference to the incident in a discussion on fighting terrorism. Speaking on the CBS "Morning News" show, Wright said:

> About a year-and-a-half ago, unbeknownst to the public, a man entered the United States House of Representatives gallery and was prepared to explode himself and send shards of glass that would have been very destructive, killing a lot of people. (cited in Associated Press 1986)

The man was arrested "in the nick of time," the House Speaker added. What made Wright's disclosure more startling was his assertion that it was "connected with one or another faction of the Palestine Liberation Organization." Needless to say, the matter was quickly dropped, and no retractions were ever made, even though Wright's statements were reported by a major wire service and published in at least one major U.S. newspaper.[72]

Anti-Arab racism is not unique. One need only compare U.S. attitudes toward Japan, and those, say, toward France under Charles De Gaulle, to appreciate how one culture (in this case our own) can harbor strikingly different attitudes toward different peoples. U.S. frustration with a defiant France under De Gaulle did not spill over into diffuse anti-French feelings. In sharp contrast, U.S. frustration with Japan has more than once erupted into ugly displays of anti-Japanese racism. The argument that Japan today poses a more serious

---

72. Although the Associated Press (1986) story mentioned Rubinowits's nationality and the fact that he had been deported to Israel, many readers would not have necessarily noticed the contradiction between those facts and Wright's false allegation, since the wire story did not draw the connection between the two disparate facts.

threat than De Gaulle's France only begs a comparison of U.S. attitudes toward Japan and Germany, the United States's other major economic competitor.

Japan is an industrial giant, sufficiently able to command respect and deference, however grudgingly conceded. But what of the Arabs, Muslims, and Middle Easterners generally? How will they be able to contend with the deeply embedded racism toward them? Until the assassination of JDL founder Meir Kahane, it seemed as though the ideologically motivated violence of Jewish extremists groups had begun to dissipate in recent years owing to a clampdown by law enforcement authorities. Similarly, jingoistic violence and hostility seemed to be on the wane in the late 1980s as the Reagan administration's war on international terrorism receded. With the advent of the present decade, it appeared that the era of unchecked anti-Arab racism and attendant hate crimes, violence, and intimidation was slowly becoming a thing of the past. The Gulf crisis of August 1990, and the ensuing war changed all that. The crisis reminded many Arab-Americans that anti-Arab racism continues to lie just beneath the surface of society. And, that as long as anti-Arab racism remains serviceable to government leaders, politicians, entertainers, the mass media, and cultural institutions, it will continue to resonate unchecked and unchallenged at the popular levels of society.

REFERENCES

Abraham, Nabeel. 1986. "The Real Target of the Airport Atrocities." *Middle East International* (Jan. 24): 14–16.
———. 1989. "Arab-American Marginality: Mythos and Praxis." In *Arab Americans: Continuity and Change,* ed. Baha Abu-Laban and Michael Suleiman. Belmont, Mass.: Assoc. of Arab-American University Graduates Press.
———. 1991. "The Gulf Crisis and Anti-Arab Racism in America." In *Collateral Damage: The New World Order at Home and Abroad,* ed. Cynthia Peters. Boston: South End Press.
ACLU. 1992. "No Peace for 'L.A. Eight'." *Civil Liberties,* Summer-Fall.
ADC. n.d. "The Jewish Defense League: A Cult of Racism and Terror, and A Threat to Arab-Americans." *ADC Issues,* no. 9.
———. 1986. *Insider's Report.* Washington, D.C.: American-Arab Anti-Discrimination Committee. June.
———. 1987. *Insider's Report.* Washington, D.C.: American-Arab Anti-Discrimination Committee. May.

————. 1991a. *1990 ADC Annual Report on Political and Hate Violence.* Washington, D.C.: American-Arab Anti-Discrimination Committee. Feb.

————. 1991b. "Hate Crimes Chronology, Update." Washington, D.C.: American-Arab Anti-Discrimination Committee. Feb. 6.

ADL. n.d. "A Decade's Perspective 1979–1989." *1988 ADL Audit of Anti-Semitic Incidents.* New York: Anti-Defamation League.

————. 1983. *Pro-Arab Propaganda in America.* New York: Anti-Defamation League.

————. 1985. "Meir Kahane: In His Own Words." New York: Anti-Defamation League. October.

————. 1987. "The Hate Movement Today: A Chronicle of Violence and Disarray," (Special Report). New York: Anti-Defamation League.

————. 1988a. *Hate Groups in America.* New York: Anti-Defamation League.

————. 1988b. *Extremism on the Right: A Handbook.* New York: Anti-Defamation League.

AIPAC. 1983. *The Campaign to Discredit Israel.* Washington: American Israel Public Affairs Committee.

Applebaum, Elizabeth. 1990. "No More Mr. Nice Guy." *Detroit Jewish News,* Feb. 23.

Aruri, Naseer. 1985. "The Middle East on the U.S. Campus. *The Link.* New York: Americans for Middle East Understanding. May-June.

Associated Press. 1986. "U.S. Deported Israeli with Bomb in Capitol," *Detroit Free Press,* Jan. 9.

————. 1987. *New York Times,* Nov. 4.

Baker, Bob. 1986. "Anti-Arab Violence Represents 17% of Racial, Religious Attacks in 1985." *Los Angeles Times,* Mar. 1.

Bassiouni, M. C. 1974. *The Civil Rights of Arab-Americans: "The Special Measures."* Information Paper no. 10. Belmont, Mass.: Association of Arab-American University Graduates.

Campbell, Colin. 1985. "Middle East Scholars Upset by a List." *New York Times,* Jan. 30.

————. 1986. "Attacks on U.S. Arabs: The Middle Eastern Link." *New York Times,* July 20.

Chomsky, Noam. 1986. *Pirates and Emperors: International Terrorism in the Real World.* New York: Claremont and Amana.

————. 1991. *Deterring Democracy.* London & New York: Verso.

Christison, Kathleen. 1987. "The Arab in Recent Popular Fiction." *Middle East Journal.* Summer.

Churchill, Ward, and Jim Vander Wall. 1988. *Agents of Repression.* Boston: South End Press.

————. 1990. *The Cointelpro Papers: Documents from the FBI's Secret Wars Against Dissent in the United States.* Boston: South End Press.

Cole, David. 1993. "It's Alive and Well at the INS." *Nation,* Feb. 15.

Committee for Justice. 1990. "Fouad Rafeedie Case." *Call for Justice.* Newsletter of the Committee for Justice. Los Angeles, Calif.: Committee for Justice. Spring.

Cook, Christopher. 1989. "Jewish Group's Letter in Flap Similar to '87 Appeal." *Detroit Free Press,* Feb. 12.

————. 1991. "Fearful of Curbs on Freedom, Arabs Fight Antiterrorism Bill." *Detroit Free Press,* May 17.

Corn, David, and Jefferson Morley. 1988. "Beltway Bandits." *Nation,* Oct. 10.

Criley, Richard. 1990. *The FBI v. The First Amendment.* Los Angeles: First Amendment Foundation.

Crutchfield, James. 1981. "Reported Milliken Slur Angers Arab Americans." *Detroit Free Press,* Dec. 18.

Cummings, Judith. 1985. "F.B.I. Says Jewish Defense League May Have Planted Fatal Bombs." *New York Times,* Nov. 9.

Eberwein, Cheryl. 1988. "Arab Businessman Faces Harassment." *Dearborn Press & Guide,* Mar. 24.

Fikes, Brad. 1990. "Sling Slime, Not Mud." *The Star-News.* Chula Vista, Calif. May 30.

Findley, Paul. 1984. *They Dare to Speak Out.* Westport, Conn.: Lawrence Hill.

Fredrickson, G. M., and D. T. Knobel. 1980. "History of Prejudice and Discrimination." In *Harvard Encyclopedia of American Ethnic Groups,* ed. Stephen Thernstrom. Cambridge: Belknap Press.

Friedman, Robert I. 1986. "Nice Jewish Boys with Bombs. *Village Voice,* May 6.

————. 1987a. "Who Killed Alex Odeh?". *Village Voice,* Nov. 24.

————. 1987b. "PACmen." *The Nation,* June 6.

————. 1988a. "Kahane's 'Good Jewish Boys.'" *Nation,* Jan. 16.

————. 1988b. "How Shamir Used JDL Terrorism." *Nation,* Oct. 31.

————. 1990. *The False Prophet: Rabbi Meir Kahane, From FBI Informant to Knesset Member.* Brooklyn: Lawrence Hill.

————. 1993. "The Enemy Within." *Village Voice,* May 11.

Gelbspan, Ross. 1991. *Break-ins, Death Threats and the FBI: The Covert War Against the Central America Movement.* Boston: South End Press.

Ghareeb, Edmund. 1983. *Split Vision.* Washington, D.C.: Arab-American Affairs Council.

Goldman, Ari. 1989. "B'nai B'rith Apologizes for Letter Containing Anti-Arab Statements." *New York Times,* Feb. 10.

Gurr, Ted Robert, ed. 1989. *Violence in America.* Vol. 2, *Protest, Rebellion, Reform.* Newbury Park, Calif.: Sage Publications.

Hagopian, Elaine. 1975–76. "Minority Rights in a Nation-State: The Nixon Administration's Campaign against Arab-Americans." *Journal of Palestine Studies,* Autumn-Winter.

Hallow, Ralph. 1990. "Arab-Baiting 'Appalls' GOP Campaign Chief." *The Washington Times,* June 4.

Hamm, Steve. 1986. "Anti-Khadafy Backlash Stings Foreigners Here." *New Haven Register,* May 11.

Harris, John W. 1987. "Domestic Terrorism in the 1980s." *FBI Law Enforcement Bulletin.* Oct.

Hentoff, Nat. 1986. "You Can't Tell a Terrorist by the Cover of Her Book." *Washington Post,* June 21.

————. 1987. "The FBI Tries to Build a Gulag." *Village Voice,* Apr. 28.

Hersh, Seymour M. 1987. "Target Qaddafi." *New York Times Magazine,* Feb. 22.

Hitsky, Brian. 1982. "Taxpayers Revolt." *The Dearborn Heights Leader,* Mar. 18.

Hoffman, Bruce. 1986. *Terrorism in the United States and the Potential Threat to Nuclear Facilities.* U.S. Department of Energy. Santa Monica, Calif.: Rand Corp.

Huard, Ray. 1990. "Congress Hopeful Demands Apology From GOP Rival." *San Diego Tribune,* May 30.

Hundley, Tom. 1987a. "State Had Most Cases of Arab Harassment." *Detroit Free Press,* Apr. 3.

————. 1987b. "Detroit's Arabs Keep Sense of Community," *Detroit Free Press,* July 5.

INS. 1986. "Alien Border Control (ABC) Committee, Group IV—Contingency Plans." Memorandum, Investigations Division. Washington, D.C.: Immigration and Naturalization Service. Oct. 31.

Jabara, Abdeen. 1987. "Terrorism Hits Home but Very Few Seem to Care." *Orange County Register,* Calif., Jan. 11.

————. 1993. "The Anti-Defamation League: Civil Rights and Wrongs." *Covert Action.* Summer.

Johnston, David. 1991. "Crime Bill Would Establish Alien Deportation Tribunal." *New York Times,* June 1.

Kahane, Meir. 1981. *They Must Go.* New York: Grosset & Dunlap.

Kass, John. 1990. "'No Arabs' Sign Removed; Apologies to Be Sent Out." *Chicago Tribune,* Apr. 5.

Kessler, J. S., and J. Schwaber. 1984. *The AIPAC College Guide: Exposing the Anti-Israel Campaign on Campus.* Washington, D.C.: American Israel Public Affairs Committee.

Kotler, Yair. 1986. *Heil Kahane.* New York: Adama Books.

Lee, Felicia R. 1989. "Arabs Feel Anger Flare in New York." *New York Times,* Aug. 6.

Lerner, Steve. 1986. "Terror Against Arabs in America." *New Republic,* July 28.

Lewis, Anthony. 1987. "Is This America?" *New York Times,* Feb. 10.

————. 1988. *New York Times,* April 14.

————. 1993. *New York Times,* Sept. 20.

Lutz, Chris. 1987. *They Don't All Wear Sheets: A Chronology of Racist and Far Right Violence—1980–1986.* Atlanta: Center for Democratic Renewal/ Natonal Council of Churches.

Magnusson, Paul. 1976. "Two Sought in Shotgun Slaying in Dearborn." *Detroit Free Press,* June 6.

Marshall, Rachelle. 1989. "The Decline of B'nai B'rith: From Protector to Persecutor." Washington, D.C.: *Washington Report on Middle East Affairs,* Apr.

McCaslin, John. 1986. "Terrorists Trained Abroad are Known to Live Here." *Washington Times,* Mar. 27.

McGee, Jim. 1993. "Jewish Group's Tactics Investigated." *Washington Post,* Oct. 19.

McGraw, Bill. 1986. "Anti-Arab Sentiment Worries Local Leaders." *Detroit Free Press,* Dec. 13.

Michalak, Laurence. 1984. "Cruel and Unusual: Negative Images of Arabs in Popular American Culture." *ADC Issues.* Washington, D.C.: American-Arab Anti-Discrimination Committee, Jan.

MSN. 1991. "Domestic Repression and the Persian Gulf War." *MSN News,* Special Edition, 7(1). New York: Movement Support Network.

Mydans, Seth. 1991. "Free Speech is at Issue as Palestinian Fights Deportation." *New York Times,* Dec. 8.

Nation. 1987. "The Untouchables." Editorial. Mar. 21.

New York Times. 1991. "No Terror Court for the U.S." Editorial, June 20.

———. 1993a. 'Exorcising McCarran-Walter's Ghost." Editorial, Oct. 4.

———. 1993b. "Inquiry Into a Jewish Group's Methods is Dropped." Nov. 17.

O'Reilly, Kenneth. 1989. *"Racial Matters": The FBI's Secret File On Black America, 1960–1972.* New York: Free Press.

Orfalea, Gregory. 1988. *Before the Flames.* Austin: University of Texas Press.

Palermo, D., and G. Jarlson. 1985. "Bomb Kills Leader of Arab Group in Santa Ana Office." *Los Angeles Times,* Oct. 12.

Pell, Eve. 1990. "Kicking Out the Palestinians." *Nation,* Feb. 5.

Pinsky, Mark I. 1986. "The 'Quiet' Death of Alex Odeh." *Present Tense,* Winter.

Prater, Constance. 1988. "FBI Enters Ethnic Slur Probe in Dearborn Hts." *Detroit News,* June 16.

Reyes, D., and L. Jones. 1985. "Odeh Becomes Victim of the Violence He Decried." *Los Angeles Times,* Oct. 13.

Ridgeway, James. 1985. "American Arabs and the Jewish Right." *Village Voice,* Nov. 17.

Rimawi, Bonnie. 1986. "A Rash of Death Threats and Arson Followed Bombing of Tripoli." *Guardian,* New York, July 9.

Robinson, John. 1986. "Kennedy Rapped on Rejected Check." *Boston Globe,* Apr. 22.

Ryan, Sheila. 1987. "Palestinian Deportation Case Continues." *Mideast Monitor* 4(2).

Said, Edward W. 1978. *Orientalism.* New York: Pantheon.

———. 1981. *Covering Islam.* New York: Pantheon.

Samhan, Helen Hatab. 1987. "Politics and Exclusion: The Arab American Experience." *Journal of Palestine Studies,* Winter.

Schidlovsky, John. 1986. "Arab-Americans Fear Growing Hostility." *Baltimore Sun,* Aug. 10.

Shaheen, Jack. 1984. *The TV Arab.* Bowling Green: Popular Press.

Shea, Terence F. 1986. "'Arab-Bashing' Described to Conyers' Group." *Detroit News,* July 17.

Slade, Shelly. 1981. "The Image of the Arab in America: Analysis of a Poll on American Attitudes." *Middle East Journal,* Spring.

Soble, Ronald. 1987. "Deportation Bid in Arab Case Focuses on Magazines." *Los Angeles Times,* Feb. 17.

Stuart, Reginal. 1985. "Arab Office Fire Termed Suspicious." *New York Times,* Dec. 1.

Suleiman, Michael W. 1988. *The Arabs in the Mind of America.* Brattleboro, Vt.: Amana Books.

Tal, Rami. 1990. "Kahane Wants A Half-Million Dollars." *Yedioth Aharonoht,* Feb. 12. Trans. Israel Shahak.

Terry, Janice. 1985. *Mistaken Identity.* Washington, D.C.: American-Arab Affairs Council.

Thornton, Mary. 1986. "Arab Americans Ask Rights Inquiry." *Washington Post,* Feb. 12.

Thurtell, Joel. 1985. "Cultures Clash Over Islamic Gathering." *Detroit Free Press* June 6.

Tivnan, Edward. 1987. *The Lobby: Jewish Political Power and American Foreign Policy.* New York: Simon and Schuster.

Turque, Bill. 1986a. "Arabs Facing a Wave of Bias." *Dallas Times Herald,* Oct. 12.

———. 1986b. "Immigrants Fear Anti-Arab Feeling Growing." *Dallas Times Herald,* Oct. 12.

U.S. Congress. House. 1988. Committee on the Judiciary. Subcommittee on Criminal Justice. Hearing. *Ethnically Motivated Violence Against Arab-Americans.* 99th Cong., 2d sess., July 16, 1986. Serial 135.

White, George. 1982. "Detroit's Arab-American Community: Thriving and Active." *Christian Science Monitor,* Jan. 5.

Winkler, Karen J. 1985. "Political Tensions of Arab-Israeli Conflict Put Pressure on Scholars Who Study Middle East." *Chronicle of Higher Education,* Mar. 27.

Young, David. 1975. "Arabs in U.S. Accuse FBI of Spying on Them." *Chicago Tribune,* July 13.

Zogby, James. 1982. Letter to the Editor. *Christian Science Monitor,* Jan. 14.

Contributors

NABEEL ABRAHAM received his doctorate in anthropology from the University of Michigan with a concentration in Near Eastern and North African ethnology. His extensive field work on political factionalism among Yemeni immigrant workers in Detroit formed the basis of his doctoral thesis, which he is currently revising for publication. He joined the staff of Henry Ford Community College (Dearborn, Michigan) in 1985, where he teaches anthropology. He has also served as visiting professor at other universities, including the University of Michigan and the University of Algiers, and as research associate at the Center for Urban Studies at Wayne State University. A fluent speaker of Arabic, Dr. Abraham has traveled extensively throughout the Middle East, and writes and lectures on the Middle East, U.S.-Arab relations, and Arab-Americans. He is a frequent commentator for the news media and is a contributing editor to *Lies of Our Times*, the monthly publication of the Institute for Media Analysis in New York City. In addition to several scholarly articles and encyclopedia entries he has coedited *Arabs in the New World: Studies on Arab-American Communities* (1983) and *The Arab World and Arab-Americans: Understanding a Neglected Minority* (1981).

LOUISE CAINKAR is Fulbright Research Scholar at the Center for Strategic Studies at the University of Jordan. Her current work is documenting the social history of the Palestinians and Jordanians who were expelled from Kuwait after the Gulf War, particularly those who have resettled in Jordan. She is the founder, and until 1922 the executive director, of the Palestine Human Rights Information Center–International.

Dr. Cainkar received her doctorate in sociology from Northwestern University; her research has centered on Arab culture and society, Palestinians, and human rights. Her book *Gender, Culture and Politics Among Palestinian Immigrants in the United States* is forthcoming from Temple University Press.

ALA FA'IK is a pioneer in the study of Aráb-American theater. He has a doctorate in directing from the University of Michigan; his dissertation dealing with theatrical forms in medieval Islamic culture grew out of his interest in cross-cultural relations in the performing arts. His master's degree in theater is from the

University of Missouri, and he has a bachelor's degree in theatre arts from Baghdad University. He is an actor, director, and teacher of film, television, and theater.

Since 1976 Dr. Fa'ik has been directing plays for U.S. audiences, including *Wayzeck, The Master Builder, The Death of Bessie Smith, The Diviners, Amadeus,* and *Orpheus Descending,* as well as the original productions of *Aliens, Scoundrels,* and *The Amber Beads* in Ann Arbor.

YVONNE YAZBECK HADDAD, professor of Islamic history at the University of Massachusetts, Amherst, has an extensive record of teaching, research, and publications on contemporary Islam, with particular reference to Muslims in North America. Dr. Haddad received her B.A. from Beirut College for Women and her Ph.D. from Hartford Seminary. She has traveled extensively in most of the Arab world and the Muslim nations of South and Southeast Asia. She is past president of the Middle East Studies Association of North America and of the New England Region, American Academy of Religion. She is associate editor of *Encyclopedia of the Modern Islamic World.*

Dr. Haddad's publications deal with Islam in the modern world, Islamic revival, the Qur'an and Qur'anic exegesis, women in Islam, and Muslims in North America. Her most recent books are *Mission to America: Five Muslim Sects in North America* (1993), *Christian-Muslim Encounters* (1994), and *Muslim Communities in North America* (1994).

ÉVA VERONIKA HUSEBY-DARVAS was born in Budapest, Hungary, but fled her homeland in her mid-teens as a refugee and migrated to the United States. From that experience she developed an abiding interest in the relationship between identity and social change, with special reference to how various forms of migration affect individuals and communities. Dr. Huseby-Darvas has conducted research in East Central Europe and in North America; she received her doctorate in cultural anthropology from the University of Michigan. She teaches at both the Dearborn and Ann Arbor campuses of the University of Michigan, and lectures on immigrant and refugee experience in general and on the changing roles, identities, and predicaments of migrant women in particular. Her publications cover such topics as Hungarian ethnic radio in Detroit and Windsor (Canada), oral autobiographies of Hungarian émigrés, migration and gender, Yugoslav women refugees, and immigrant women as agents of continuity in a Hungarian-American community.

ALIXA NAFF, after a long career in corporate management, earned a doctorate in the history and politics of the modern Middle East, with a second major field in American social history. She has taught at the university level, including at the American University in Cairo. In 1976 Dr. Naff joined the Middle East Educational Trust in Washington, D.C. as executive director to produce visual and print materials on the Middle East; a documentary on Arab-Americans resulted from this. The paucity of data on these Americans inspired her Arab American Study Project, which she conducted under the auspices of the National

Center for Urban Ethnic Affairs. From this study she published an in-depth study entitled *Becoming American. The Early Arab Immigrant Experience* (1985) and *The Arab Americans* (1987), an illustrated history for high school students and young adults in general. She has also published articles and lectured widely.

Dr. Naff is the donor of a unique collection of immigrant Arab artifacts and archival materials to the Smithsonian Institution, part of which was exhibited in its National Museum of American History.

RONALD R. STOCKTON is a professor of political science at the University of Michigan–Dearborn. He is past president of the Michigan Conference of Political Scientists and is a research associate of the University of Michigan Center for Middle Eastern and North African Studies. He is a frequent traveler to the Middle East, and publishes on Middle Eastern topics in the *Middle East Journal,* the *Journal of Palestine Studies,* and the *Armenian Review.* He frequently speaks to teacher workshops, on the secondary and postsecondary levels, and is the author of *The Israeli-Palestinian Conflict,* a curriculum unit for high schools published by the University of Michigan Center for Middle Eastern and North African Studies.

MICHAEL W. SULEIMAN is University Distinguished Professor of Political Science at Kansas State University in Manhattan, Kansas. He received his Ph.D. in political science from the University of Wisconsin. He has written widely on American attitudes toward the Middle East and on Arab politics, women in the Middle East, political socialization in the Middle East, and the Arab-American community. He is also a frequent guest lecturer and speaker. Among his publications are *Political Parties in Lebanon* (1967), *The Arabs in the Mind of America* (1988), and, with Baha Abu-Laban, *Arab-Americans: Continuity and Change* (1989).

Dr. Suleiman is currently working on a comprehensive bibliography on Arab-Americans and on a book detailing the social and political history of Arabs in America.

Index

Acculturation, 18
American Arab Association
  (AMARA), 81
American Druze Political Action
  Committee (ADPAC), 81
American Lebanese League (ALL), 81
American-Arab Anti-Discrimination
  Committee (ADC), 48, 53, 54, 81,
  176–78, 182–85, 204
Americanization process, 30–34, 45,
  74, 75–79, 83–84
Anti-Arab bias, 52–53, 160, 195–99
Anti-Arab racism, 155–60
Anti-Arab violence, 167–68; 174–75
  causes, 179 ff., 186
  government policies, 165–67, 169–
    70, 171–72
  ideological racism, 180–87
  jingoism, 160–61, 170, 193–94
  media hype, 161–65, 168–70
  nature of, 177–78
  xenophobia, 188–93
Anti-Defamation League (ADL), 156,
  184–87
Antiochian churches, 66
Arab identity, 61, 63–65, 79
Arab-American identity, 60, 79 ff.
Arab-American Institute (AAI), 48,
  54, 189
Arab-American: definition, 37, 61, 63
Arab-American theater. See Theater
  in United States

Arab press in United States, 33–34,
  39
  Al-Ayam, 40
  Al-Bayan, 34
  Al-Hoda, 33–34, 40, 42
  Al-Mushir, 40
  Kawkab America/Amrika, 33, 39–
    40, 42
  Meraat al-Gharb, 34, 40
  The Syrian World, 34
Arabs, American images of, 126–30
Assimilation, 15, 17–18, 39–41, 43,
  45, 76–77, 84, 91, 92, 96
Assyrian church, 66, 69
Association of Arab-American Uni-
  versity Graduates (AAUG), 47–48,
  54, 80

Boas, Franz, 14–15

Center for Democratic Renewal
  (CDR): report on racial violence,
  155 ff.
Chaldean Church, 66, 69–70
Christian sects in Near East, 66–69
Christian sects in the United States,
  31–32, 69–73
Coptic Church, 66–67, 71
Cultural pluralism, 15, 17

Eastern churches, 66–70, 83
Erikson, Erik, 18–19

Ethclasses, 89–90

Federation of Islamic Associations
  (FIA), 74, 82

Gender and ethnicity, 86
Gender and politics, 88
Gulf of Sidra, 166–67, 169
Gulf War, impact on racial bias,
  204–6

Hitti, Philip K., 25

Immigrants, European, 11–14, 19 ff.
Immigration
  census statistics, 24
  motivation for, 62, 96
  economic, 12, 23, 26–27
  political and economic oppression,
    96
  social ideal, 13, 46
Islamic Society of North America
  (INSA), 75

Jackson, the Rev. Jesse, 49–50
Jewish Defense League (JDL), 157
  ff., 163 ff., 180–83

L.A. Eight, 199–202

Maronite Church, 66, 69, 70
Melkite Greek Catholic Church, 66,
  69, 70
Melting pot, 15–18
Millet system, 65–66
Muslim sects, 73–74
Muslim sects in the United States,
  73–76
Muslim Student Association (MSA),
  75
Muslims in United States, 32, 74–77

National Association of Arab-
  Americans (NAAA), 48, 54, 80,
  207

Odeh, Alex, 157, 163 ff.
Orthodox Church, 69–71
Ottoman society, 65–66

Pack peddling, 23, 28–30
Palestinian women
  emigration patterns, 87–88, 96–97,
    102
  marriage patterns, 94–95, 99–101
  patterns of adaptation, 91–92
  political life, 102–3
  sexual mores, 94–95, 99–101
  social classes, 89–90, 103–4
  social values, 89
  survey, 86–104
  middle class, 90–96, 101
  lower class, 96–101
  values, 92–94, 98–99
Palestinians, 46, 86
  in Chicago, 87
Peddling. *See* Pack peddling
Political activity, 42, 43, 49–60, 80–
  83, 102–3
Political identity, 32, 37–38, 45, 48–
  60, 88
  questionnaire survey, 48–59
Protestant missionaries, 68–69
Protestant sects, 66, 68, 70–73

Racism defined, 155
Ramallah, 87
Religious affiliations, 49, 63, 65
Religious revivalism, 64–65

Sectarian rivalry, 64–65
Sojourner (concept), 38, 89
Stereotypes, 119–20
  anti-Arab themes, 130–49, 194–96
  generic archetypes, 120
  of Arabs, 126–29
  of Blacks, 122–23
  of Japanese, 124–25
  of Jews, 123–24
Syrian immigrants, 23 ff., 47
  as Ottoman subjects, 24 ff., 38
Syrian Orthodox Church, 67

Theater in United States, 107–9
    artistic quality, 117
    for general audiences, 113–17
    themes, 109
    social commentary, 109–10
    musical productions, 111–13

    drama, 114–17

Uniate churches, 71, 83
United Muslims of America, 81

War, Arab-Israeli 1967, 79
Women. *See* Palestinian women